May ~~~~ 1974

To Jo Ann –

With Best Wishes,

Donald [signature]

D0389259

Cape Cod

A GUIDE

Cape Cod

A GUIDE

by DONALD WOOD

Little, Brown and Company · Boston · Toronto

COPYRIGHT © 1973 by Donald Wood

ALL RIGHTS RESERVED. NO PART OF THIS BOOK MAY BE REPRODUCED IN ANY FORM OR BY ANY ELECTRONIC OR MECHANICAL MEANS INCLUDING INFORMATION STORAGE AND RETRIEVAL SYSTEMS WITHOUT PERMISSION IN WRITING FROM THE PUBLISHER, EXCEPT BY A REVIEWER WHO MAY QUOTE BRIEF PASSAGES IN A REVIEW.

FIRST EDITION

T08/73

The author is grateful to the Dennis Historical Society for permission to quote from *Master Mariners of Dennis* by Neva O'Neil. Copyright © 1965 by the Dennis Historical Society.

The town maps in this book are reproduced by permission of the copyright owners, The National Survey, Chester, Vermont. The map on page 2 was drawn by Merwin H. Freeman and is used with his permission.

Library of Congress Cataloging in Publication Data

Wood, Donald, 1926–
  Cape Cod.

  1. Cape Cod--Description and travel--Guide-books.
2. Cape Cod--History. I. Title.
F72.C3W6 1973   917.44'92'044   73-6959
ISBN 0-316-95163-3
ISBN 0-316-95164-1 (pbk.)

Published simultaneously in Canada
by Little, Brown & Company (Canada) Limited

PRINTED IN THE UNITED STATES OF AMERICA

TO
MY WIFE

CONTENTS

Introduction

Founded on the Puritan ethic, nurtured on rugged individualism and tempered by salt spray, the Cape and Cape Codders have come to be known as a world and race apart from those west of the Cape Cod Canal. There were times when outsiders might have felt inclined to cut the bridges and set them adrift, and most Cape Codders would have been delighted at the prospect. The last fifteen or twenty years have witnessed great changes. The outsiders now outnumber the Codders on their home ground. Later generations of Cape folk have mellowed, perhaps because they began visiting Boston and points west more frequently than Hong Kong and Calcutta. At the same time, the outsiders have come to appreciate the Cape for its geographical wonders and its people for their cultural heritage.

Modern Cape Codders, the outsiders of yesterday, still consider the Cape a world apart. Strangely enough, the geological origins of Cape Cod bear out this difference. A sandy spit curving 70 miles into the Atlantic, the Cape was respectfully referred to as the "strong right arm of Massachusetts" in years past. About 20 miles wide at its western shoulder, the Cape narrows down to an average 8-mile width to the elbow at Chatham and abruptly turns north in a slender forearm to the curved fist of Provincetown. Through its whole length, geological Cape Cod consists of sand, gravel, silt, clay and boulders, with no solid bedrock for many feet below the surface. Most of New England was already shaped to its present-day landscape long before Cape Cod came into existence. Fifty to seventy thousand years ago, great ice sheets made their final invasion of the northeastern United States and left the ragged outline of the Cape we know today. Endowed by man and nature with outstanding scenic, historical and recreational resources, the Cape today might better be called the matchless right arm of Massachusetts.

This book presents both the historic and geographic attractions of the Cape. We'll follow what seems to be a natural path: from the earliest settlements in Sandwich and the Bay Shore towns down Cape to Provincetown and then back along the south shore to Bourne and the Cape Cod Canal. The Cape has something for everyone, from the antique buff to the sun worshiper and those in between: history, historical landmarks and antique homes for those interested in tracing the thread of the old Cape; amusements, beaches, campgrounds and golf for those seeking the pleasures of the new.

We often cite hours and dates of operation and other statistics of a highly variable nature. For those facts that have changed by the time you read this book, our apologies. We sincerely hope you enjoy your visit and will return again soon.

Cape Cod

A GUIDE

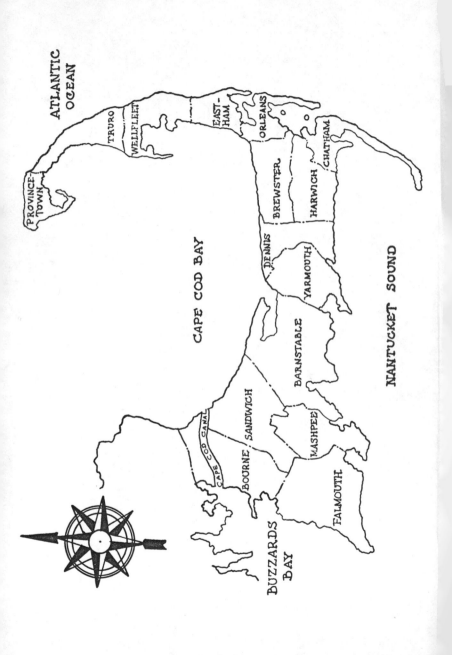

CHAPTER I

The Cape—Then and Now

"Time is but the stream I go a-fishing in," said Thoreau, and many visitors to the Cape enjoy the same kind of fishing. From the Cape Cod Canal to that point in Provincetown where a man may stand and put all America behind him lies the Cape and its people, unique in American history and culture and blessed by nature with some of the most beautiful seascapes in the country. Today's blend of historic treasures and resort facilities makes the Cape hard to beat.

To fully appreciate the Cape and its virtues, a knowledge of its history is invaluable. The old times have gone, the Cape Cod regional accent has been absorbed and is almost imperceptible now; but the legacy of the old Cape Cod remains and is pervading and visible no matter where we turn.

Cape history began in 1630 when William Bradford of Plymouth received a patent to annex the Cape to the Plymouth Colony. Before that one could go back through the Indians, the explorers, the Vikings, the ice ages and beyond. But ours is a modern history as time goes, and the new Cape Codder was modern man. He was fighting for a cause: religious freedom, security, independence, or perhaps merely fame and fortune. Whatever it was, the Cape attracted many of the best men and very few of the worst that the world had to offer.

By 1630 tiny Plymouth was getting crowded. In a village in a wilderness, two families are company, three a crowd. New settlers felt they were too late, much like the real estate buyer of today; prices were up and all the worthwhile acreage gone. The patent of 1630 opened a vast new area and the rush was on.

The Cape had many attractions: a trading post on the Manomet River, acres of salt marsh for cattle feed, unlimited forests, streams, ponds and harbors, and, most important, land for the landless. Edmund Freeman of Saugus was the first of the town builders, as opposed to the itinerants who had speckled the Cape for years. He and his "ten men from Saugus" chose the nearby trading grounds of the Manomet, present-day Sandwich. Almost immediately new recruits began to arrive, and hard on their heels came new leaders to establish settlements in Mattakeese and Nauset, later incorporated as Yarmouth, Barnstable, and Eastham.

Sandwich, Yarmouth, and Barnstable became towns of the colony in 1639, Eastham in 1646, and on them rested the early civilization of the Cape. All the others developed from these four towns, some by partition and some by resettlement of dissatisfied factions. Eastham, whose colonists had so weakened Plymouth by their departure, was, in turn, the town most damaged by expansion on the Cape.

The first Cape settlers were faced with a wilderness relieved only by a few Indian clearings. Men from England, many of whom had never performed manual labor, found that the use of an ax and hoe was a necessity for survival. They were inept at times, but thanks to helpful Indians and divine Providence they learned, and not only survived but prospered. After long hours of hard work, it is amazing how much energy they reserved for bickering — if it wasn't land it was religion, and if all else failed the government in Plymouth served the purpose. No one was ever too busy to trade the Indians off their land, spreading the gospel as they did so.

Early crops surpassed expectations, and Cape colonists were happy and well established in their new towns within a very few years. Corn was their principal crop, and each season the settlers converted a few more acres of woodland into farmland. The struggle was over and the settlements began to take on the appearance of established villages. Even in the earliest years, form and substance were of great importance. This was no western saga in which a man's past was his own business. In the Plymouth and Cape settlements, the gradations of class and the warning out of undesirables were accepted facts of life. Village titles ranged from the regal Squire to the respectable Mister and the common Goodman or Yeoman. Wealth and ability helped but were not conclusive. Democracy as we know it had no place in the early Cape settlements. Slaves were not uncommon, black and sometimes white, and were limited here only due to the straitened circumstances under which many of the wealthier colonists left England. John Gorham of Barnstable managed to keep a few slaves, and when he died his will lists "his Negro girl Peg and half the use of the man Cezar" among his assets.

As the towns were being settled, the farmers found a fine fall and winter crop to supplement their fortunes. Whales were incredibly abundant off the coast and often became stranded and washed ashore. Stripping and boiling down the blubber was highly profitable and a pleasant diversion from the chores of farming. The government yoke was always there, however, with town, colony and crown all claiming a share of each whale.

Many a whale sighted close in, apparently in trouble, would somehow manage to avoid the bars and shoals and slip out to sea again. Pursuit was inevitable and initial efforts were more in keeping with sheepherders than whalemen. Small boats surrounded their prey and drove them ashore. Skills improved and the harpoon came into use as individual boats probed the Bay for free-swimming whales. As long as the supply of whales held out, shore whaling was profitable and popular all over the Cape.

By 1680, half the citizens had farms of 30 acres or more, a pair of oxen for plowing, a horse for occasional visits to town, and cattle and sufficient sheep to provide milk, meat and clothing. Mills had been built to grind the surplus corn; cobblers, tanners, building contractors and tavern keepers turned the farming villages into towns.

The new Cape Codders could not, however, stray far from the watchful eye of the Plymouth government, the source of all authority and the arbiter of any dispute. The highest authority was the governor, elected annually by the "freemen," members of the church with a landed estate; each town also elected two deputies. The governor, his assistants, and the deputies formed the all-powerful General Court. The government may have been strict, dictatorial, and cumbersome, but there wasn't an ounce of corruption in it.

By 1657, the executive power of the Plymouth Colony began to shift to the Cape. Thomas Prence of Eastham was appointed governor, with Thomas Hinckley of Barnstable his lieutenant. In 1680 Hinckley became governor in his own right and steered the colony through some of is most trying times. After sixty years of relatively autonomous government, the Crown dispatched the officious Sir Edmond Andros to take over the colony and time marched backward. Land titles were declared no better than the "scratch of a bear's paw," and had it not been for the fall of James II, the first blows for independence might well have fallen a hundred years earlier in history. Andros was, fortunately, as expendable as his sovereign and dispatched just as unceremoniously. The accession of William III in 1689 calmed the waters in New England, due more to the Crown's ignorance than its intent. The English learned nothing from the Andros incident; the colonists learned much. A century later the English Parliament was still debating the degree of subservience due from colonials, while the colonies were molding bullets and stockpiling powder.

The Crown managed to inflict another blow in 1691.

The Plymouth, Massachusetts Bay, Maine, and Nova Scotia colonies were consolidated into one province. Local pride was damaged and the outcries were loud and clear, but the merger had substantial merit. The individual colonies had long been hard pressed to support themselves and their governments. The new province took the name of Massachusetts Bay and served a purpose the Crown did not foresee. As the petty regional grumbling died away, a common bond, a united feeling was born. At long last, men on this side of the world began to see themselves as an integral part of a common front rather than relatively independent English colonists off to find peace or to make their fortunes in an outpost of the Empire.

From 1670 to 1770 the Cape towns expanded and prospered, with a series of off-Cape wars to keep things stirred up. These wars were largely remote nuisances, except that they interfered with fishing and marine trade. They occasionally achieved local importance when the few Cape casualties were counted or the exploits of Cape soldiers reported.

By 1675 King Philip, chief of the Wampanoag Indians, son of Massasoit, had taken enough from his sharp-trading Massachusetts friends. Spurred by summary justice to his people, he led a conspiracy — King Philip's War. Off-Cape towns were sacked and burned, but the Cape Indians remained peaceful and Philip was finally cornered and dispatched. So ended tribal Indian life in New England.

Next came the interminable French and Indian Wars from 1690 to 1763, with treaties made and broken in Europe at the expense of colonial manpower and money. Several Cape Cod officers distinguished themselves in these campaigns, particularly the Gorham family of Barnstable.

Great Britain ruled the seas at this time. To protect their Canadian outposts, the French had built most of their settlements inland, along the rivers where warships couldn't reach them. Whaleboats could, however, and

whaleboat units became an integral arm of the provincial
forces. Who but a Cape man could command whaleboats?
Lieutenant Colonel John Gorham of Barnstable was
chosen. In 1690 the fleet made its first appearance: 40 or
50 boats, with about a dozen oarsmen to the boat. Each
boat could carry 10 or 12 soldiers as well, the predecessors of modern assault landing craft. The young Cape
Codders, reluctant to shoulder a musket in the foot-
slogging infantry, felt more at home in the whaleboat
fleet. French gunboats preyed constantly on their fishing
vessels and Cape men enjoyed considerable satisfaction
striking back at the river ports.

Success did not come easily. The whaleboats performed
honorably but the initial Canadian expedition ended in
disaster and retreat. Other whaleboat expeditions met
with limited success before the Treaty of Ryswick in 1697
temporarily halted the war. Fighting broke out again in
1703, with the whaleboats recalled again under Colonel
Gorham. Occasionally raids along the Canadian and Nova
Scotian coasts were carried out until the next hiatus in
1713. During the ensuing ten-year lull Gorham died, but
his son and two grandsons carried on the family tradition.
Shubael Gorham and his son David commanded a foot
company; the second son, John, commanded the whaleboats. All three ranked as colonels and served with distinction in the siege of Louisburg, Nova Scotia, in 1745.

Peace was short-lived, as war broke out again in 1755.
For the first time the mother country sent over substantial
contingents of regulars to show the colonials how a war
should be conducted. The British redcoats fought the
Indians in the classic European style of battle and were
slaughtered. Instead of proving their invincibility to the
ragged colonials, they showed nothing but mindless valor,
and a myth was shattered. The flexible leadership and
tactics of the colonial officers left the professionals
amazed, but only a few learned from it. Cape Codders
learned what they needed to: British soldiers put on their
pants one leg at a time just like any other man. In an in-

eptly fought war, the British and their colonials eventually emerged the inglorious victors, and Canada, fought over for almost a century, finally passed into British hands in 1763.

Toward the end of the French and Indian Wars, deepwater whaling began to come of age on the Cape. As shore whaling died out, Barnstable and its neighboring bayside towns sent out very few deepwater whalers, leaving to Truro, Wellfleet, and Provincetown the major development of long-voyage whaling on the Cape. The deepwater whalers rapidly developed into barrel-bottomed, wide-beamed floating factories of the sea; the tryworks were built into their decks. Stable and stout, they rode heavy seas like a cork, and cruises up to four years were not uncommon. Whaling crews were a hard and motley lot; miserable quarters, poor food, constant dangers, and long voyages made discipline far more important than seamanship. It was a grim industry played for high stakes. The merchant ships were floating palaces compared to conditions on a whaler.

Truro sent out one of the first deepwater whaling vessels in 1758. Others followed, cruising the coast of Africa; they soon rounded Cape Horn and entered the South Pacific. Wellfleet and Provincetown were not far behind. Almost the entire economy of Wellfleet was based on whaling before the Revolution. The Revolutionary War ended whaling in Truro and Wellfleet, but Provincetown resumed the chase and in 1876 still had seventeen whaling vessels at sea. The last whaling skipper out of Provincetown was Captain John Cook, who kept at it until 1916. Not even Provincetown in its heyday could match Nantucket at its prime. To the Cape's everlasting credit, it was a Cape Codder, Captain Ichabod Paddock of Yarmouth, who in 1690 was asked by Nantucket "to instruct the people in the art of killing whales." Captain Paddock was pleased to oblige.

Toward the end of the French and Indian Wars, financial chaos swept the Cape, and the mother country fueled

the fires with repressive legislation. Each restrictive measure by the Crown was met with increasing bitterness by
its colonial subjects. In 1761, the Writs of Assistance —
in effect unlimited search warrants — enraged the colonials, and their advocate general, James Otis of West
Barnstable, resigned his position to take up the cause.
His eloquent plea before the superior court fell on deaf
ears, but the seed of resistance was planted. The effects of
his speeches and writings were immediate throughout the
colonies. Everyone took sides, Loyalist or Patriot, and for
the first time the doctrine of patriotism meant not loyalty
to the British Crown but separation from it. Otis was a
national leader, and in John Adams's words, "His orations
breathed into this nation the very breath of life."

Tempers frayed easily on the Cape. Extreme Patriots
argued as vehemently with their moderate supporters as
they did with the Loyalists. Extremist Colonel Freeman of
Sandwich and moderate Captain Crocker of Barnstable
engaged in a typical political conversation of the time.
Captain Crocker expressed his opinion that routing tea
out of old women's larders was unworthy of the high
cause of patriotism. Freeman replied that such a statement was Toryism. Shortly thereafter, the extreme Patriots showed their patriotism by pulling up the fence in
front of Crocker's home. So it went. The Loyalist Abigail
Freeman operated a general store in Barnstable. She, in
her usual outspoken fashion, not only kept her stock of
tea but also freely delivered a piece of her mind. Tarred,
feathered and ridden on a rail, Abigail kept her views to
herself in the future.

In 1774, fifteen hundred citizens marched to the Barnstable Court House and succeeded in preventing the opening of His Majesty's Court. The Loyalists retaliated a few
days later by beating up Colonel Freeman, the Patriot
leader. The Cape was in a vulnerable position and Cape
men had much to think about before espousing the Patriot cause. Shipping was the mainstay of the economy
and war would mean ruin for many and unemployment

for most; the situation gave pause to all but the most rabid Patriots.

In 1776 all Cape towns were requested to give instructions to their representative at the Continental Congress with regard to independence. Barnstable alone failed to cast its vote in favor — nor did she vote against. The Loyalist leader Edward Bacon so intimidated the moderate Patriots that his Tories carried the day. Equivocation by Barnstable was not, however, sufficient to stem the tide, and the Declaration of Independence soon revolutionized life on Cape Cod.

Succeeding events confirmed the fears of Cape Codders. The British blockaded the Bay and captured many who ventured outside the harbor for fish or tried to run the gauntlet. Constant demands for fighting men, food, beef, and blankets created a desperate situation. Fishing and trading schooners rotted in the harbors under the watchful eye of the British fleet in the Bay. Resolve hardened and the Cape fought back.

Efforts were concentrated on the sea, logically enough; 21 privateers were commanded by Cape men and Cape crews served on many more. Captured seamen were impressed in either the British navy or their whaling fleet. Minor shore raids took place periodically for provisions, and the only sizable British landing, at Falmouth in 1779, was easily repulsed. An occasional British ship fell victim to the treacherous bars and shoals, and it was a happy day on the Cape when the 64-gun *Somerset* struck the bar and beached at Truro in November 1778. The local "mooncussers" had picked the wreck clean as usual by the time the government representatives arrived to take charge.

The condition of the Cape at the end of the Revolution was dismal indeed. Shattered but triumphant, the Cape Codders weathered the storm and began to rebuild. With most of its vessels rotted or captured and traditional English markets closed to the newly independent nation, Cape skippers refitted what ships they could, regained their sea legs, and looked to the West Indies and the Pacific. Just as the fledgling Cape merchant marine was hitting its stride, another bombshell burst — the War of 1812.

It was an unpopular war on the Cape, blamed on an inept southern administration; several Cape towns paid out protection money and took a "live and let live" attitude. Barnstable, perhaps to atone for its earlier vote on independence, chose to fight. Cannon were hauled down from Boston but the town was never seriously challenged. Whaleboat fleets were organized to trade with New York by the old water route stretching almost across the Cape at Scusset Creek in Sandwich. These blockade runners were responsible for what supplies were available in Cape kitchens during the war. A handful of Cape masters took to the sea in privately armed vessels, but most were content to sit at home and belittle the administration. Despite New England's apathy the war ended, and Cape shipmasters sailed forth to trade with the recent enemy.

The end of hostilities in 1815 ushered in the most prosperous era in the history of the Cape. Ashore and at sea, the Cape was bursting with energy. Manufacturing and salt-making, together with marine-related shore industries of sailmaking, ship chandlery and shipbuilding, brought a heady commercial prosperity that has never been equaled since.

While the Bay towns sent out relatively few long-voyage whalers, they were in the thick of the competitive packet trade to Boston. As time passed these sailing packets, noted for their speed and luxury, were cheered on with fierce town pride as the sporting events of the day. Two or three packets hailed from each of the village ports along the Bay; they were generally immaculate and quickly replaced when the least bit out of date. Sailing time to Boston ranged from 6 to 24 hours; the round-trip fare was $1.50, and passengers were catered to as on a holiday cruise. Grudge races were common, and the prime requisite of any new vessel was speed — the ability to beat the next town's current champion.

In 1840 the reigning sloop in the mid-Cape was Yarmouth's *Commodore Hull*. Barnstable countered with the new sloop *Mail* and the race was on. Neck and neck all the way, the *Mail* nosed out the *Commodore Hull* by three lengths at the finish, and a substantial amount of money changed hands back home.

The packets sailed from every little creek and harbor along the coast. These ports were suitable for fishermen, small whalers, West Indies trading vessels and the packets; but no harbor on the Cape, except Provincetown, was suitable for the deepwater trade. Many a packet captain and crewman left the Cape to man the long-voyage ships from Boston, New York, Philadelphia and Baltimore. The schooling of the packet trade provided hundreds of experienced seamen just as the country was beginning to emerge as a maritime power to be reckoned with. Cape captains and crews were in great demand; their experience combined with their hardheaded Yankee virtues made them excellent traders throughout the world. Typhoons, pirates, mutiny and diplomacy were all in a day's work for the merchant captains. It seems hard to believe, but the fabulous clipper ships, the graceful champions of sail, were manned to a great extent by Cape Codders on the quarterdeck, yet no clipper ever swung alongside in a Cape Cod harbor.

Clipper ships were the aristocracy of sail. Designed and built primarily in Boston and New York, the clippers of the 1850s sailed forth and quickly captured the maritime leadership of the world. They were the finest ships afloat and were entrusted to only the most experienced captains. Many Cape Cod skippers were rated at the top in this exacting profession: Captain Eldridge of Yarmouth's *Red Jacket*, Captain Hatch of Eastham's *Northern Light*, Captain Sears of Dennis's *Wild Hunter*, Captain Dillingham of Brewster's *Snow Squall*, and Captain Hallet of Yarmouth's *Phantom*, to name a few.

It is said that most Cape Codders knew the sea route to Hong Kong better than the land route to Boston in this era. Daniel Webster once told of a trial at the Barnstable

Court House in which an important issue hinged on the depth of a remote harbor in the Hawaiian Islands. Webster noticed smiles among the jurymen and suggested to the judge that he request those who knew the harbor to stand up. Seven of the twelve rose to the occasion.

By the late 1850s a few people began to realize that the days of sail were numbered, and American supremacy at sea was on its way out almost as quickly as it had arrived. Slowly at first, steam began to take the wind from the clippers' sails. Great Britain and the United States were both introducing steam-driven vessels to compete with the clippers when, in 1856, Congress withdrew support and the field was left to the British. The opening of the West and the accompanying expansion of the railroads drew tremendous amounts of American capital and our merchant marine was doomed as a fading glory. The Civil War prolonged the agony, but each year brought fewer and lighter cargoes. One by one the Cape captains furled their sails for the last time and came home to live. They brought home much more than their fortunes. Each village had its share of these strong-willed and worldly wise giants and village affairs have not experienced a dull day since. When they died they passed on a salty tradition that becomes painfully evident each year in each town right about town meeting time.

As the war clouds approached again in the 1850s, the Cape knew what was coming. Cape Codders were of two minds in earlier wars, but the Civil War found them united.

When President Lincoln issued a call for volunteers, the Cape responded with an enthusiasm which, coming from a maritime community, was surprising. The Cape contributed twenty-five hundred soldiers and about a half million dollars to the cause. Much of her merchant marine remained at sea carrying supplies, and the excitement of war masked the problems brewing for the seagoing Cape. Whaling was in its last days, commercial fishing was transferring to Gloucester and Boston, and commerce and capital were moving westward. Cape Codders blamed their troubles on the war, but when the war ended the bad times came, just as they would have anyway.

Over the next thirty years the population of the Cape shrank from 36,000, to 27,000 as families, young ones in particular, moved inland. Small-scale fishing and farming plus a large measure of Yankee self-reliance kept abject poverty at a minimum. Occasional bright spots, such as the cranberry industry and even bootlegging in the Prohibition era, brought in some needed cash here and there. It was not until 1930 that the Cape's population finally struggled back to its Civil War level.

The railroad opened up the West but almost finished off Cape Cod. When the rails came down the Cape in the 1850s, the packet trade folded as passengers and freight took to the trains. But the railroad did bring many passengers *to* the Cape as well, the summer people, as they were called. There was only a trickle in the first few years. They built their homes on the fashionable south shore, arrived on the Fourth of July and left on Labor Day. The stories of Cape Codders and its summer people are both numerous and humorous — always the stolid native willing to take anything from the off-Cape foreigner, at a price. Up went the "Rooms for Rent" signs and the roadside stands. When the antique craze hit, Cape Codders changed their signs to "Antiques" in season and back to their usual "Junk" shortly after Labor Day.

Sand roads, semi-isolation, and a cantankerous populace supported a sleepy Cape, broken only by the affluent summer people in slowly increasing numbers. Things began to liven up when the canal bridges went up in the thirties; roads were straightened and blacktopped, and the tourists of the forties "discovered" the Cape. From 1940 to 1970 the resident population boomed from 37,000 to 97,000, making Barnstable County currently one of the fastest-growing in the nation. Today on an average summer day there will be 250,000 to 500,000 visitors on the Cape. This tremendous growth has changed the character of the Cape, of course, but a lot of the old shines through to complement the new.

Cape Cod today consists of fifteen towns, each comprised of several villages. These villages are a somewhat confusing anomaly to the visitor, for they often have undefinable boundaries, no political significance, and no common bond except perhaps pride and a post office. Each town generally has a village within it by the same name, and more than one flustered visitor isn't sure if he is talking about Barnstable town or Barnstable village when a conversation is over. When an old-timer refers to the village of Yarmouth he is more than likely talking about the area from the firehouse east on Route 6A, whereas many of the residents are under the impression they live in Yarmouth Port.

Nebulous or not, many of the villages have strong bonds of local pride and they have been known to fight any remaking of their theoretical boundaries. The hamlet of Hyannis Port was up in arms in 1972 to exclude a new housing development that met with their disapproval. With no legal definition of village boundaries, the practical decision rests with the post offices — they decide between themselves which one can most conveniently serve an area. In this case mail delivery was RFD from Hyannis, so that *should* settle that one.

Village streets within a town are often a bit perplexing. Union Street in Yarmouth becomes Station Avenue as soon as it bumps into South Yarmouth — both villages are in the same town, of course. Route 28 west of Hyannis has an old name that changes each time you pass through another village: Marstons Mills Road, Hyannis Road, Falmouth Road. Luckily, it is better known as Route 28. Route 6A through Yarmouth is perhaps the best example. From the Barnstable line to the firehouse is commonly known as Hallet Street. From there to the Dennis line it is just as well known as Main Street. Route 6A and the Cranberry Highway are official names for the same stretch. If none of these suit you as a mailing address, how about the King's Highway, as it was known before crowns became unpopular, or perhaps Grand Army of the Republic Highway, the name that took its place? Choose what you will, it won't matter to the postmaster. He knows everyone on the street anyway.

We also have our superhighway, Route 6 or the Mid-Cape Highway, a well-landscaped ribbon that bisects the Cape from the Sagamore Bridge to Provincetown. Don't expect to see anything from it — not to belittle its wooded setting — but it's a dandy way to get from here to there. If you're looking for the scenic route, try Route 6A along the Bay shore.

As you read this book and travel up and down the highways of the Cape, you'll encounter the expressions "up Cape" and "down Cape," "upper Cape" and "lower Cape." When the Pilgrims landed at Provincetown they explored "up the Cape," and so it has been ever since. To many people it seems the reverse of what it should be, but nothing is going to change it. "Up Cape" is toward the mainland, "down Cape" toward Provincetown. "Upper Cape" towns, then, are those nearest the mainland, such as Bourne, Sandwich, Falmouth, and Mashpee. "Lower Cape" towns definitely include Eastham, Wellfleet, Truro, and Provincetown. The rest may be considered "upper," "mid," or "lower" Cape depending on your point of view. I always considered Yarmouth a mid-Cape town until I heard a Truro man refer to it as upper Cape. These regional designations are sometimes as flexible as village boundaries.

A good map of the Cape is essential to any visitor. Many of the villages, clearly dotted on the map, are so small that you can pass through them and never know you've been there.

Good maps are hard to find. If you wish to explore the nooks and crannies of the Cape I suggest you equip yourself with a set of town maps. Almost every town has an information booth in the summer season and most provide relatively good complimentary town maps. The F. J. Miller Company publishes a set of four maps covering the Cape, and several other commercial maps are available from Cape bookstores and other shops. The Cape Cod Chamber of Commerce distributes a general map of the Cape and oil company maps are available, but neither are particularly good. The best overall map is the Cape Cod Vacation Map published by The National Survey, Chester, Vermont. It is available free from its fifty advertisers. The Cape Cod Chamber of Commerce also receives limited supplies and can secure more at 25 cents each.

The old saw, "If you don't like the weather, wait a minute," is appropriate to the Cape. There is never a month when you can't find a nice day to play golf or picnic on the beach. Few if any Cape Codders own, much less use, an umbrella. When the rain persists it's more than likely accompanied by a wind that would undoubtedly blow the darned thing inside out anyway. The wind is the Cape's blessing and its scourge. If the wind is west to south — and there is a lot of this in the summer season — good weather usually prevails. But if it backs around to the east, look for rain, fog and dismal days. If the wind is from the west to north quarter, it'll be cold and icy in winter, but cool and beautiful in summer. Then again, we have our no'theasters. They are a part of life and the less said about them the better. As a resort area, our beautiful summer weather is our glory. But what about the rest of the year?

Those who live on the Cape year round are in general agreement that our fall weather is unsurpassed anywhere. From Labor Day until well into November the weather is generally cool, clear and sunny. Beaches that were too crowded to enjoy before Labor Day still have a few weeks of fine swimming left. After that they are perfect for some of the most memorable walks you'll ever take. Shells and driftwood, breakers and dunes — it's soothing yet invigorating in the clean, cool and crisp air of the Cape.

Our fall foliage may not be as dramatic as some in New

England, but try Route 6A from Sandwich through Brewster on a sunny afternoon in the autumn. The blazing red maples, yellow elms and tawny oaks of the Cranberry Highway frame some of the most picturesque old homes, ancient Capes and stately captains houses that you'll see anywhere.

The vast majority of the vacationing public — families with school-age children and the college crowd — are pretty well limited in their choice of vacation dates. For those with a flexible schedule I heartily recommend Cape Cod in Indian summer. The Cape is at its uncrowded best, many points of interest are still open, and the weather is glorious.

As the leaves fall and an unaccustomed sharp chill comes to the air, the age-old resort area question comes to mind, "What in the world do you do in the winter?" A crusty old Cape Codder might well reply, "We fumigate the place and go on living!" Actually, the winter, or off-season, is when Cape residents relax, look around, and begin to appreciate the beauty and opportunities that surround them.

They say it snows very little on the Cape and they are right; I have gone through more than one winter in which I needed no more than a broom to sweep the snow off the front walk. Then again, on March 13, 1897, the *Yarmouth Register* reported that the snow had finally disappeared for the first time since December. Take your choice; we get less than Boston or New York but we do have snow!

The winter climate on the Cape is not ideal, but it's certainly better than most. The golfers are out one day and holed up like moles the next. Our family has a traditional beach picnic each year after Thanksgiving; bundled up next to a blazing fire it's great fun. Even in the dead of winter, crisp, clear days will draw many outdoors for a walk on the beach or the National Seashore trails, or a round of golf.

Dozens of lakes and ponds dot the Cape like the measles, and they come into their own in winter. The cran-

berry bogs are flooded and they and the more shallow
ponds are great for ice skating — an old-fashioned kind
of skating with lots of beach fires, kids, hockey sticks and
ladies balancing themselves with brooms and old chairs.

For many, winter is the social season on Cape Cod. The
resident population of the Cape today is a pretty intelligent and cosmopolitan group from every stratum of society. They all have one thing in common: they are on
the Cape because they want to be! Almost no one lives on
the Cape because he was transferred here or his particular skill demands it. Those earning a living on the Cape
could usually do better, in dollars, elsewhere. But here
they are, young and old, rich and poor, working and retired, with one thing in common — they are here because
they want to be. The social life can be what you want it
to be, a party every night or merely friendly chatter over
the hedge. Age, background and position are of little
value on today's Cape; interests, hobbies and civic affairs
are much more important.

Year-round Cape residents are avid students, joiners
and hobbyists, perhaps because of the large proportion of
retired people. In 1972 approximately one quarter of our
citizens were sixty or older, and their Social Security and
Medicare checks, not to mention private pensions and the
like, accounted for more than 10 percent of the Cape's
gross income. Adult education courses in any conceivable
subject are offered by the Community College and the
high schools. Many are so enthusiastically received that
there is a waiting list from one year to the next. Arts and
crafts are extremely popular and clubs on the Cape cover
almost every subject of interest.

Spring is a different story. I will be the first to admit
that spring has seen greater glories elsewhere. The summer is fun, the fall is glorious, the winter is better than
most, but the spring — ugh! It has been said that winter
ends and summer begins on the Fourth of July. Spring *is*
late, but it's not as bad as all that. Friends from New
York, Boston and Connecticut all remark how their tulips

and daffodils are all gone and here ours are just getting started — in May! Our spring is late, brief, and except for those few glorious days, most uninteresting.

In 1956 a local weekly newspaper broke a story that kept the Cape boiling for ten years and still simmers on the back burner even today. The story announced that plans were going forward to create a Cape Cod National Seashore. Battle lines quickly formed. Seashore proponents argued for the protection of the towns from overdevelopment; opponents feared the loss of tax revenue and argued for home rule. By September 1959 a formal bill was introduced in the U.S. Senate and on August 7, 1961, the establishment of the Cape Cod National Seashore was written into law.

The bounds of the National Seashore cover 27,000 acres in six towns: Chatham, Orleans, Eastham, Wellfleet, Truro and Provincetown. The federal government now has title to 18,200 acres, the towns 2,100 acres, and private owners about 7,000 acres. Those private owners whose land was improved with a private residence before September 1959 — about 500 homes on 1,300 acres — may continue their ownership ad infinitum, subject to the strict zoning laws enacted for all National Seashore property. The balance will be purchased for the National Seashore over a period of time. Most owners will be permitted twenty-five-year or life tenancy, but the end is inevitable. Town-owned property, primarily beaches, cannot be taken without the town's consent. The National Seashore is well on its way toward assuring this and future generations the opportunity to enjoy the outstanding scenic, historical, and recreational resources to be found on Cape Cod.

Most Cape residents today would agree that the National Seashore has been in their own best interests as well. There is no doubt that visitors are pleased with it. Except for room and board and a small beach parking fee, one can easily fill a two-week vacation by taking advantage of the free services and facilities it offers.

The current beach parking fee is $1 per car per day, or for $10 you may purchase a Golden Eagle pass, which also entitles you to visit any other national park during the calendar year. Foreign nationals and senior citizens are admitted free. The Cape Cod National Seashore offers beaches, nature trails, bicycle paths, over-sand vehicle routes, museums, films, illustrated evening programs, craft instruction, surf and shellfishing demonstrations, and surf rescue exhibitions. You can follow the nature trails yourself, or take guided tours conducted by staff members well versed in the history and ecology of the area. Among those available on a scheduled basis in summer and early fall are bird walks, children's field trips, seashore tours, sketching trips, sunset campfire walks, and night prowls. Brochures are available that provide current information on any of these activities.

Town-owned beaches are maintained and administered by the individual towns, and each one has different rules. Parking at town beaches is free in only a few towns; most charge a daily fee and offer seasonal parking stickers. The seasonal price ranges widely, from a dollar or two up to $20 or $30 in some of the mid-Cape towns. Some offer limited one- and two-week parking stickers at a reduced price. Check with each town's Information Booth or at the Town Hall for detailed information. In all fairness to the towns, there is only one that meets its beach expenses by revenue from parking fees.

Shellfishing regulations also vary widely in each town. Most will charge a visitor from $2 to $5 for a family shellfishing permit. Regulations concerning open and closed shellfishing areas, days they may be taken, and family limits are variable and you should request a copy of the current regulations when you secure your permit. You'll find soft shell clams, sea clams, quahogs, scallops and razor clams a lot of fun to gather and mighty tasty fresh from the sea. Quahogs, pronounced *co*-hogs, are what many call "cherrystones" or "little necks." Call them anything, but don't call them clams.

Cities and towns across the nation are becoming choked with their own debris, the air above filled with noxious vapors and their waterways and lakes polluted. The air is clear and clean on the Cape, ponds and streams are relatively unpolluted, the streets are free of litter, and the town dumps — well, where else can you see a million seagulls at one time? In most localities, the town dump is merely where you or the garbage collector dumps the trash. Not so on the Cape, where the town dump is also a social center (Ours has been toned up in recent years by changing the name of the entrance from Dump Road to Old Town House Road. Yarmouth doesn't want just anybody's trash — you have to have a ticket to get in!)

You don't need a ticket to visit the Cape, yet, and the Cape Cod Chamber of Commerce is always standing by to help the visitor. There are three information centers covering the whole Cape and nearly every town has its own in season. The headquarters of the Cape Cod Chamber is located just off Exit 6 of the Mid-Cape Highway (Route 6). It is open all year and is well equipped for just about any information or assistance a visitor is likely to require. In addition to its mid-Cape headquarters, the Chamber of Commerce maintains two seasonal booths at the Cape Cod Canal, one on the mainland end of the Sagamore Bridge, the other on the Cape side of the Bourne Bridge. It publishes the *Sportsman's Guide to Fresh and Saltwater Fishing* for fishermen and *A Wonderful Way of Life* for those interested in living permanently on the Cape. Requests for information, maps or booklets should be addressed to the Cape Cod Chamber of Commerce, Hyannis, Mass. 02601.

The old Cape Cod of shipwrecks and whales seems a bit distant now, but the shadows of the past still fall across the narrow land to remind us that things may not have changed so much after all. Recently a Cape fishing boat went aground on Old Man Shoals, was pounded apart by the sea, and the two-man crew lost. Modern "mooncussers" stripped the beached wreck. Not long ago, a 25-foot white whale was spotted in the Hog Island channel of the canal. Occasional whales are still washed up on Cape beaches, but nowadays it's a job for the garbage collector rather than the tryworks.

That about completes the circle. Now let's take a look at each of the towns, its history and character, and the points of interest you can expect to find.

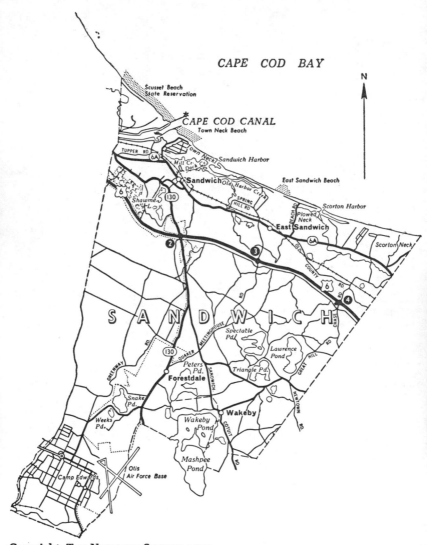

CAPE COD BAY

N

Scusset Beach
State Reservation

CAPE COD CANAL
Town Neck Beach

TUPPER RD.

6A

Mill Cr.
Dock

Town Neck

Sandwich Harbor

Sandwich

Old Harbor Cr.

East Sandwich Beach

130

SPRING
HILL RD

Shawme L.

Scorton Harbor

Plowed
Neck

East Sandwich

2

3

6A

Scorton Neck

COUNTY

S A N D W I C H

RD.

6

RD.

4

CHASE

MEETINGHOUSE

Spectacle
Pd.

Lawrence
Pond

GREENWAY

130

QUAKER

Peters
Pd.

SANDWICH

Triangle Pd.

GREAT HILL RD.

NEWTOWN RD.

Forestdale

Snake
Pd.

Wakeby

Weeks
Pd.

Wakeby
Pond

COTUIT

RD.

Mashpee
Pond

Camp Edwards

Otis
Air Force Base

Copyright, THE NATIONAL SURVEY, 1973
Chester, Vermont

CHAPTER II

Sandwich

The first settlers in Sandwich came "to worship God and make money" — not a bad combination if done honestly on both counts. Sandwich men have never been known to shirk their responsibilities in either regard, at times with a vengeance. With ups and downs aplenty, Sandwich has managed to keep the faith.

By 1627 the Plymouth Colony had established the Aptucxet Trading Post at the headwaters of the Manomet River. Traders found that vessels that sailed up Scusset Creek required only a short portage to the river, providing a water link between Plymouth and the Connecticut River and New York — the forerunner of the Cape Cod Canal.

In 1630 the Plymouth Colony secured a patent that included the entire Cape in its domain. New settlers to Plymouth and Massachusetts Bay were looking for new worlds to conquer. One, Edmund Freeman of Saugus (now Lynn), was the first of many to choose Cape Cod. The governor's consent was given in 1637 and Freeman and nine others set out to establish a settlement for sixty families across the Scusset. The "ten men of Saugus" slogged through the woods and began to clear the land and build their homes at the present site of Sandwich.

Sandwich, or Manomet as it was then known, had quite a bit to offer: salt hay from the marshes for the cattle, lumber from the thick forests, herring in the creek for food and fertilizer, and a navigable stream to the Bay.

A score or more families from Plymouth, Duxbury and Saugus followed almost immediately, and others filtered in as the town grew and prospered. Two years after Edmund Freeman and his fellows arrived, the settlement was incorporated and named Sandwich after the English town that many had so recently left.

Soon after the first families arrived a church was founded, with the Reverend William Leveridge as minister. The good Mr. Leveridge was the first of a long line of Sandwich shepherds to fail to measure up to the standards of his flock. His views questionable and his sermons boring, he was harassed sufficiently to find Long Island more inviting. Other parsons followed, contentious every one, with Quaker missionaries from Rhode Island adding to the turmoil. Men who left England dedicated to religious freedom established Congregationalism as the orthodox religion. True to the mother country's tradition, the Puritans wanted not only to enjoy their own freedom of religion, but also to prevent anyone else from enjoying his.

The first Quaker missionaries were warned out of town quite quickly, but not before converting several families. Stephen Wing, Sandwich's first Quaker, was one of those who considered the orthodox Congregationalism insufferable and the long-winded parson a jackass. When the missionaries called on him to "quake at the word of the Lord," he quaked. Within the year seventeen families of Sandwich joined him in his new faith. Similar troubles boiled throughout the colony. The government held that theirs was the one true faith. Those who disagreed, whether Episcopalians or Quakers, were heretics. There was considerable sympathy for these "heretics," but the authorities managed to find men, righteous men and rascals, to inflict the penalties of imprisonment, whipping, fines, excommunication and disenfranchisement. Charles II ordered all persecution to cease in 1665, but it took

more than thirty years for the idea to begin to filter down
to Sandwich. As late as 1715 the orthodox Reverend Cotton was voted the privilege of pasturing his horse in the
Quaker cemetery.

The early men of Sandwich were no more free to choose
their occupation than they were to choose their religion.
They had to be farmers or starve. Every family was self-
supporting. Most had some cattle and sheep, and family
members milked the cows, sheared their own sheep, spun
the wool, and made their own clothes. Cultivated land
yielded fine crops of corn, beans, and onions; the salt flats
were generous with clams; the Bay teemed with fish and
lobsters; and game was abundant in the forests. Beef,
ham and mutton were available for special occasions but
far too valuable for everyday fare. Corn was the accepted
medium of exchange; corn in the crib was their money in
the bank. It is said that there was not £500 cash money
in the whole Plymouth Colony in 1675.

Soon after their arrival the colonists were also farming
the beaches, as dead whales washed ashore. By 1653 the
town fathers saw the need to regulate this gift of the sea
and declared the beach common land and the proceeds to
be divided equally among the householders of the town.
The omnipresent Plymouth government had other ideas,
demanding one hogshead of oil from each whale. Farmers
soon tired of waiting for stranded whales and devised
ways to force the whales ashore. What began as a diversion from farming rapidly developed into an industry
of its own. As long as the supply of whales held out, shore
whaling was highly profitable. The young found it an
exciting occupation after the dreariness of farming, and
the fledgling Cape Cod whaleman was born.

The constant activity of scores of whalemen soon
chased the whales out of the Bay, and by the 1750s only
an occasional whale was sighted close to shore. Now was
the time to follow them to deep water. Sandwich, without
a decent harbor, was at a disadvantage and sent out only
two vessels. Nor did Sandwich figure very large in the

two other major maritime industries of the Cape: large-scale fishing and the deepwater merchant marine. Sandwich had its share of fishermen, and hundreds of its men paced the quarterdeck and manned the sheets of clippers and whalers. But most sailed from other ports.

Sandwich did, however, attract two large manufacturing industries to the Cape. The Boston and Sandwich Glass Company, of Sandwich glass fame, came in 1825, closely followed by Keith and Ryder, transport manufacturers, in 1826. They made everything from stagecoaches and prairie schooners to railway freight cars in their 102 years of operation. Sandwich also produced its captain of industry, Gustavus Swift, who rose from selling pigs on the Cape to found the Swift and Company empire, the great meatpacking house in Chicago. His success was predicated on the idea that "all parts of the hog were used except the squeal."

Sandwich today is a sleepy little town of 5,300 souls who enjoy what they have and hope to keep it that way. The town covers 42.6 square miles and consists of six villages: Sandwich, East Sandwich, South Sandwich, Wakeby, Forestdale and Farmersville. Sandwich is representative of the very old Cape and has much to offer the visitor tracing the threads of history.

SHAWME LAKE

A painter would find it difficult to improve on the sylvan setting that forms the focal point of Sandwich village. Rimmed by drooping willows over soft green banks, Shawme Lake (pronounced *Shawm*) is the jewel of one of the handsomest villages in the country.

Long ago there was merely a brook running from a small pond in the woods to the Bay. To secure water power, the early settlers dammed the brook in the vicinity of the present Town Hall and Shawme Lake was created. Shortly thereafter, another dam was placed between Shawme Lake and the original pond, creating Upper Shawme Lake. The lower pond is most familiar to visitors.

Town Hall, Dexter's Grist Mill, the Hoxie House, and the old cemetery all grace its shores. The First Church of Christ with its Christopher Wren steeple, the Sandwich Glass Museum, the John Pope House, and Thornton Burgess's birthplace are all within a stone's throw. There are also many other fine old homes overlooking the lake (almost all from a respectable distance I am pleased to say). Look closely between Town Hall and the entrance to the mill and you will find fish ladders up which a small-scale herring run takes place each spring. The townspeople are justifiably proud of the ducks, geese and other wildlife that have been enticed to settle about the old pond.

From the Hoxie House grounds, look across the lake to the old cemetery — the resting place of Cape Cod's first settlers — on a beautiful spit of land projecting into the lake. Its burial records go back to 1663, when the town purchased the land for £3.7.4, $8.08 at current exchange rates. The oldest marker now standing is dated 1680. The Reverend Thomas Tupper, one of the "ten men from Saugus" lies here, as do the two wives of Richard Bourne, famed minister to the Mashpee Indians. Many of the earliest headstones have crumbled away or become illegible.

DEXTER'S GRIST MILL

Just behind the Town Hall, straddling the brook feeding Shawme Lake, stands Thomas Dexter's Grist Mill. The town records of June 26, 1654, refer to an agreement with "Tho. Dexter to go on to build the mill new againe." The mill continued in service until the latter years of the nineteenth century, when modern milling methods gradually replaced the old water-driven grist mills.

When the last miller, William Nye, closed down for lack of trade, the mill lay idle until it was restored by the town in 1961. During the restoration it was necessary to remove post-seventeenth-century additions in order to portray an authentic, working grist mill of the 1650s. The mill machinery is of the earliest type used in this country;

the water wheel, drive shaft and gears are made of wood and are driven by water power from the Mill Pond. A miller is on hand daily to demonstrate how corn was ground in Thomas Dexter's day. Corn meal ground at the mill is for sale and recipes are available for those who wish to do some old-fashioned baking. A nominal admission fee is charged and the mill is open from mid-June to the end of September.

CAPE COD'S OLDEST HOUSE (1637)

High on a knoll overlooking Shawme Lake in the center of Sandwich sits the Hoxie House (1637). To reach it take Route 130 toward Forestdale from the Town Hall area. It's only a few hundred yards away, by the lake to your right.

The Hoxie House is generally considered to be the oldest house on the Cape. Proof is difficult and the often-reported 1637 chimney brick is yet to be found. There is, however, no doubt that it *is* very old. The house is named after Captain Abraham Hoxie, a whaling captain who owned the house in the middle 1800s. Other reliable records report the house as early as 1688, when it was occupied by the Reverend John Smith, his wife and thirteen children. This was another gentleman "whose tolerant principles had rendered him obnoxious to the majority," and he took his leave to New York.

There are many interesting features in this classic salt box home of the 1600s: gunstock corner posts, chamfered beams, wide board floors, tiny windows, thick walls and great sill seats for the youngsters in the days when chairs were at a premium. The restoration has maintained the seventeenth-century character of the house, and the furnishings loaned by the Boston Museum of Fine Arts are representative of the period. The admission fee includes a guided tour highlighting the most interesting features. Hoxie House is open to the public from about mid-June to the end of September.

THE BOSTON AND SANDWICH GLASS COMPANY

In 1825 Deming Jarves came down from Boston to propose a new industry for the town. It wasn't the sand that attracted the glass-maker to Sandwich. Too much iron in the Cape Cod sand caused odd-colored glass and bubbly textures. Jarves saw the prime requisite of a glass works in the great oak and white pine forests — fuel to keep the furnaces hot! In that same year the factory went up, skilled workmen were brought in, and production was begun.

The Boston and Sandwich Glass Company was a sizable operation in its day. The company built homes for the expatriate workmen, set up company stores, operated its own water transportation system and ran what amounted to a major lumbering industry. The company owned and operated 2,000 acres of forest land to keep the fires going. At the peak of production in the 1850s, the plant employed 500 men and boys and turned out $600,000 worth of glass per year. Most of the glass was inexpensive and practical: tableware, lamp chimneys, candlesticks, and novelties.

Every known type of glassware was produced here; pressed and lace glass originated here. Exceptional colors and tones were developed and it is said that the golden ruby, jade green, sapphire blue and opalescent tints from Sandwich have never been equaled. Presentation pieces and spare-time creations of the Sandwich craftsmen were often etched, engraved, cut, and otherwise decorated to the highest standards of the glassmaker's art. At its prime, Sandwich, the Town of Glass, was the glass capital of the world, complete with fortunes for some and an envied reputation for all.

As interesting as the spectacular ascent of the industry, and even more rapid, was its decline. The immediate cause of the shutdown of the factory in 1888 was a disagreement between management and labor over wages. This merely hastened the inevitable. Other more mechanized factories were fast gaining ground in Pittsburgh and Chicago and the craftsmanship of Sandwich was rapidly becoming obsolete. Sandwich glass has not always been the collector's dream. Modern (1900) styles in glass relegated much of the Sandwich artisans' work to the attic or cellar, even on the Cape. It took another thirty years before the antique collectors and glass buffs began to stir some interest, and once underway, the quest for its possession has never diminished. Counterfeiting is rampant and it takes an expert to differentiate a fake from the genuine article. Glass being subject to breakage, and considering the artistry of the French, English, Belgian and American "gaffers" at Sandwich, the future value of Sandwich glass appears quite secure.

There is now very little at the site of the factory. A bronze tablet was placed and dedicated on July 15, 1951, which depicts the old factory complex in relief. To reach it take Jarves Street across Route 6A to the end, where it joins Factory Street. The bronze tablet is mounted in a small park area there.

SANDWICH GLASS MUSEUM

The Sandwich Historical Society's Glass Museum is located directly across from the Town Hall on Town Hall Square in the center of Sandwich village. Admission fees are charged to further the work and objectives of the society. The museum is open from April to about the end of November.

Founded in 1907, the Sandwich Historical Society took an early interest in the collection and display of Sandwich memorabilia, antiques, and of course the products of its most illustrious manufacturing industry of the past, the Boston and Sandwich Glass Company.

In 1922 the society moved an old building (1813) to the present site of the Glass Museum; it is now the entrance and lobby of the museum. It is reported that this structure was originally used as a barn or stable and was the object of one of the more romantic legends of Sandwich. The tale concerns a parishioner of another faith who constructed his barn to face the entrance of the Congregational Church, thereby conveying his rather odorous opinion of the Congregationalist faithful. As to whether or not this particular building is the original "spite barn" remains a bit cloudy.

The same year the Sandwich Women's Club presented the society with the colonial doorway that now graces the front entrance. The structure was thoroughly renovated over the years, a second floor laid and additional land acquired for parking. A new fireproof wing, the Deming Jarves Memorial Wing, was completed in 1957. The Craftsman wing was added in 1959, the Pratt wing in 1961, and a large new addition was completed in 1972.

The museum today consists primarily of many outstanding private Sandwich glass collections on loan to the society. The absence of distinguishing or identifying marks on Sandwich glass has always plagued collectors. Only by diligent study and careful comparison is it possible for the society to live up to its aim not to display any questionable glass. Many of the prize pieces of the collections are the "end of the day" or "offhand" creations of individual workers on their own time. These pieces are rare and quite beautiful, for many of the men were true artists. They spent many evenings at the glass house making trinkets and ornaments for their homes and for their wives and sweethearts. These items are generally one of a kind, not subject to counterfeiting, and readily recognizable by experts as genuine Sandwich glass. Presentation pieces, fashioned for Presidents, princes and famous personalities, also highlight many of the best qualities of the Sandwich glassmaker's art.

The museum also offers a faithful reproduction of the glass plant as it looked in 1850 and a diorama of how glass was made in its heyday. The diorama is a model, scaled one inch to the foot, built by faculty and students of the Massachusetts Institute of Technology around 1940. The scene depicts glassblowers or "gaffers" in action, some using the blowing iron or pontil rod, others using glass molds, and an apprentice is placing tumblers in the annealing kiln to gradually cool the finished glass.

Many other items are worth seeing here, including glassblowing tools and molds, the bell from the old glass factory, and a map of Cape Cod constructed of bits of Sandwich glass. There are also numerous antiques and memorabilia, including a musket with a history and a case of trinkets from one of the renowned seagoing wives of the mid-1800s.

The musket was presented to the society as *the* musket that shot the last wolf in the Sandwich woods. Other muskets have been known to dispute the claim. Wolves were a major problem in the area for over two hundred years, so much so that it was once proposed to build a wall across the Cape to keep them out. The bounty on them ranged upwards of £2, a lot of money in those days. The last wolf was probably killed in about 1846.

Hannah Rebecca Burgess was the sea captain's wife who bequeathed a case of souvenirs from her many voyages to the Sandwich Historical Society. Her husband, Captain William Howes Burgess of the clipper *Challenger*, was a Brewster man who met his Sandwich bride while his ship was under construction nearby. After many voyages, including crossing the equator eleven times in four years, she and her husband were bound for France with a cargo of guano. Captain Burgess suddenly became seriously ill with the nearest medical attention 22 days' sail away in Valparaiso, Chile. Hannah, the only competent navigator aboard, was equal to the task. The captain was not, however, and died at age twenty-seven only two days from port. The captain's remains were returned and buried in the West Sandwich (Sagamore) cemetery. The grave is marked by a tall column facing Route 6A. Hannah lived to be eighty-three and now rests beside her husband.

JOHN POPE HOUSE (1699)

Around the corner from Town Hall, on Grove Street at the corner of Academy Street, stands the 1699 home of John Pope, a monument to Sandwich cussedness. John's father, Seth Pope, was a common peddler thought not to be sufficiently upright and worthy, and therefore warned out of town lest he become a public charge. Seth was not one to take the insult lightly and left no doubt behind as to his opinion of the town and town fathers.

New Bedford proved more tolerant of Seth's talents and he prospered economically, socially, and politically. In 1699 he returned to Sandwich and "purchased nearly all the land in the village." He built fine homes for his sons and announced his revenge. His children could stay if they chose, but as for him, he "would not live in the damned town," and off he went again.

The house is privately owned and is not open to visitors.

THORNTON BURGESS'S BIRTHPLACE

It may be news to children today, but their parents and grandparents will well remember Peter Rabbit and his briar patch. Peter Rabbit, created by the English writer Beatrix Potter in 1903, later became a childhood chum of millions of American youngsters through the gifted pen of Thornton W. Burgess (1874–1965).

Burgess, the creator of Jerry Muskrat, Reddy Fox, Sammy Jay, and many other entertaining animal friends, was born at 6 School Street, a short way in from Main Street on the right. After many moves within Sandwich, Burgess graduated from Sandwich High School and moved to Somerville to find a trade. Brief encounters with book-keeping and sales convinced him he was not cut out for the business world, and he was delighted to land an office boy's position with a small publisher in Springfield in 1895.

Within a few years his children's stories began to appear, but it was not until he had a young son of his own to entertain that Peter and his friends scampered out of the brambles and into the hearts of the children of America. His first book was a collection of stories, *Old Mother West Wind,* published in 1910. He is most famous for his *Bedtime Stories,* among the best sellers of his day. His Sandwich boyhood memories of forests, fields, marshes and brambles provided the setting for his little animal heroes. A master storyteller and a competent naturalist, Thornton W. Burgess captured young imaginations by presenting homespun natural history in fable form.

FIRST PARISH MEETING HOUSE • YESTERYEARS DOLL MUSEUM

In 1638 the first settlers of Sandwich chose the site for their meeting house a short way up Main Street where the old First Parish Meeting House stands today. Parts of the original building are still there — split in half and widened, split front to rear and lengthened, and finally raised and a new ground floor built underneath. To see the original beams you have to visit the attic, a hair-raising experience. The last renovation was in about 1833, but there is no doubt that sections of the structure go back to close to two hundred years before that.

This church received a gift from Titus Winchester, a Negro slave freed on the death of his master in 1784. Titus then shipped out on a whaler and willed his estate to buy a clock and bell for the church. Since the meeting house was then also used as the town hall, there was a difference of opinion as to who had the rights to the clock and bell when the new town hall was built in 1834. A hurricane resolved that dispute in 1854 by destroying the tower. The present clock and bell tower was a gift of Jonathan Bourne, a whaling tycoon born in Sandwich.

The stained-glass windows in the meeting house were donated by Deming Jarves of the Boston and Sandwich Glass Company. One can only presume that they are the only Sandwich stained-glass church windows on record.

The First Parish Meeting House is now operated as a

private nonprofit museum. Yesteryears Doll and Miniature Museum, which houses antique dolls, dollhouses, doll furnishings, and other doll accessories from all over the world. It is undoubtedly a rare collection.

Yesteryears Doll Museum is open from 10 A.M. to 5 P.M. from Memorial Day to Columbus Day and occasional weekends earlier and later in the season. An admission fee is charged.

HERITAGE PLANTATION

In 1917 Charles Dexter and Paul Frost, a famous landscape architect, created a spectacular garden, profuse with rhododendrons and azaleas, on Dexter's estate in Sandwich. In more recent years the 76-acre estate has been expanded and developed to include many museums and replica buildings of early America.

In addition to the gardens and grounds, which are served by free jitneys that you can hop on and off at convenient locations, the plantation offers a replica of a round stone Shaker barn, a working windmill of 1800, a replica of Washington's "Publick House" of 1783, an old barn general store and an arts and crafts building full of old treasures. Each structure houses a different collection of great interest.

The round Shaker barn is copied from the original one built in Hancock, Massachusetts, in 1826. It displays an exceptional collection of antique automobiles in mind condition. Thirty-five stand on the two floors of the museum at any one time, with one set aside for children to climb aboard. Old-time one-reelers of Charlie Chaplin and the Keystone Kops are shown and a diorama reenacts the auto racing of the early 1900s. The barn has room for only part of the total collection and changes are often made during the season.

The 1800 windmill was moved to the site in sections from Orleans in 1967. Rather than trust the winds, the mill is now operated electrically to demonstrate the grinding of corn to visitors.

The "Publick House" is a replica of the Continental Army's first social installation built at Washington's cantonment at Windsor, New York, in 1783. The original building served as church, activity center and reception hall for the post. Quite fittingly, the Publick House at Sandwich now serves as a military museum, featuring antique firearms, collections of miniature soldiers depicting units from 1621 to 1900, and a complete collection of flags flown over America — from the "Raven Flag" of the Vikings to the Imperial Russian flag once flown over Alaska.

An old barn serves as a general store for visitors and a relatively new building is devoted to the arts and crafts of yesteryear. One wing features a collection of early American paintings, wood carvings, scrimshaw, glassware, trade signs, weathervanes, tinware, cigar store figures and ceramics. Another wing houses an extensive collection of early American tools and a workshop. The central attraction is an operable, antique carrousel, c. 1912, a free ride for the children and a pleasant reminder for the older folks.

Several musical pageants are held on summer weekends. Scot's Highlanders, fife and drum bands, symphony orchestras and other attractions appear on the Parade Grounds from time to time. Picnic grounds are also available. Charming trails and paths abound for those who merely wish to wander through the beautiful grounds. By the Publick House is Upper Shawme Lake, the little pond in the hills dammed and enlarged by the first settlers.

Heritage Plantation is open from 10 A.M. to 5 P.M. from May to mid-October. An admission fee is charged. To reach the plantation follow Grove Street out from Town Hall Square; plan on spending several hours here.

SADDLE AND PILLION

In the early days many couples rode two to a horse, the husband in the saddle and the wife on the pillion behind. Edmund Freeman and his wife, Elizabeth, rode together through a happy life of fifty-nine years of marriage. When Elizabeth died in 1676, Edmund buried her on a knoll near their home, using as a headstone a large circular flat rock resembling a pillion. Beside it he placed another stone shaped like a saddle. When Edmund died at ninety-two he was buried under the saddle as he had requested.

To reach the Saddle and Pillion take Route 6A to the westerly of the two entrances to Tupper Road. A hundred yards in on the right, at a break in the stone wall, is a sign and path leading to the graves in a charming wooded bower.

A bit farther down Tupper Road on the left is a historical marker on the site of the homestead of the Reverend Thomas Tupper, another of the "ten men from Saugus," whose descendant Sir Charles Tupper was premier of Canada in 1863.

THE GREEN MONSTER

The Canal Electric Company's Sandwich facility, looming on the skyline off Tupper Road over by the canal, has been not-so-affectionately dubbed "The Green Monster" by local residents. A monster it is, capable of producing 560,000 kilowatts of electricity per hour, or the equivalent of seven times as much power as is required to meet the present maximum load requirements of all Cape Cod. An expansion program is underway to triple the capacity of this key link in the New England power chain. By far the largest Sandwich taxpayer, about 40 percent at present, Canal Electric may be contributing as much as 60 percent of Sandwich's tax revenue by 1977. (A monster like that can't be all bad.)

The plant is not open to the general public but group tours may be arranged for interested organizations.

THE SANDWICH FISH HATCHERY

A few yards east of the junction of Main Street and Route 6A is the tree-lined entrance to the Sandwich Fish

Hatchery. It's open to the public free of charge from 9 A.M. to 4 P.M. daily throughout the year.

In 1912 the Commonwealth of Massachusetts purchased two hatcheries from the privately owned Sandwich Trout Company. The other, still in operation, is located on Old County Road in Sandwich but is not open to the public. Both are managed by the Division of Fisheries and Game in the State Department of Natural Resources.

These hatcheries raise three species of trout to stock the lakes, ponds and streams of Barnstable County and some surrounding areas: rainbow and brown trout primarily for the lakes and ponds and brook trout for the streams. The hatcheries have produced as much as 149,000 pounds of trout per year but presently operate on a yearly quota of about 100,000 pounds. These are two of the few hatcheries in the area that keep their own brood stock and take their own eggs. Spawning season, from late October to early December, is an excellent time to visit; you can watch the men take the eggs and prepare them for hatching.

Hatchery staff choose only the best trout as brood stock. Along about late October the fish start indicating a readiness to spawn, digging in the gravel and fattening up in general. An experienced hand can tell by feel if a particular trout is ready or still a week or two off. As they ripen, groups of males and females are netted and placed in tubs of shallow water, just deep enough to keep the fish comfortable but easy to control. Experienced "strippers" then remove the eggs from the females and sperm from the males by an expert squeeze and squirt into a pan or pail. The eggs and sperm are mixed in a ratio of two female trout for each male. As the pails become full they are thoroughly washed with fresh water. The eggs soon expand to about twice their original size and take on a firmer consistency so that they bounce like a rubber ball. After sterilization by a chemical process, the eggs are placed in troughs and stored under controlled conditions until they hatch, normally about 55 days later. Each female trout produces one to two thousand eggs once a year. For breeding purposes, four- to five-year-old rainbow and brown trout females are chosen and two- to three-year-old brookies. The brood males are one or two years younger.

The 100,000 pounds of trout produced here will average down to about 100,000 to 150,000 brook trout, 30,000 to 35,000 brown and about 40,000 rainbows. Some stocking in this area's reclaimed ponds is done in the fall with four-inch fingerlings. Most are held over until the spring. Brook trout sent to the area's rivers and streams in the spring are one year old, six to nine inches long and weigh an average of a quarter pound. Rainbow and brown trout released in the lakes and ponds are generally two years old, nine to twelve inches in length, and weigh in at about three-quarters of a pound.

SANDWICH STATE GAME FARM

On the way toward Barnstable on Route 6A, about a half mile after Old County Road on the right, is the long driveway leading to the State Game Farm. It's a treat for the whole family, particularly from May through October. The game farm, founded in 1914 on 135 acres of woods, ponds and marshlands, has been under the genial management of Game Bird Culturist John A. Prouty since 1937. A nature-lover's delight, there is much to see; most visitors miss half because they don't realize what is available.

Its primary function is to raise about 20,000 cock pheasants and 4,000 quail per year to stock state wildlife areas and other good cover land in southeastern Massachusetts. It is quite correct that the hunters then take over. Before we rise in arms at this use of the taxpayers' money, we should remember that this is all paid for by the sportsmen themselves — hunting licenses bring revenue for the game farm, fishing licenses for the fish hatchery. Without the hunters and fishermen, these facilities probably would not exist.

Sandwich game farm raises both pheasants and quail

from their own brood stock. Each year about 3,500 pheasants and 300 to 400 quail are carried over the winter for this purpose. Pheasants begin laying eggs about mid-March, quail about a month later. Eggs of specifically strong parent stock are marked and segregated to form the brood stock for the following year.

Incubation of both pheasant and quail eggs takes 23 days. If you visit the farm in April or May, ask to see the incubators in the basement of the main office and the building next door. From about the first of May until late June you can be sure of finding some young chicks. The newborn quail are about the size of a bumblebee — little furry balls of down. Baby pheasants are about the size of ordinary chicks. Both are given about 24 hours to dry off after hatching and are then whisked off to the brooders.

Pheasants spend about seven weeks in the heated brooders and are then turned loose in open range pens. As these pens are not covered, it is first necessary to remove the ten primary flight feathers from one wing to keep them grounded. By five or six weeks later, about midsummer, these feathers have grown back and the birds are returned to a covered pen to be fitted with a leather strap called a brail and returned to the open ranges. (The brail prevents flight but allows the pheasants to develop normally.) Two or three weeks before the birds are to be released they are again returned to covered pens and the brail removed to allow them to regain full use of their wings.

Quail are kept in brooders for about three weeks and are then taken to the small rearing pens that you see about the grounds.

Pheasants and quail are released when about twenty-five to twenty-six weeks old. All of the quail currently go to Miles Standish Wildlife Area in Carver and the Crane Wildlife Area in Falmouth. Most of the pheasants are released in areas throughout southeastern Massachusetts that provide good open cover able to support the birds. A small proportion of the cock pheasants are released in gun club areas under the Sportsman's Rearing Program. These pheasants are turned over to the clubs when six to eight weeks old and raised by the organization until their release during hunting season.

As hen pheasants are illegal hunting game in Massachusetts, only cock pheasants are released. Hen chicks, other than brood stock, are generally sold to other breeders.

Cock pheasants and quail are released in groups on a scheduled basis throughout the hunting season, from October 20 to the end of November. From December until the next cycle of eggs in the spring, the birds at the farm are limited to the brood stock.

What's the biggest problem? Raccoons — one raccoon in a pheasant range can make an awful mess. Those electric fences are to keep the raccoons out rather than to keep the birds in.

Prouty has provided several other wild friends at the farm to please children. Particularly popular are the deer in one of the pens and some horned owls in cages. The ponds host a large variety of ducks and geese: eider, red heads, canvasbacks, blue bills, blue and green wing, hooded mergansers, pintails, widgeons, teal, blue geese and snow geese. In the spring, their nests and eggs may be almost anywhere, so watch your step.

The game farm is open Monday through Friday from 9 A.M. to 4 P.M. year round. It is also open occasionally on weekends in summer; check to see if the gate is open.

BENJAMIN NYE HOMESTEAD (1685)

On Route 6A in East Sandwich going toward Barnstable, Old County Road angles off to the right. About two-thirds of a mile in on the left is the Nye house, built by one of the early settlers of Sandwich.

Town records show that Benjamin Nye built a grist mill nearby in 1669. His old mill pond, now called Nye Pond, is across the road. When this mill was built there was but one other on Cape Cod. Later in the 1600s he built a fulling mill nearby and his son Jonathan built a carding mill, using the first carding machinery on the Cape. Six generations of Nyes were millers here before the grist mill was torn down in 1867.

The homestead is a restoration and preservation project of the Nye Family of America Association. The Nye family traces its lineage from a tenth-century Danish king, Harald Blautand (Bluetooth), through Benjamin and the eight generations that have lived in the Sandwich homestead and their hundreds of descendants now spread throughout the country.

Nye house has undergone three major structural changes. The original building was a small two-story Cape with two lower and two upper rooms and a large central chimney. In about 1710 rooms were added to the rear of the lower floor; in about 1780 the roof was raised and extended and more rooms added to make the full colonial we see today.

The upper floor of the old home is still being restored. The aim of all restoration work has been to show the transitions the house has undergone in almost three hundred years, both architecturally and in its furnishings.

The treasures in the house, including many furnishings and documents belonging to the early Nye families, are too numerous to detail here. One word of caution: don't miss the chimney room! The four fireplaces and Dutch oven are served by two separate chimneys. The backs of these chimneys are about four feet apart at the base and form an inner room entered through a small door beneath the stairs. Also note the interior wood window shutters. The Nye family says the chimney room was for winter warmth and the shutters to reduce drafts, but I smell the blood of an Indian! Cape Indians proved to be peaceful, but remember, this house was built only a few years after King Philip's conspiracy in which many off-Cape towns were sacked. I'm not convinced that Benjamin Nye was too sure of peaceful relations with his Indian neighbors at his lonely outpost when he built his home in 1685.

Many of the surrounding houses on Old County Road were also built by Nye and his sons, most dating from the eighteenth century. The Nye homestead is open from 10 A.M. to 12 noon and 1 to 4 P.M. daily except Mondays and from 1 to 4 P.M. on Sundays from June to October. A nominal admission fee is charged.

OLD QUAKER MEETING HOUSE

The Friends Meeting House in East Sandwich is the oldest continuous Quaker meeting house in America. To reach it take Quaker Meeting House Road north off Route 6A, across the railroad tracks, bear left a few yards on Gilman Road, and you will see the entrance. The first meeting house on this site dates from 1658. The present one is the third, constructed in 1810 complete with his and her privies in the rear and an old cemetery for tombstone buffs. A service is held at 11 A.M. the first Sunday in August. Visitors are welcome.

Quakers in Sandwich, as in all of New England, were persecuted unmercifully. Thrashed and fined in the name of righteousness, it was a wonder they survived. One well-to-do Quaker, William Allen, was plundered of everything of value and then imprisoned, leaving his wife, Priscilla, almost destitute. The Sandwich marshal, George Barlow, finally took the last copper kettle and asked:

"Now, Priscilla, how will thee cook for thy family and friends, thee has no kettle?"

And Priscilla answered: "George, that God who hears the ravens when they cry, will provide for them. I trust in that God, and I verily believe the time will come when thy necessity will be greater than mine."

The Quakers were made of stout stuff. An old and broken George Barlow, persona non grata around the town, sought the Allens' charity many times and was never refused.

Almost directly behind the meeting house and cemetery on Spring Hill Road is the home of Stephen Wing, the first Quaker convert in Sandwich. Stephen settled in Sandwich and built his home in 1641. One of the two living rooms dates back to 1637. Its walls are 18 inches thick, built as a fort to protect the community from Indian attack. Still owned by the Wing family after 330 years, the homestead is open to the public during July and August. No admission is charged, but donations to maintain the property are gratefully accepted.

When you leave the area go back and rejoin Route 6A the way you came in. Directly across on the southeastern corner of Quaker Meeting House Road is a tiny home. Despite the additions — which have a certain jerry-built charm of their own — the original structure to the left is perhaps the most quaint on the Cape. It is a bow roof quarter Cape dating from about 1650. The home originally stood on County Road as part of a larger Cape and served for about a century as the home of Quaker leaders. It is now privately owned and not open to the public.

SHAWME-CROWELL STATE FOREST

Camping and travel trailer facilities are available only a short ride west on Main Street at the Shawme-Crowell State Forest. There are 265 type II campsites on a first-come, first-served basis. Community sanitary facilities and hot and cold showers are available for each group of campsites. Each site has its own fireplace and picnic table and is limited to one family with a maximum of two tents or one recreational vehicle.

The campgrounds are generally open from mid-April to mid-October. There are no ponds or streams in the forest, but good fishing is available nearby and camp receipts entitle campers to use nearby Scusset Bathing Beach. There are excellent views of Cape Cod Bay from some of the highland campsites.

Should the campgrounds be full when you arrive, the supervisor will enter your name on a waiting list for the following morning. Those on the list must return at 9 A.M.

the next day or lose their place. Campsites are $3 per day, with a maximum stay of two weeks in season.

CAMPSITES AND TRAILER PARK

A privately owned and operated camping, recreational vehicle and cottage park, Peters Pond Park is located on Cotuit Road in the Forestdale section of Sandwich.

The park includes 375 camping and trailer sites, private sandy beaches, ample facilities for most sports and a general store with a complete line of staples. Peters Pond Park covers 87 wooded acres with extensive frontage on 137-acre Peters Pond, a fine spring-fed lake excellent for trout fishing, swimming and boating. The season runs from April 15 to October 1. Mini-bikes, motor scooters, pets and open fires are prohibited. Electrical, water and sewerage hookups, tent platforms, rowboats and cottages are available at extra charges. Reservations are generally required. A brochure is available from Box 446, Sandwich, Mass. 02563.

PUBLIC GOLF COURSES

There are two 18-hole golf courses in Sandwich open to the public.

Round Hill Country Club is located in East Sandwich off the service road between Exits 3 and 4 on the Mid-Cape Highway. On the south side of Exit 3 you will see the service road just a few yards from Route 6. Follow in alongside the highway about a half mile to the entrance. Round Hill is a 6,605-yard, par 72 course. A fine clubhouse, locker room, dining and bar facilities are provided. Golf carts, tennis courts, driving and putting practice areas, and golf lessons are also available. The views from the clubhouse and parts of the course are exceptional.

Holly Ridge Golf Club is located off Boardley Road in South Sandwich. Look for signs from Cotuit or Farmersville roads. Holly Ridge is a 2,968-yard, par 54 course. A pro shop, snack bar and air-conditioned cocktail lounge are available.

PUBLIC SWIMMING BEACHES

There are three public swimming beaches in Sandwich, two salt and one fresh. Windshield sticker permits for town residents and guest cards for resident guests, such as house guests and renters, are available without charge at the Town Hall. Motel operators also have guest cards for their customers. Those without stickers or cards must pay a parking fee at the beach.

Saltwater buffs may enjoy Town Beach in Sandwich or East Sandwich Beach. To reach Town Beach from Route 6A, take Tupper Road a short way, turn right over the railroad tracks on Town Neck Road, and follow it to the end. One of the Cape's remaining Coast Guard stations is located nearby. East Sandwich Beach may be reached by taking Route 6A toward Barnstable, going left at Beach Road to the end and then left again to the parking area at the end of the pavement.

Snake Pond in the Forestdale area has a fine, sandy swimming beach maintained by the town. To reach the pond take Route 130 from Sandwich center for about five miles to Snake Pond Road (Otis Air Force Base sign), then right about a half mile.

Registered voters and taxpayers of Sandwich may also use Barnstable's Sandy Neck Beach without charge. As the only way to get to Sandy Neck by land is through East Sandwich, Barnstable's generosity makes sense. Nonresidents and guests may visit this beach by paying the usual parking fee. The entrance to Sandy Neck is a quarter mile before the Barnstable town line on Route 6A.

CAPE COD BAY

NANTUCKET
SOUND

Copyright, THE NATIONAL SURVEY, 1973
Chester, Vermont

CHAPTER III

Barnstable

Each town on the Cape has a distinctive character and charm of its own — except Barnstable. The Town of Barnstable is representative of the whole Cape — old and new, good and bad — all rolled into one.

The town extends from the Bay on the north to the Sound on the south. The difference is that of two different worlds: from the pastoral beauty of West Barnstable and the historic charm of Barnstable village in the north to the commercial bustle of Hyannis, the suburban resorts of Osterville and Centerville and the white-tie social enclaves of Hyannis Port and Cotuit in the south. The difference is primarily due to geography. The settlers were looking for salt hay; the summer residents for a suntan. Long, beautiful beaches attracted the "summer people" in droves and enabled the Bay side to doze through the worst of it. As a result, both sides have their advantages, and owe them in large part to each other.

Joseph Hull, a parson elbowed out of Weymouth, was the first to settle in Barnstable together with a small group of followers. Some months later, in October 1639, the Reverend John Lothrop moved in with a larger group of Congregationalists, and it wasn't too long before the unfortunate Hull was elbowed out again. The new settlement was incorporated and named almost immediately. There seems no doubt the town was named after Barnstaple, England (spelling was not a strong point of the day).

Barnstable flourished under the competent leadership of Reverend Lothrop; the united group set about their work without the religious squabbles of Sandwich or the land bickering of Yarmouth. With common goals and problems, however, the pattern of progress was the same. Farming and self-preservation were the first priorities; shore whaling, fishing, commerce and trades such as cobbling, tanning and milling were the luxuries.

The Barnstable of the 1650s included the area we now know as Falmouth, and a settlement at Saconesset (Succonessitt) was established in 1660. Many of these settlers were Quakers, who achieved a measure of religious freedom by no longer being underfoot. Even so, the settlers at Saconesset were required to travel the 18 miles to Barnstable for Sunday church meeting.

The south side of present-day Barnstable remained a wilderness of pine forests and quiet beaches.

Shore whaling soon became big business in Barnstable, as it did all up and down the Bay. Sandy Neck was a fine base of operations and common grounds were set aside for tryyards and whaling. The tremendous quantities of firewood required for boiling whale blubber at these tryworks were a major factor in the deforestation of large areas of the Cape.

In about 1660 a Barnstable man, Nicholas Davis, traded the current Sachem out of a piece of real estate on Lewis Bay, and later constructed a small building there to store his trading goods to and from Rhode Island and New York. Over the next thirty or forty years about a dozen families had made scattered settlements on this coast between Hyannis and Cotuit. It wasn't many more years before the Indians had been traded out of other large tracts and the development of the south shore was on its way. Some say it has done pretty well ever since.

After twenty-five years of commuting to the Barnstable

Meeting House, Saconesset was sufficiently well established to warrant incorporation and town status in 1686. It was not until 1693 that its name was officially changed to Falmouth. This was the first of a series of partitions to divide the vast areas of the original four towns into the fifteen we know today. The Cape towns were of increasing importance and population as the seventeenth century wore on, and in 1685 they achieved county status within the Plymouth colony and Barnstable was named the county seat. A courthouse was constructed and much of the legal and minor administrative chores transferred to the Cape.

The story of the Cape during the various wars has been told elsewhere in this book, but one of their aftereffects deserves mention here. The wars disrupted the economic life of the Cape and degrees of financial chaos followed each one. In addition, whales moved too far out and the government moved too close in to suit many people; there was much grumbling and many people emigrated. The best-known case is that of the Gorhams of Barnstable, the famed Indian fighters and whaleboat commanders. Colonel Shubael was instrumental in securing land grants for the descendants of soldiers in King Philip's War and he personally led the settlers in founding a new town. In 1736 they emigrated to what is now Gorham, Maine, and it was from there that he and his sons returned to command the Cape men in their whaleboats at the siege of Louisburg in 1745. Bankrupt and exhausted, he died in 1746.

As the county seat, Barnstable has always been at the political, commercial, and social center of life on Cape Cod. By that we mean the Town of Barnstable; the village is the political center, Hyannis the commercial center, and the south shore the social.

In the heyday of the Cape, all was well in Barnstable. At the two hundredth anniversary celebration in 1839 a speaker said, "We see no beggars, no idlers, no sots. The population of the town is over four thousand, its poor house has eighteen tenants. The population of the county is thirty-two thousand, in its jail there are three prisoners, and those three are foreigners!"

Today Barnstable is the largest town on the Cape, with a population of 20,000 covering 60 square miles from the Bay to Nantucket Sound. Its villages are Barnstable, West Barnstable, Cummaquid, Marstons Mills, Hyannis, Hyannis Port, Centerville, Osterville, Cotuit, and Santuit.

SANDY NECK

By the time the last vestiges of glacial ice had melted, the Atlantic Ocean had risen sufficiently to enter Cape Cod Bay and Nantucket Sound. The work of the waves and currents began to mold the shoreline of the Cape and gave it the form we know today.

Ocean currents curling down the coast of the Bay carried sand from the bluffs of Manomet south and east along the smooth coastline. As the currents approached Barnstable Harbor the sudden deep water caused much of the drifting material to be released, creating sand bars and finally a barrier beach almost completely across the mouth of the harbor. Now seven miles long and still growing slowly, Sandy Neck is one of the most beautiful beaches on the Bay side, with rolling dunes, a natural sanctuary for wildlife, and uninhabited except for a few summer cottages and fishing shacks at its tip. There are no improved roads, and the summer residents at the tip, mostly permanent village residents incognito, generally commute across the harbor.

The Cummaquid Indians used to gather on Sandy Neck for lobster, oyster and clam feasts, the shells of which are still uncovered as storms and waves reshape the beach. When shore whaling was at its prime, the neck was common land for town whalers. When the whalemen went to sea, four areas were set aside as tryyards available to any townsman to boil blubber into oil. The right is still available to Barnstable men but the location of the old tryyards is a bit hazy.

To reach Sandy Neck, take the well-marked entrance road a quarter mile across the Barnstable town line in East Sandwich. Sandwich owns the road, Barnstable the neck. If you have a yen to walk beach and dunes, try Sandy Neck. The scenery is exceptional.

THE GREAT MARSHES OF BARNSTABLE

The "hay grounds" of Barnstable attracted the first settler, cattle-raising pastor Joseph Hull. Nowhere in Massachusetts are there more extensive salt marshes than at Barnstable. About four miles long by two miles wide, the Great Marshes look out over Sandy Neck. No longer used for cattle feed, the marshes continue to fill a vital ecological requirement for marine and bird life. They can also be credited with an important negative value in preventing the large-scale development of shore lots so prevalent elsewhere on the Cape. Thus the landscape has been preserved — vivid green in summer and a tawny brown in fall.

A salt marsh takes hundreds of years to form. Clay and silt are washed in on the tides, building mud flats behind barrier beaches such as Sandy Neck. When the mud flat is high enough, saltwater grass, known as "spartina," gets a foothold and traps increasing quantities of clay and silt until the land surface is built up to the level of average high water. The tide will not be denied, however, and channels are kept open through the marsh. These tidal creeks carry the ebb and flow through the marsh, covering great areas of it around the time of the highest spring tides.

When entering West Barnstable from Sandwich on Route 6A, a beautiful view of the Great Marshes is on your left. Other excellent views will occur periodically most of the way into Barnstable village. Salt marsh land is firm, if a bit soggy in places, and wonderful for a nature walk. Beware of the mud flats, however; a changing tide has forced more than one man to swim for his life.

"MAD JACK" PERCIVAL

At the corner of Routes 6A and 149 is the old West Barnstable cemetery. Many of Barnstable's earliest citizens rest here, their monuments long since crumbled and unrecognizable. A more recent (1862) grave is that of Captain John Percival of naval fame.

John Percival was born on Scorton Hill, about a mile away toward Sandwich. He went to sea at fourteen, rising through the ranks to serve as an aide to Admiral Nelson in the Battle of Trafalgar (1805) and fought valiantly in the naval engagements of the War of 1812. His last voyage was in command of the U.S.S. *Constitution*, "Old Ironsides," on its 495-day, 52,279-mile voyage around the world in 1844–1846. An eccentric but able skipper, "Mad Jack" rests in good company with two eighteenth-century Captains Crocker just abaft his port beam.

WEST PARISH MEETING HOUSE

In 1616 a group of reformers in England gathered to form a new congregation. An attempt at compromise, this new group never repudiated the Church of England, but it was not in close communion with it either. This splinter group came to be known as the Congregationalists, and in 1632 a meeting was raided and the leaders jailed. The leaders, including the Reverend John Lothrop, were released on condition that they leave the country.

In September 1634 Lothrop and thirty parishioners arrived in the Plymouth Colony. The new settlers and those who had so recently preceded them conflicted to the extent that the new arrivals were soon looking for greener pastures. In 1639 they were given permission to settle in Mattakeese, now the town of Barnstable.

They were not the first settlers, but Lothrop, by strength of character and weight of numbers, soon took control. He was a wise and tolerant guide and Barnstable prospered. His second home, built in 1644, is still standing as part of the Sturgis Library in Barnstable.

After Lothrop's death, the church floundered; for the next three hundred years it drifted from strength to weakness and back again. As Barnstable grew, the dispersed congregation demanded local parishes; with considerable trepidation, east and west parishes were formed.

Work began on the West Parish Meeting House in 1717, and two years later, on Thanksgiving Day 1719, the first service was held. Only four years later the building was enlarged by cutting it in half, pulling it apart, and adding eighteen feet in the middle. The 5½-foot gilded cock weathervane on the bell tower was added then.

By 1852 the church needed major repairs and the decision was made to "modernize" the structure. A new exterior over the old and a belfry and spire in place of the bell tower transformed the church into a typical nineteenth-century colonial. The old church stayed alive over the next hundred years but did not flourish.

In the 1920s the historic and architectural significance of the West Parish Meeting House began to be recognized. Over the next twenty-five years interest grew but the funds did not. By 1950 the parish faced a crisis — either extensive repair or restoration. By 1953 sufficient funds had been raised to begin restoration. For those involved over the many years, it was a labor of love. Bit by bit, piece by piece, the old building was painstakingly restored to stand as it stood 250 years before.

The West Parish Meeting House is a memorial to the sturdy spirit that built it and the unflagging devotion that restored it. Visitors are always welcome. The Meeting House is located a little less than a mile from Route 6A on Old Meetinghouse Way (Route 149) in West Barnstable.

JAMES OTIS, THE PATRIOT

On the north side of Route 6A, about a quarter mile east of the junction of Route 149, is a boulder and bronze plaque marking the homestead of "The Great Advocate" James Otis, of Revolutionary War fame. His plea before the Superior Court in 1761 was credited by John Adams as the spark by which "the child Independence was born." Often called the Patrick Henry of the North, the fiery leader of colonial opposition to the Crown was incapacitated in a political brawl in 1769 and was killed by a bolt of lightning in 1783.

CAPE COD COMMUNITY COLLEGE

In September 1970 Cape Cod Community College opened its new 116-acre campus on Route 132 in West Barnstable, between Route 6A and Exit 6 on the Mid-Cape Highway.

The college offers two-year transfer, general and career programs, all leading to the Associate in Arts degree. Extensive evening and summer programs offer courses toward degree and certificate and a wide range of adult education, career, and community service courses are also available.

SACRAMENT ROCK

Less than a mile east of the junction of Routes 6A and 132, on the left, is a fragmented boulder with a bronze historical marker. In October 1639, the newly arrived John Lothrop and his congregation celebrated communion at this site.

LOTHROP HILL

John Lothrop (1584–1653), minister and driving force behind the Barnstable settlement, lies buried in the beautiful cemetery down Route 6A just east of Governors Way.

This cemetery, known as Lothrop Hill, is the earliest marked cemetery in Barnstable. According to Lothrop's diary, Patience Cobb was "buried May 4, 1648, the first that was buried in our new burying place [Lothrop Hill] by our meeting house." Earlier dead were buried in the "Calves Pasture." The field at the end of Scudder Lane, formerly Calves Pasture Lane, was the site of the burying ground for the first nine years of the settlement. The graves were unmarked and are lost to history.

CROCKER TAVERN

The old Crocker Tavern, located on Route 6A in Barnstable village about a quarter mile west of the Court House, was built by Cornelius Crocker in 1754. The property is owned by the Society for the Preservation of New England Antiquities and is open to the public Tuesday, and Saturday afternoons from 1 to 5 P.M. during the summer season. A nominal admission fee is charged.

Cornelius Crocker operated a public house, or tavern, in this building until his death in 1784. His daughter Lydia, widow of Captain Samuel Sturgis, inherited the property and added the eastern wing sometime after 1791. She continued the business and the house became known as the Sturgis Tavern or Aunt Lydia's Tavern. After Lydia's passing at age eighty-six the old house was used as a residence by Crocker descendents until willed to the society in 1927. An accompanying bequest of $10,000 was provided to support it as a historic museum. The house is furnished with Crocker family furniture and is a fine example of a large two-story colonial of the eighteenth century.

STURGIS LIBRARY

John Lothrop built his second home in 1644. It is still standing as part of the Sturgis Library in Barnstable village, the oldest library building in the United States.

The Lothrop house was a two-story half-Cape, 21 feet across the front and 29 feet deep. The chimney was on the west side with an oven projecting through the wall. In 1782 it was enlarged by the Sturgis family. Captain William Sturgis, born and raised in the house, became one of Barnstable's most famous skippers. In command of the *Atahualpa*, he shot his way out of a Chinese pirate attack in Macao Roads, only to be reproved by the owners for "taking the cannon with him in the first place"; and they made him pay the freight!

Captain Sturgis willed the house, his book collection, and $15,000 for the establishment of a free library in 1863. One room is now called the Lothrop Room, as it originally served as the minister's study. It was also used as the church meeting room until a formal church was built.

Sturgis Library has recently been greatly enlarged by a new wing. The library is proud of its rare histories and genealogies of early America and the original Lothrop Bible printed in 1605.

BARNSTABLE COUNTY COURT HOUSE

In 1685 the Plymouth Colony was divided into three counties, Plymouth, Bristol, and Barnstable. The Town of Barnstable became the county seat for the Cape and a courthouse was constructed. The first recording of a deed in the new county was made on October 5, 1686. In 1778 a new brick courthouse was constructed just east of the Sturgis Library. A fire on the night of October 22, 1827, gutted the building and destroyed much of the written legal history of the county to that date. Copies had been made of some of the records and a few others were rescued by patrons of nearby Crocker's Tavern, but it was many years before Cape land titles achieved a semblance of order again.

The oldest structure in the current courthouse complex dates from 1834. Several additions in the rear are of much later vintage, and the new main building was completed in 1971. The gray granite walls of the old courthouse are protected by two cannon brought from Boston by ox team during the War of 1812 to defend the salt works along the shore against British attack. No shots were fired, and the cannon lay forgotten in the sand until moved to the courthouse lawn many years later.

The Registry of Deeds is perhaps the busiest county department. In 1903, 2,500 legal instruments were recorded, rising to 8,000 in 1928 and to a rousing 40,000 in 1971. And the pace shows no sign of slackening.

THE CUSTOMS HOUSE •
TRAYSER MEMORIAL MUSEUM

When shipping and commerce flourished on the Cape, a U.S. Customs port of entry was a necessity. A Customs House was established in 1789 with General Joseph Otis, a brother of patriot James Otis, appointed as collector by George Washington. In 1856 a brick, "fireproof" building was erected in Barnstable village and served as the port of entry for the county until 1913. From then until 1959 it served as the village post office.

This old Customs House, just east of the traffic light at the corner of Route 6A and Phinney's Lane, is now a museum dedicated to the preservation of articles of historic interest that reflect the spirit and character of the men and women of Barnstable. It is called the Donald G. Trayser Memorial Museum in honor of the editor, historian, and driving force behind the Barnstable Historical Society.

Trayser museum is a hodgepodge of treasures — early Indian tools and crafts. Victorian home furnishings, fine marine paintings, silver work by early Barnstable craftsmen, dolls, and documents. The carriage house in the rear contains other memorabilia, including a horse-drawn hearse and early farm and carpentry tools.

The old County Jail, built in about 1695 and the earliest known in Plymouth Colony, has been moved next door to the Trayser Museum. Of heavy oak post and plank construction, the cells are small and their walls are adorned with designs of ships and schooners scratched by the prisoners. Time has been hard on the old jail, but grants of federal and town funds have been secured to restore the structure to its old colonial "splendor." The original site of the building was on Old Jail Lane, Barnstable village.

Visiting hours are 1 to 5 P.M. Tuesdays through Saturdays during July and August. A nominal admission fee is charged.

BARNSTABLE HARBOR

At the foot of Mill Way and Commerce Road lies Barnstable Harbor, one of the most picturesque on the Cape. It's a fine place to visit on a summer day if only to watch the boats, put-puts to 60-foot yachts, as they cruise in and out.

The marina provides about 150 slips (no moorings), mostly owned by the town. All the slips have been booked solid for years, but the harbormaster does keep five or six berths open for the larger transient vessels.

Primarily a sportfishing marina, four or five charter boats are available in season. A town-owned concrete launching ramp is available free of charge. The channel is open to a minimum six-foot draft at low tide. Detailed harbor information is shown on Coast and Geodetic Survey Chart 339.

SACHEM IYANNOUGH'S GRAVE

In 1860 a Barnstable farmer, David Davis, turned up a copper kettle and other Indian artifacts while doing his spring plowing. More careful excavation with a spade soon turned up the bones of the Sachem himself. The grave has been authenticated and the bones now rest in the Pilgrim Hall Museum at Plymouth.

In 1621 young Sachem Iyannough had a golden opportunity to delay if not demolish the colonization plans of the Plymouth Colony. Instead he chose friendship, gave provisions and assistance as required, and received scant thanks for his aid. He died at the age of twenty-six hiding in the swamp in fear of Captain Miles Standish, who had massacred a group of Indians rumored to be conspiring against the colony. Iyannough left another legacy to the Cape in his name. Corruptions of time and tongue have given us the village names of Hyannis and Wianno, a fitting honor for the friendly host of Barnstable.

Across the street and a little east of the Cummaquid Post Office on Route 6A, a slate marker commemorates the grave of Iyannough, Sachem of the Cummaquid Indians and friend of the early settlers. To reach the site follow the driveway to the right down a cleared trail about three hundred yards back into the woods.

KENNEDY ICE SKATING RINK

In 1957 the Kennedy family gave the Town of Barnstable the Joseph P. Kennedy Jr. Memorial Skating Rink on Bearse's Way in Hyannis. The rink is used for youth and amateur hockey and public skating. A nominal admission fee is charged and skate rentals are available. The rink is open from mid-November to mid-March and times are set aside for public skating at least once a day.

SUNSET HILL

Sunset Hill is a fine place to enjoy a sunset or to admire a beautiful view. From Hyannis take Scudder Avenue almost to the end, then turn right on Irving Avenue. A few hundred yards on your right is Saint Andrew's-by-the-Sea, one of the most attractive of the newer churches on the Cape, and a bit beyond is the lookout area on Sunset Hill.

The lookout is in the middle of the posh Hyannis Port residential area and also serves as the parking lot of the Hyannis Port Golf Club. The fairways are beneath you and Nantucket Sound all around. The spit of land ahead, joined at your left by a narrow causeway, is Squaw Island. Edward Kennedy's home there is almost completely hidden by the large home at the left. The older Kennedy Compound is behind you, a little past the corner of Scudder and Irving avenues.

JOHN F. KENNEDY MEMORIAL

About a half mile past the docks on Ocean Street in Hyannis is the John F. Kennedy Memorial, Cape Cod's tribute to its most illustrious summer resident.

The fieldstone monument, faced on either side with the

presidential seal and a bronze medallion of the late President, overlooks Lewis Bay. An attractive terrace surrounding a reflecting pool invites meditation. Soft lights illuminate the fountain at night and reflect on the Bay where the Kennedy family sailed while vacationing in Hyannis Port.

Shortly after the memorial opened in 1966, coins of all denominations began appearing in the pool. The total collection stands at over $18,000 and the funds are earmarked for youth activities in the town.

A quotation of President Kennedy, "I believe it is important that this country sail, and not lie still in the harbor," is engraved around the pool.

THE OCTAGONAL HOUSE

Coming up one-way South Street in Hyannis, the octagonal house is on the right after High School Road. It was built in 1850 by a clipper ship captain with some different and definite ideas on architecture.

Captain Rodney Baxter of Hyannis was one of the foremost sailing masters of his day. His Atlantic crossing in the clipper *Flying Scud* was made in 19 days, 20 hours, a record passage for a loaded vessel in its day.

The octagonal house is constructed of concrete with walls 18 inches thick, a novel experiment in 1850. There are two large, relatively square rooms on each floor and a few smaller oblong rooms; the remaining triangular nooks and crannies are used for closets and other service areas. True to his plan, Captain Baxter built an octagonal barn as well.

COLONIAL CANDLE COMPANY

In 1909, a young Hyannis housewife named Mabel K. Baker hand-dipped bayberry candles on her kitchen stove to make Christmas gifts for her friends. As her fame spread, a business grew, so that by 1926, forty-five skilled employees produced thirty-seven colors of hand-dipped and molded candles at a clip of 5,000 to 10,000 per day and shipped them all over the world. Today the Colonial Candle Company factory produces from 125,000 to 150,-000 candles a day: flower tapers, table candles, fancy molded candles, and some of the most beautifully decorated candles imaginable. The firm has also developed complete candle-making kits for the home craftsman.

The making of hand-dipped candles hasn't really changed much since Pilgrim times. Complimentary tours are available daily, except on Saturdays, Sundays and holidays, from 9 A.M. to 12 noon and 1 to 3 P.M. at the factory at the east end of Main Street in Hyannis. Signs from their parking lot clearly point the way. You tour the actual factory, and see the stringing of the wicking on the old wooden frames, the frames hand-dipped in wax vats, the ends clipped and beveled; one more dip, then they're wrapped, packaged, and off they go. It takes 12 to 15 dips for a small flower taper and 30 to 40 dips for a standard table candle.

The fancier shapes, sizes and designs are generally molded. Except for liquid wax piped in from storage tanks, little automation is possible. The rough candles from the molds are then hand-machined, painted, and decorated. The firm has a gift shop on the premises and a "Seconds Shop" nearby in which surplus and slightly imperfect products are sold at substantial discounts.

THE MELODY TENT

Theater in the round under a canvas tent is an established part of Cape Cod summer theater. For over twenty years the Cape Cod Melody Tent has been bringing outstanding summer stock theater to Hyannis. Located at the end of Main Street just after the rotary at the west end of Hyannis, the Melody Tent's season runs from late June to Labor Day. Individual or season subscription tickets are available from Boston, Cambridge, Falmouth and New Bedford ticket agencies as well as by mail or at the box office in Hyannis.

Productions at the Melody Tent are primarily proven

Broadway hits featuring exceptional casts. The Melody Tent is in every sense a "star house." Recent musical comedy productions featured such stars as Jane Powell, Jan Peerce, Mitzi Gaynor, Betsy Palmer and Donald O'Connor. Special children's matinees of familiar classics, such as *Sleeping Beauty* and *The Wizard of Oz*, are performed by professional New York casts. Sundays are reserved for special events such as singing groups, concerts and instrumentals.

Performances of the weekly Broadway hits are generally scheduled Monday through Saturday evenings at 8:30, with Wednesday and Thursday matinees at 2:30. The special children's features take place most Wednesdays at 11:00 A.M. The timing of Sunday attractions and other special events is variable.

Should you be interested in a program of the season's productions, write to the Cape Cod Melody Tent, Hyannis, Mass. 02601, in the late spring.

ETHNIC DANCE FESTIVAL

A new dimension has been added to the Cape's performing arts theater. The Ethnic Dance Arts Company, headed by the internationally known dance star and choreographer, La Meri, has established itself as an annual attraction on the Cape Cod bill of fare.

The Ethnic Dance Festival presents colorful dance programs at the Village Hall on Route 6A, Barnstable Village, next to the County Court House, during July and August. Called the United Nations of the Dance, the festival engages the most renowned dancers from all over the world to participate. Lavishly costumed and artistically directed by La Meri, the festival is one of the Cape's leading contributions to the American cultural scene.

BOAT CRUISES

Cruises to Martha's Vineyard and Nantucket, sightseeing cruises around Hyannis Harbor, and deep sea fishing excursions are all available from the Ocean Street docks in Hyannis. Reservations are not needed.

Martha's Vineyard is only 90 minutes from Hyannis. A quaint and charming island with magnificent seascapes and picturesque villages, the Vineyard is wonderful for a one-day excursion or a visit of several days. Hyannis Harbor Tours offers a choice of vessels, each making three round trips a day during the busy summer season. Spring and fall schedules are a bit slimmer but you can usually count on at least one vessel a day from May to mid-October. Two-and-a-half hour conducted bus tours of the entire Vineyard can be arranged after you board ship. Free parking is provided for one day excursionists. The first vessels leave the pier about 9:30 A.M. daily; others at midday and late afternoon during the season. All vessels are modern and well equipped; snack and beverage bars, enclosed lounges, and deck chairs are standard equipment.

Nantucket was one of the greatest New England whaling towns and abounds with traditional interest. It is served by one vessel daily from the Ocean Street docks and another vessel from the Pleasant Street docks of the Steamship Authority just a short distance away. The Steamship Authority Vessel is the only one from Hyannis equipped to carry automobiles. Both services operate from May to October. A bus sightseeing tour is available at Nantucket on the same basis as at Martha's Vineyard. Be sure to see the famed whaling museum — but keep in mind that a Yarmouth man taught them the trade.

Hyannis Harbor sightseeing cruises leave the Ocean Street docks every half hour from 9 A.M. to 7:30 P.M. during the summer season. Special moonlight cruises are also very popular. Schedules from May 1 to mid-June and from Labor Day to the end of October are variable but you can count on one or more cruises each day if the weather is good. Each vessel has an enclosed lounge for inclement weather. It's an interesting one-hour trip; points of interest are explained by the captain and it's a fine way to get at least a little taste of the sea.

Deep sea fishing cruises are available from May 15 to

October 15 from Pier 1. There are two sailings a day, morning and afternoon. Each cruise lasts four to five hours and they guarantee safety, comfort and fish. Rods and reels may be rented on board, bait is furnished free. Beverages may be purchased aboard and box lunches are available at the dock. Anyone who brings in a tautog in excess of 19 pounds receives a $100 reward.

Ocean Street is the left turn at the only traffic light on Main Street in Hyannis. Follow it for about half a mile and you can't miss the docks. The Steamship Authority docks are one block farther east on Pleasant Street.

HYANNIS ANTIQUES FAIR

Cape Cod, long a collector's happy hunting ground, has played host to the Hyannis Antiques Fair for a quarter of a century. Running from Friday through Tuesday in mid-July, the fair has been held at the National Guard Armory on South Street, Hyannis.

Approximately fifty dealers from all over the East display their wares for buyers and browsers each year. The fair covers a wide range of items and prices. It is generally open from 2 to 10 P.M. and charges an admission fee.

MARY LINCOLN HOUSE (c. 1840)

Centerville is doubly fortunate in having both an active historical society and many generous patrons. This combination has resulted in an exceptionally fine museum for the village.

Tinsmith Clark Lincoln built his home next to his tinshop on Centerville's Main Street in about 1840. His daughter, Miss Mary, inherited the home and lived there for many years. After her death the property was acquired by the historical society, named the Mary Lincoln House, and opened to the public in 1955. Clark Lincoln's old tinshop is still next door, long since converted into a charming private home.

In recent years a wing was added to the home, made possible by a bequest of Miss Mabel Phinney of Centerville. Visitors to the Mary Lincoln House are given a guided tour. Admission is free but donations are gratefully accepted.

With assistance from donors such as Miss Phinney, financier Charles Ayling, the Marsden estate, and many others, the society has been able to amass some outstanding collections. The Dorothy Waterhouse Room contains one of the finest displays of period costumes to be found in a small New England museum. Other rooms contain excellent collections of Elmer Crowell bird carvings, Sandwich glass, dolls, quilts, Dodge MacKnight paintings, and antique furnishings and memorabilia from Charles Ayling's home.

The tour ends at the Down Under Shop, a treasure chest of bric-a-brac donated for sale to support the museum. The Mary Lincoln House is open from 2 to 4:30 P.M. on Thursdays and Sundays during the summer season. Group tours at other times may be arranged by appointment. The museum is located across from the post office in the center of the village.

CROSBY BOAT YARD

Well over a century ago, Horace Crosby designed a rather radical fishing boat for the Cape's fishermen. The Crosbys had been building fine boats for years by then, but most laughed when they saw this one; it had a square stern, wide beam and a single mast well forward. The laughing stopped as soon as the sea trials were underway, for the Crosby boat quickly proved itself fast, safe, seaworthy, and dependable. The consensus was, "quick as a cat, b'gosh," and the famed Crosby Cat was born.

Until the turn of the century, the Cat was a working boat, primarily for fishing. The pleasure boat skippers finally realized it was also a fine family sailer and the Crosby Cat became world-renowned. Lighter, simpler, and less expensive boats have now priced the cats out of the market, but the old ones are in great demand. A catboat association still meets at Mystic, Connecticut, each year and the Crosby Yacht Building and Storage Company built its last catboat as recently as 1969. (They will still build them on special order but the cost of handcrafted wood boats puts them out of reach of most buyers.)

Fourth-generation Crosbys now operate competing building, storage, service, and docking facilities around West Bay in Osterville. It's a friendly competition, both have their hands full, and there are fifth-generation Crosbys ready to carry on. The Crosby Yacht Building and Storage Company does most of the wood boatbuilding now, primarily Wianno senior class sailboats. These are 25-foot knockabouts, very popular among yachtsmen on the Cape. Boatbuilding is limited to the winter months, so if you want to see one under construction, that's the time to go.

Crosby Yacht Building is located just off West Bay Road, Osterville. Cousin Chester's place is around the corner on Bridge Street. Visitors are welcome at any time.

CAPTAIN JONATHAN PARKER HOUSE (c. 1795)

The Osterville Historical Society and Museum at the corner of West Bay and Parker roads is a charming house that once belonged to Captain Jonathan Parker.

The Parker House now bears little resemblance to the original, probaby a half-Cape, as only two of its original rooms remain intact. All the others have been altered or added over the past 175 years.

Each room represents either a different period or a different specialty. The early eighteenth, late eighteenth, and early nineteenth centuries are each illustrated by complete room collections of the period. Other rooms contain exceptional marine artifacts, documents, and antique children's toys. Many feature collections of early American antiques from friends of the society.

Visitors are given a booklet explaining the features of special interest in each room. The museum is open to the public each Thursday and Sunday from 3 to 5 P.M. from the last Sunday in June to the end of September. Admission is free.

DOTTRIDGE HOMESTEAD (c. 1800)

On Main Street in Cotuit village you will find the Dottridge Homestead, restored and opened to the public by the Historical Society of Santuit and Cotuit.

Samuel B. Dottridge was born in London in 1786, the son of an innkeeper down by the docks. In the early 1800s, press gangs roamed the streets kidnaping able-bodied young men for the British navy, and it is believed that Samuel was sent abroad to escape. At any rate, he was living in Brewster in 1805, and was apprenticed "to learn the art, trade or mystery of an house carpenter." Fulfilling his indenture on his twenty-first birthday in 1807, he received a suit of clothes "in a handsome and decent manner as is customary in such cases."

In 1808 Samuel married Abigail Chase, and they purchased a three-room house built some years before, probably about 1800. Opportunities on the south shore beckoned the young couple, and in about 1811 they moved to Cotuit Highground, bringing their home on skids drawn by yokes of oxen. The Dottridges settled on what is now Ocean View Avenue, facing the sea.

Moved several times over the years in the near vicinity, the homestead was given to the historical society and now serves as the historical museum for the two villages. It is of interest that Santuit was the original Cotuit; its name was changed to accommodate a second post office in the area.

The old home is authentic in every detail and all furnishings date from the 1800–1850 period. In keeping with Dottridge's position, the furnishings reflect only those items that a relatively poor carpenter might have in his home. Several items were fashioned by Dottridge himself. Wide board flooring, rafters spliced with pegs, and other fine examples of original workmanship grace this attractive Cape cottage.

Behind the house is a museum of Cape and early American memorabilia, including a collection of wooden tools, household items, and a variety of souvenirs brought back by sailing captains.

The Dottridge Homestead is open to the public Thursdays from 3 to 5 P.M. and Sundays from 4 to 6 P.M. from late June to mid-September. Admission is free.

COTUIT OYSTERS

Captain William Childs, born in Cotuit in 1819, went to sea for twenty-four years before deciding that there might be more money in those delicious local oysters. In 1857 he, his son Samuel, and two sons-in-law, Ezra Gifford and Ezra Hobson, set up their shanties and went into business. They soon prospered and became one of the largest oyster shippers on the Cape. In those days the oysters were packed in barrels, hauled by wagon to West Barnstable, and then carried by rail to Boston, New York, and other markets.

In 1894, Samuel and the two Ezras went into business for themselves and moved their shanty to the Little River area. In 1908 another group formed the Cotuit Oyster Company and about 1920 also moved their business to Little River. Ezra Gifford, Jr., kept up the independent operation until his death in 1940, and his son Herbert continued until 1954. The Cotuit Oyster Company continues to thrive at the foot of Little River Road.

No longer do the oystermen merely rake in nature's bounty. For many years, Cotuit oysters have begun life in Long Island Sound. The company purchases both seed oysters and the three- and four-year-olds. The adult oysters are summered in Cotuit waters and ready for the market in the fall. Seed oysters are the very young, ¼ inch to 2 inches long, and they require about four years to mature. A female oyster produces up to a half billion eggs in a season but the survival rate is almost as minute as the egg.

The purity of the Cotuit water and its chemical content are given credit for the exceptional flavor of the Cotuit oyster, known and in demand throughout the world. You won't find pearls here; the edible oyster never produces a valuable pearl. The lining of its shell lacks the mother-of-pearl that gives the true pearl its beauty.

Oyster harvests at Cotuit begin in early September and it is interesting to watch the men dredge the oysters up, sort them for size, and pack them for shipment.

The story is told of a lady who was asked the secret of her longevity on her ninety-fifth birthday. "Well," she replied, "I dunno', 'cept it might be they fed me oysters when I was a baby."

MARSTON'S MILL

The first fulling (finishing rough cloth for use) mill in America, Marston's mill, was built in 1689 and rebuilt after a fire in the 1800s; it served the area for over two hundred years. Long idle, it came down in a gale in 1930, but the dam, herring run, and a beautiful setting remain. The site is just a few yards in on Route 149 off Route 28.

Thomas Macy built the mill, but old Ben Marston generally gets the credit. Marston arrived in 1738, took over the mill, and prospered sufficiently so that the village bears his name. His son went to Yale, and became the wise and respected Judge Nymphas Marston of Barnstable.

Old Ben and Judge Nymphas were poles apart politically: Ben was a Whig revolutionary, Nymphas a Loyalist to the Crown. Judge Nymphas was one of the key men who gave Barnstable the dubious honor of being the only Cape town not to vote for independence in 1776. Ben was an ardent patriot, however, and when some young soldiers shot up his dining room in a noisy celebration, Ben assured the boys it was all right "if they would carry out their zeal in shattering the ranks of the enemy."

PUBLIC GOLF COURSES

There are two 18-hole and two 9-hole golf courses in Barnstable open to the public.

On the north side is the venerable Cummaquid Golf Club, claiming to be the first course built on the Cape

(1895) and one of the oldest golf clubs in the country. Cummaquid is a semi-private course. The public is invited to play so long as the course is not overcrowded or being used for tournament play. Cummaquid is a 6,190-yard, par 71 course. It is located off Route 6A in Cummaquid near the Yarmouth line.

Downtown Hyannis has an 18-hole layout, Fiddler's Green, at the Dunfey Hyannis Resort on the west end rotary at the end of Main Street. Fiddler's Green is a 2,833-yard, par 54 course.

The Santuit Golf Course is a 9-hole, 2,635-yard, par 34 course located about a half mile south of Route 28 on Newtown (Old King's) Road. Tennis courts are available to the public in the summer season.

Cotuit Highground Country Club is located on Crocker Neck Road off School Street, Cotuit. One of the few seasonal courses, open from early April to late November, Cotuit Highground is a 9-hole, 2,504-yard, par 28 course.

PUBLIC SWIMMING BEACHES

Visitors to Barnstable must pay a parking fee at the beach or purchase a sticker from the town offices. The major Barnstable saltwater beaches on the south side are Craigville Beach at the end of Main Street, Centerville; Veterans Park behind the Kennedy Memorial, Hyannis; Kalmus Park Beach at the end of Ocean Street, Hyannis; and Loop Beach at the end of Ocean View Avenue, Cotuit. Saltwater beaches on the north side are Sandy Neck in West Barnstable and Mill Way Beach by Barnstable Village Harbor. The town maintains freshwater beaches at Hathaway's Pond, Barnstable; Hamblin's Pond, Marstons Mills; Lake Wequaquet, Centerville; Joshua's Pond, Osterville; and Lovell's Pond, Santuit.

N

CAPE COD BAY

Bass Hole

Chase

Garden

6A

Yarmouth

Mill Pd

Follins Pond

Yarmouth Port

Kelly Bay

Dinahs Pond

CENTRE ST.

ST.

WILLOW

Dennis Pond

Greenough Pond

7

8

6

RD.

STATION

Y A R M O U T H

River

Little Sandy Pd.

Horse Pond

Long Pd.

South Yarmouth

ISLAND

Plashes Pd.

RD.

WEST YARMOUTH

Big Sandy Pond

Seine Pd.

Bass

W. Yarmouth

28

Bass River

Hyannis Park

SOUTH SEA AV.

SHORE DR.

Bass River Beach

Lewis Pd.

S.

Sea View Beach

Lewis Bay

Sea Gull Beach

Great Island

NANTUCKET SOUND

Point Gammon

Copyright, THE NATIONAL SURVEY, 1973
Chester, Vermont

CHAPTER IV

Yarmouth

Retirement on the Cape is the dream of many, and Yarmouth is the choice of a large proportion of them. Yarmouth's first elderly resident came the hard way. At the age of seventy-five, the Reverend Stephen Bachiler of Lynn set out on foot in the winter of 1637–1638 with a few of his followers to start a new settlement and church in the eastern section of the land of the Mattakeese.

Bachiler was a stormy old cuss, continually at odds with the Church of England and authority in general. As a town builder he was a dismal failure. Friendly Indians helped his little group through the first year, but he and his followers had suffered enough. They left in the spring of 1639 to continue their battle with authority elsewhere. Excommunicated for unchastity in 1640, Bachiler took on three more wives before passing on in England shortly before his hundredth birthday.

Hard on the lively Reverend's heels came the first permanent settlers of Yarmouth: Anthony Thacher, John Crowe, and Thomas Howes were stable and hardworking men, more interested in building estates than engaging in religious squabbles. Predictably enough, their major concern was the division of land. New settlers arrived and the town was quickly incorporated. The miscellaneous collection of settlers had little in common except for their new town and their conflicting land claims. Instructions from the Plymouth court were at first vague but quickly clarified. The fiery Captain Myles Standish was sent down to straighten things out as he saw fit, and he did. By the time he left everyone was dissatisfied, but they all knew just where they stood. The good captain's reputation for decisive, iron-fisted, summary justice was not tarnished in Yarmouth.

Anthony Thacher quickly emerged as the leading citizen of the new town. Thacher, father of nine, had lost his wife and five of his children in England. In 1635, with a second wife and the four remaining youngsters, he set sail for Massachusetts. They arrived safely and took a coastal vessel from Ipswich to Marblehead. A storm struck off Cape Ann, and of the ship's company of twenty-three only Thacher and his wife survived. A scarlet coverlet was the only worldly possession they saved from the wreck. A son, John, was born in Marblehead in 1638, and the family moved to Yarmouth a year later. John Thacher grew up to be an army officer, a terror to hostile Indians and a dashing darling to the ladies. His twenty-one children managed to preserve the Thacher line still prevalent in Yarmouth today. Colonel John's old home in Yarmouth Port across from the post office is now maintained by the Society for the Preservation of New England Antiquities and is open to visitors during the summer season.

By 1641 Yarmouth, Sandwich, and Barnstable were all solidly established and overworking the Plymouth court with their petty legal disputes. A local court was appointed to settle cases involving not more than 20 shillings, with John Crowe (later Crowell) as the Yarmouth representative. This first court on the Cape led to the establishment of circuit courts in 1811; but perhaps of more historical interest, the selection of the town representatives for the court led, twenty years later, to the selectman system of local government we have today.

Before the turn of the century the aggressive settlers of Yarmouth had traded the Indians out of all their land on the north side and were rapidly squeezing them out on the south. In 1715 a large tract was reserved for the Indians around Long Pond and Bass River in what is now South Yarmouth. Over the years the area became known as Indian Town, and it was here that the last wigwams of the praying Indians of Yarmouth were in evidence as late as 1779.

Yarmouth settlers, of diversified interests and backgrounds, generally wanted more elbow room than the closely knit communities of Sandwich and Barnstable. Old Yarmouth covered a wide expanse and new settlements sprang up along the Bay shore and inland. In 1721 the East Parish of Yarmouth was formed in the area of Dennis. Distance from the meeting house was the usual argument for promulgating new parishes, but dissatisfaction with the establishment and the spirit of independence were always in the air. In fact, almost all of the early new parishes sooner or later incorporated as new towns. Dennis took the step in 1793, the fathers of the new parish becoming the leaders of the new town.

The Quakers that came to Yarmouth generally congregated in the southern part of the town. In 1802 a meeting house was constructed near Follins Pond and replaced in 1809 by the Friends Meeting House that still holds services each Sunday on North Main Street. The area then known as Friends Village is much of the South Yarmouth of today.

Ever since Anthony Thacher had been licensed to "draw wine" in 1643, the good citizens of Yarmouth had debated the question of intoxicating spirits. The second temperance society in the United States was organized here, and in 1817 the town voted to allow only one ordinary "for the accommodation of travelers," on the tavern keeper's bond not to sell to his neighbors. Alcohol for medicinal purposes was excluded from the restrictions, and one might logically conclude that patent tonics did a good business in some households.

At about the same time, the townspeople of Yarmouth and other Cape villages sought to advance their intellec-

tual and social graces, and many a Lyceum Hall was constructed, such as the one on Hallet Street in Yarmouth
Port. Centers of light and learning, these self-improve-
ment societies also engendered museums, libraries, and
historical societies in many towns. Religion and politics
were forbidden; however, debates, lectures, readings, and
displays covered a wide range of other topics. The Lyceum
Hall in Yarmouth Port is now used only as a book de-
pository, primarily due to the lack of parking facilities,
but in its day it was the center of culture for the prosperous community.

In 1836 the town welcomed the ingredient required to
keep things stirred up — the *Yarmouth* Register com-
menced publication from its new plant on Railroad Avenue. Under the leadership of N. S. Simpkins, the fledgling
paper took out after Andrew Jackson, Martin Van Buren,
and the editorial policy of the *Barnstable Patriot,* and it's
still going strong. Now located a few doors up from the
Lyceum Hall, the *Register* continues in hard pursuit of
the establishment.

Whether the uplift of the lyceums or the thunder of
the *Register* had anything to do with it, we can't say, but
the 1840s produced a village improvement society under
the leadership of Amos Otis that changed the face of the
north side. Otis loved trees and he possessed admirable
foresight. Under his direction a mile of elm saplings were
planted on either side of Hallet Street (Route 6A) in Yarmouth Port. A century later this street was considered
one of the most beautiful in the nation, a cathedral of
stately elms forming a tunnel of green foliage and cool
shade. Regrettably, the elms are falling fast; Dutch elm
disease and age take several more as each year goes by.

No longer a cathedral perhaps, the old street still retains much of its charm. The old King's Highway here is
lined on both sides with a larger number of beautiful old
homes than can be found elsewhere in a single group.
Captain Asa Eldridge of the *Red Jacket* lived here, as did
Captain Ebenezer Sears, Colonel John Thacher, Genera

Hamblin, and many other famed Yarmouth men. The four authentic old half-Capes in a row west of Summer Street are some of the most-photographed homes on the Cape. Some say half-Capes were built as a dowry for unmarried daughters; those who married enlarged the home as the family grew. The unlucky spinster at least had modest independence in her tiny home. Gone is the Chandler Gray House from the corner of Wharf Lane, torn down in 1899. It was here that the women of Yarmouth melted their pewter in March 1776 to mold bullets for their men to use in the defense of Dorchester Heights.

By 1854 the Old Colony railroad had reached Yarmouth and soon attracted the Methodist camp meetings, long popular on the lower Cape. A grove was purchased on Willow Street in 1863 and can still be identified by the Y.C.G.A. sign out front. Camp meetings were annual gatherings, a sort of evangelical clambake. From a tent community, the Yarmouth Camp Ground became quite a summer cottage village, with Grove Hall headquarters and meeting grounds. The area hasn't been used for a camp meeting for years. The dozens of cottages whose architecture can only be described as "early Methodist" are privately owned now.

The seagoing trades declined rapidly as the railroad inched its way down the Cape. In May 1871 the *Register* announced the sad news to Yarmouth, "No Boston packet this year!" Old Yarmouth curled up and took a snooze for the next many years. Sure, in 1871 Mrs. Hervey Snow arranged for two kerosene street lamps by her home, and in 1894 there was talk of putting in two miles of macadamized road. And yes, in 1913 the first electric lights came to West Yarmouth. There was no great hurry and the summer people could write home their standard joke about "how they take in the Yarmouth sidewalks at nine o'clock." But times slowly changed and an era came to an end.

South and West Yarmouth were quick to join in the post–World War II tourist boom that encompassed so much of the south coast. Yarmouth has had another more recent boom as the most popular retirement center on the Cape. Centrally located at mid-Cape, with the resort pleasures of the south coast and the historic charm of the Bay side, the retirement home popularity of Yarmouth shows every indication of continuing. Luckily, large-tract grid housing developments have so far been excluded. Those that exist are generally small, with trees left intact and land contours followed so that the new homes rapidly blend into their surroundings.

Yarmouth today is wide awake again, so much so that it is one of the fastest-growing towns in the Commonwealth. Its population of 12,000 covers 24 square miles from the Bay to Nantucket Sound, and includes the villages of Yarmouth Port, Yarmouth, South Yarmouth, West Yarmouth and Bass River.

COLONEL JOHN THACHER HOUSE (c. 1680)

Born in 1638, John Thacher came to Yarmouth as an infant, the surviving child of Anthony Thacher, one of the original settlers of the town. When John married Rebecca Winslow in 1664, his father built a home for the couple near the corner of present-day Thacher Street and Thacher Shore Road in Yarmouth Port. In 1680 the home was moved to its present location at the corner of Thacher Street and Route 6A across from the post office. The original home consisted of the eastern section only; the western wing was added some years later.

Rebecca died in 1683 and the dashing Colonel John spent many grief-stricken weeks lamenting her death with pages of sad verse. It wasn't long, however, before he began to take notice of a handsome young woman he had long known as a child of his friends, the Gorhams. The Colonel's son was paying court to the young lady at the same time. A bargain was struck, five pounds and a yoke of oxen passed from father to son, and forty-six-year-old Colonel John Thacher pursued and won his young bride in 1684.

The Colonel and his wives were blessed with twenty-one children. Thachers have played a major role in Yarmouth since the founding of the town, and this old house has sheltered many generations of them. Judge Peter Thacher, Judge George Thacher and Colonel Thomas Thacher all occupied the ancestral home over the years. Miss Mary Thacher gave this house to the Society for the Preservation of New England Antiquities at the same time that she donated the Winslow Crocker property next door. The Colonel John Thacher House is open to the public Tuesday through Saturday, 11 A.M. to 4 P.M., June through September. A nominal admission fee is charged.

John's father, grantee Anthony Thacher, had his homestead at the end of Church Street across Thacher Shore Road, about 150 yards past the intersection. A historical marker indicates its approximate location.

WINSLOW CROCKER HOUSE (c. 1780)

Across from the post office on Route 6A in Yarmouth Port stands the beautiful Winslow Crocker House, owned by the Society for the Preservation of New England Antiquities. Winslow Crocker was a Barnstable man and the old house spent most of its many years about nine miles west on Route 6A in West Barnstable.

Not much is known about Crocker. His son Watson inherited the home on his father's death in 1821. Watson Crocker's two wives presented him with a dozen youngsters, and it is believed they were all born in the big house. The youngest, George Fenelon Crocker (1847–1941) inherited the home and never married. In his later years he lived in one room with his two dogs and kept the balance of the house unfurnished. It is assumed that the other eleven children divided up the family's possessions as they grew up, married, and moved away. Recent visitors to the old homestead who knew "Fen" Crocker personally tell how he built small gunning boats in one front parlor and stored apples in the other.

In 1935 Miss Mary Thacher purchased the house and

had it moved to its present location. Due to the size of the house and the cathedral of elms along the highway, it was necessary to dismantle and rebuild the house board by board. When the huge chimney was rebuilt, 13 feet wide at its base, brick was salvaged from the original so that each of the six fireplaces could be refaced and the chimney above the roof surfaced with the original material.

Miss Thacher put the old home in apple pie order, furnished it with her collection of period antiques, and donated it to the society on condition that she would retain life occupancy. After Miss Mary's death in 1956, the society opened the Winslow Crocker House to the public.

This gracious home is a magnificent example of colonial architecture, authentic and unspoiled. Of particular interest is the lavish use of fine pine paneling and wainscoting. Seven of the eleven rooms are finished in this style. Also intriguing is the gun room snuggled behind the fireplaces. In the early days it was the one place sure to keep your powder dry. There are wide board pine floors throughout, exceptional wrought-iron hardware, and even a slight bow to the roof.

The Winslow Crocker House is open to the public Tuesday through Saturday, 11 A.M. to 4 P.M., June through September. A nominal admission fee is charged.

CAPTAIN BANGS HALLET HOUSE (1840)

This attractive Greek Revival home is a short way in on Strawberry Lane on the Yarmouth Port village green. When Captain Bangs Hallet bought the property there was a smaller 1740 house already there. As Captain Hallet's family expanded and prospered, he had the front section removed and the new home added on to it. The rear sitting room, basement kitchen, and a small attic bedroom are all that remain of the earlier structure. It is believed that the main section of the older house was moved to nearby Summer Street, or Hawes Lane, as it was then called.

Visitors receive a booklet that gives a brief history of

the house and an inventory of the furnishings on display. Included are portraits of Bangs and Anna Hallet and many fine antiques and bric-a-brac donated by friends of the historical society.

The Captain Bangs Hallet House is owned by the Historical Society of Old Yarmouth and is open to the public Monday through Saturday from 10 A.M. to noon and from 2 to 4 P.M. during the summer season. A nominal admission fee is charged. Due to parking restrictions on Strawberry Lane, visitors are requested to park in the Botanic Trails parking area directly behind the house. The entrance sign is to the right of the Yarmouth Port Post Office on Route 6A

BOTANIC TRAILS OF YARMOUTH PORT

Thanks to a grant of 53 acres by a descendent of Anthony Thacher, the Historical Society of Old Yarmouth has been able to provide excellent marked trails through unspoiled countryside in Yarmouth Port. The area provides a fine opportunity for a delightful walk and the unhurried observation of plants, trees, and wildlife.

The gatehouse and entrance to the Botanic Trails are located to the right rear of the village post office on Route 6A. The trails are open year round, but the gatehouse, which offers trail maps and a guide to the local flora and fauna, is manned only during the summer season. Guided tours may be arranged with the curator of the Captain Bangs Hallet House next door. An admission fee is charged to assist in maintaining and improving the trails.

At present there are about a mile and a half of improved trails, with additions planned for the near future. Your walk includes Miller's Pond, a wet "kettle hole" formed by a retreating glacier. Great blocks of ice remained after most of the glacial ice had melted away, forming depressions, or the "kettles," so common on Cape Cod. There are no fish in the pond, but there are plenty of frogs and turtles to catch if the youngsters are quick enough.

The shady woodland trails of Yarmouth Port are for walkers only; bicycles, horses, unleashed dogs, and the like are not permitted. Camping, picnicking, and hunting are also prohibited.

YARMOUTH PORT VILLAGE PUMP

Years ago all of our towns had their village pump; it was a place to draw household water, to water your horse, or just to take a refreshing drink on a hot day. One of the most attractive of the few remaining pumps is at the corner of Route 6A and Summer Street in Yarmouth Port.

The pump and stone watering trough date from 1886. In 1928, Mabel Simpkins had a wrought-iron memorial erected in memory of her husband. The Simpkinses, an old and distinguished Yarmouth family, contributed greatly to the commercial and philanthropic well-being of the town. Nathaniel Stone Simpkins was the founder of the *Yarmouth Register,* the active and aggressive newspaper still serving the area.

THE NEW CHURCH

Across from the village green in Yarmouth Port is the beautiful old New Church, or Church of the New Jerusalem. The New Church was one of the most influential in Yarmouth in the latter half of the nineteenth century.

The Church of the New Jerusalem, taking its name from the Book of Revelation, bases its doctrine on the word of the Lord as interpreted by the writings of Emanuel Swedenborg (1688–1772). A successful Swedish scientist, Swedenborg received a spiritual call when he was about fifty-five and went on to write prodigiously of the revelations that came to him. His major work was a verse-by-verse interpretation of the books of Genesis and Exodus as a divine parable having a spiritual sense quite different from their literal interpretation. The New Church is often called the Swedenborgian Church.

Interest in the New Church first surfaced in Yarmouth

in 1823. By 1843 a formal church was formed by a group
that included Nathaniel Simpkins and eight other substantial citizens. Services were first held in Yarmouth
Hall and later across the street on the upper floor of what
is now the Parnassus Book Store. The present church was
built and dedicated in 1870.

Many of the leading citizens of the town belonged to
this church during the last half of the century. The roster
of Simpkinses, Hallets, Gorhams, Eldridges, Thachers,
Howes, and Hamblins reads like a "who's who" of the
town at the time.

The New Church, always well maintained, was designed by an Italian architect in a style not common to
Cape churches of the period. The church enjoys one of
the finest organs in New England and attracts exceptional
organists and soloists to their summer services. These
highly trained musicians have established a tradition of
"worship in the sphere of great music." Talented musicians also visit the old church to play for their own enjoyment and organ recitals have occasionally been presented at the church.

The ministry of the New Church in Yarmouth Port has
been in the Priestnal family, passing from father to son
for sixty years. The church is open from early July to the
Sunday before Labor Day, with services at 10:45 A.M.
each Sunday. Visitors are always welcome.

BASS HOLE

Whether it is fact or legend, Bass Hole has a claim to
its place in history. At the very end of Center Street in
Yarmouth Port is a beautiful little cove looking out on the
Bay, with Sandy Neck on the left and Chapin Beach on
the right. Noted for bass and shell fishing, with a long
boardwalk out over the marshes, it's a delightful spot at
any season. If you enjoy the story that goes with it, so
much the better.

Students of the Norse sagas have been interpreting the

manuscripts *Flatey Book, Hauk's Book,* and *A.M.* 557 for years and have come up with many different interpretations. Edward F. Gray, in his book *Leif Eriksson, Discoverer of America,* A.D. 1003, makes a strong case that Thorvald Eriksson, younger brother of Leif, spent three winters at No Mans Land off of Gay Head, Martha's Vineyard. On one voyage from No Man's Land he reportedly damaged the keel of his ship rounding the Cape, put ashore, and called the place "Keelness," our present Provincetown. He soon continued south to an anchorage, which Gray insists was none other than Bass Hole. Next to Bass Hole was the "wooded headland" of the saga, known by the Indians as Hockanom, the hilly area off to the right rear. The party went ashore to spend the night, only to be awakened by war canoes coming down what is now Chase Garden Creek, the tidal river to the right that winds back into the marshes. A fight ensued; Thorwald, mortally wounded, was carried to the headland. The saga reports him as saying, "Ye shall bury me here and place a cross at my head and another at my feet, and call it Crossness forevermore." His followers did so, returned to spend the winter at No Man's Land, and then returned to Greenland.

There are no crosses at the Hockanom headland near Bass Hole. No trace has ever been found of Thorvald or his visit, but who is to say his bones aren't there today?

Though almost as hard to believe, it's a fact nonetheless: Bass Hole was once a shipyard. In 1750, the Bray family operated a shipyard here and built fishing and trading schooners of 50 to 150 tons. The schooner *Perseverance* was launched here and a group of young people took her out before she was ballasted. The *Perseverance* capsized and Miss Anna Hawes, seventeen, was drowned. Launching a boat at Bass Hole today can be a tricky undertaking. If you don't draw more than two feet and stay within two hours of high tide you'll have no trouble — if you pay attention. Sands shift, channels change, and Bass Hole is not the harbor it used to be.

CAPTAINS ROW

Normally a shopping center, even a small one, would have no place in a guidebook. Captains Row is just that, a village shopping center, but of a different character.

A few years ago a rundown parcel of business property came on the market in the historic district of Yarmouth Port. Many legal, but to the residents unpleasant, uses could have been made of it. Instead, a few of the neighbors bought it and designed and built a small shopping court to blend completely with the surrounding colonial architecture and the historic charm of the town. In many ways they did their job too well; some visitors can't find it without assistance even when they know what they're looking for!

Captains Row is located between Pine Street and West Yarmouth Road on the south side of Route 6A in Yarmouth Port. There is a large hidden parking area in the rear. Browsers are most welcome.

CAPE COD COLISEUM

If your kids are sunburned and tired of the beaches, how about ice skating in midsummer? The new Cape God Coliseum on Whites Path off Union Street, South Yarmouth (Exit 8 on the Mid-Cape Highway), is ready and waiting.

Home of the Cape Cod Cubs of the Eastern Hockey League, the Coliseum provides ice for ten or eleven months of the year. From October to April it is used for ice events; home games of the Cubs, youth and amateur hockey and public skating. There even may be a basketball game or other event sandwiched in between. In May and possibly early June the ice disappears and trade shows, conventions and other events take over. Sometime in June the ice goes on again and, except for special events, remains through the summer and the following winter. Keep your eye on the local newspapers to determine the schedule of events available during your visit.

INDIAN GRAVES

In 1715 a large tract of land was set aside for the Indians around Long Pond and Bass River in South Yarmouth. It was known as Pawkanawkut Village, or Indian Town, and wigwams were common in the area up to the end of the Revolutionary War. The war and smallpox decimated the Indian population so that only one old squaw remained just before the turn of the nineteenth century.

Perhaps the most famous of the legendary praying Indians of Yarmouth was Deacon Elisha Naughaught. His fervor was the equal of any of his white contemporaries and he could dish up hell, fire, and brimstone with the best of them. Legend has it that he stood his ground one day when attacked by a large number of black snakes. One climbed his body and tried to put his head into the Deacon's mouth. Naughaught opened his jaws and snapped the snake's head off. The rest of the snakes fled and the good Deacon strolled home to tell his flock of his latest adventure. Deacon Naughaught died peacefully at the age of eighty-nine and is probably buried in this South Yarmouth Indian burying ground.

A short way down Indian Memorial Drive off Station Avenue you will find the Indian Monument historic marker placed by the town. One boulder is engraved "On this slope lie buried the last native Indians of Yarmouth." There are no gravestones on the slope overlooking Long Pond. Kiehtan, the red man's Great Spirit of the Western Heavens, would undoubtedly approve.

YARMOUTH HERRING RUN

Though not as spectacular as the Brewster run, the Yarmouth herring run between Swan and Long ponds in South Yarmouth has charms of its own.

The alewives, or herring if you prefer, come from Nantucket Sound up Parker's River to Swan Pond. Those originally spawned in Long Pond then make the half mile run between the two. The town has established catching pools just as the alewives leave Swan Pond and just before they enter Long Pond. The narrow shallow brook between the ponds is lined by a trail that makes a most interesting nature walk, particularly in May when the run is most impressive. Wear old shoes or overshoes as the path gets soggy in spots. It is hoped that the town will improve both the run and the trail, for they have great potential.

Long Pond is only seven feet higher than Swan and this makes a good run difficult, but not impossible. The brook sands up heavily and tides, sandbars, and lack of rainfall sometimes make the brook a real test of the ale-wives' determination. They skitter along, sometimes on their sides or half out of the water, and one gets an excellent opportunity to observe them in an unusual setting.

The Swan Pond outlet is located at the end of Clear Brook Road off Winslow Gray Road. A dirt road leads to the pond, about a hundred yards farther. The Long Pond inlet is at the corner of Winslow Gray Road and Long Pond Drive.

Should you wish further information concerning what is taking place and what to look for at a herring run, a more detailed account is given under the Stoney Brook Herring Run, Brewster, section of this book.

FRIENDS MEETING HOUSE

The "cursed sect of heretics," the Quakers, soon spread from Sandwich to Yarmouth. The government invoked the whip and the fine but they were not to be denied. In self-defense and for relative peace of mind, members of the sect formed their congregations away from the existing villages. The Yarmouth Quakers moved south and formed what was known as Friends Village, now South Yarmouth.

By 1717 the town had mellowed sufficiently to end the requirement that Quakers contribute to the support of the orthodox minister. In 1809 a new meeting house was built by David Kelley. It is still in operation at the corner of

North Main Street and Kelley Road in South Yarmouth. Sunday Services are held at 10 A.M. in the summer and visitors are welcome.

The Friends Meeting House and burying ground are models of the simple faith of their Quaker heritage. There is no pulpit, stained glass, or music. Shutters may be lowered to separate the sexes during meetings. The rope and log operation of the shutters and the 1832 clock made by Ezra Kelley of New Bedford are of great interest. The burying ground, row upon row of identical headstones, emphasizes the Quaker conviction that all are equal in God's eyes. No rich, no poor, and no epitaphs. The stark simplicity of the meeting house, burying ground and the service itself is most impressive.

JUDAH BAKER WINDMILL (1791)

At the end of Willow Street, just across River Street on Bass River in South Yarmouth, stands the Judah Baker Windmill.

Judah Baker built this grist mill in South Dennis. Captain Freeman Crowell moved the mill to West Dennis and in 1863 Captain Bradick Matthews moved it to its present site. Moving windmills was a common practice of the day; the mills were bought and sold, "dismasted" and moved as the needs of the villages ebbed and flowed.

The old grist mill shut down for good in 1891 and was purchased by millionaire Charles Henry Davis. Davis's home, "The House of Seven Chimneys," was for many years a tourist attraction. Four old houses and a barn connected by passageways produced almost 50 rooms, 21 exterior doors, 219 windows, and of course the 7 chimneys. Davis maintained the windmill and willed it to the town on his death.

YARMOUTH PLAYHOUSE

Now in its fourth season, the Yarmouth Playhouse is the only fully professional resident theater company on the Cape. Completely staffed by New York professionals and sanctioned by Actors Equity, the company at Yarmouth presents a diversified program from the first of July to about the end of September.

The playhouse also conducts a school of theater during the season by arrangement with the Cape Cod Theater Workshop. The school exposes these young apprentices to all facets of theater production, rehearsal, and performance, inasmuch as a resident company must develop each production on the job, as opposed to the imported package productions of the other professional theaters on the Cape.

The old playhouse itself has quite a history. Constructed in the off-season by fishermen on Nantucket in 1882, the building was floated on rafts to the Cape. Its home for a few years was on River Street, where it served as a general store. Since then the structure has functioned as the Eureka Dance Hall, the Standish Opera House, a Chinese theater, and a Masonic Hall. The Yarmouth Playhouse is now located on Old Main Street, South Yarmouth. From the Bass River Bridge traffic light go south about a quarter of a mile, and you'll find it on your right.

Performances are generally at 8:30 nightly except Sunday, with Wednesday matinees at 3. Season subscriptions are available. Tickets may be purchased at the box office from 10 A.M. in season or at any of the Ticketron locations.

PERFORMING ARTS ASSOCIATION

The Cape Cod Performing Arts Association was established in 1967 to promote the performance and enjoyment of fine music on the Cape. Its only criterion is excellence in programming and performance. The association is a nonprofit organization and friends and patrons are solicited.

Each summer the association presents one or two programs and possibly a workshop. In 1972 it featured the Philadelphia String Trio and lecture demonstration as a prelude to a projected two-week Workshop in Early Music scheduled for 1973.

For current information write to the association, Box
231, Yarmouth Port, Mass. 02675.

AQUARIUM

On the north side of Route 28, just west of Parkers
River bridge in West Yarmouth, is the Aquarium of Cape
Cod.

Hundreds of specimens in picture-window fish tanks
range from exotic tropical varieties to those native to the
waters surrounding Cape Cod. Alligators, squid, penguins,
harbor seals, piranha, and sharks are also featured. A
large seashell collection and other marine exhibits are of
interest. Admission fees include admittance to the indoor
stadium and dolphin pool, where a continuous aquatic
circus takes place in season. The trained dolphins, Tom,
Dick, and Harriet, and the trained sea lions are a delight
for all ages.

The aquarium is open from 9 A.M. to 9 P.M. seven days
a week from June to October. From then to April the
Aquarium is open weekends 9 A.M. to 5 P.M. and from
April to June open six days (excluding Monday) from
9 A.M. to 5 P.M. Admission fees are charged; children under 12 pay half price.

BAXTER MILL (1710)

> *The Baxter boys they built a mill,*
> *Sometimes it ran,*
> *Sometimes stood still.*
> *But when it ran, it made no noise,*
> *Because 'twas built by Baxter's boys.*

The first known publication of this bit of doggerel was
in 1880, but it was old even then. It honored John and
Shubael Baxter who built this mill in 1710. The mill is
located on the north side of Route 28 in West Yarmouth
about a quarter mile before the Barnstable line and is
open to the public in the summer season.

Baxter Mill was originally powered by an outside
wooden water wheel. In about 1860 the mill was con-

verted with the most modern improvement of the day: a metal water turbine was installed to replace the old-fashioned water wheel. The turbine rests under water and under the mill so that it can be operated even when ice or low water level conditions might stop the water wheel.

The old mill closed down in about 1900. Dustin Baker, the last miller, earned 68 cents a day at the time. As the mill deteriorated over the years it was used for many purposes. In the 1950s it was a gift shop, then a lobster stand. In 1960 it was purchased by Harold Castonguay, a civic-minded local businessman, who restored it — aided by volunteers — and turned it over to the town.

All of the original machinery was used in the restoration except the turbine which, rusted beyond repair, now graces the shore of Mill Pond for all to inspect. A replacement turbine was found on a hillside in Maine and the old mill now operates again as it did in the 1860s. The Baxter boys would be proud of their handiwork.

PUBLIC GOLF COURSES

There are two 18-hole golf courses in Yarmouth open to the public.

Bass River Golf Course, on Highbank Road in South Yarmouth, is a 6,235-yard, par 72 course. Electric golf carts, pull carts, and a practice green and fairway are available for your use.

Blue Rock Golf Course is almost next door to Bass River. The main entrance is on Great Western Road; you will also see signs from Highbank Road and North Main in South Yarmouth. Blue Rock is a 2,803-yard, par 54 course.

PUBLIC SWIMMING BEACHES

Visitors to Yarmouth must pay a parking fee at the beach or purchase a parking sticker at Town Hall. The major Yarmouth saltwater beaches on the south side are Bass River Beach at the end of South Street; Parkers River Beach, Sea View Beach, and Bay View Beach all on South

Shore Road, South Yarmouth; Thacher Park Beach at the end of Sea View Avenue, South Yarmouth; Sea Gull Beach at the end of South Sea Avenue, West Yarmouth; Englewood Beach at the end of Berry Avenue, West Yarmouth; and Colonial Acres Beach at the end of Standish Way, West Yarmouth. The sole saltwater beach on the north side is Bass Hole Beach at the end of Center Street, Yarmouth Port. The town maintains a freshwater beach on Long Pond off Indian Memorial Drive, South Yarmouth.

CAPE COD BAY

N

Sea St. Beach
Cold Storage Beach
Sesuit Harbor
Quivet Neck
Coles Pd

Corporation Beach
Nobscusset Pt.
Nobscusset Harbor
Sesuit Neck

SESUIT RD.

Sesuit Cr.

Ouivet Cr.

SEA ST.

Bass Hole Beach

BEACH ST.

Scargo L.

East Dennis

134

Bass Hole

Dennis

6A

D E N N I S

Aunt Patty's Pd.

Chase Garden Cr.

Flax Pond

Run Pd.

OLD BASS RD.

SETUCKET RD.

Grassy Pond

AIRLINE RD.

RIVER RD.

Follins Pond

Kelly Bay

6

9

DENNIS RD.

134

WESTERN

GREAT

S. Dennis

Swan Pond

River

WEST DENNIS

EAST DENNIS

Fresh Pd.

Dennis Port

Grand Cove

28

West Dennis

Bass

Kelley's Pd.

Swan Pond

LOWER

COUNTY RD.

West Dennis Beach

SOUND

NANTUCKET

Copyright, THE NATIONAL SURVEY, 1973
Chester, Vermont

CHAPTER V

Dennis

The Town of Dennis has many blessings to be thankful for and a major one is certainly its historical society, one of the most active and accurate on the Cape. All Cape towns are justifiably proud of their seagoing traditions and historical landmarks, but few have documented them with such care as the dedicated group in Dennis. Those black-on-white date markers that can be found prominently displayed on close to a hundred Dennis homes are fully reliable; each has been researched and authenticated by the society before the emblem is awarded.

In the early days Dennis was part of old Yarmouth. Thomas Howes and John Crowe, two of the original Yarmouth grantees, settled in the area we now know as the village of Dennis. A few years later, in 1641, Francis Baker settled on the north shore of Follins Pond. Richard Sears followed, settling farther east and William Nickerson of Chatham fame was not far behind. The later arrivals had to move farther up the coast and inland to find satisfactory homesteads. Nathaniel Baker, the son of Francis, soon purchased a large tract in South Dennis, the Nickersons much of the land immediately north of the Bakers, and the Searses moved well along the coast to what is now East Dennis. Most of the oldest homes in each area of the town can be traced back to these and other family groups. Large areas within villages were often better known by family names, such as Searsville in East Dennis, Baker Town in South Dennis and Crowe Town in West Dennis.

More and more settlers found their way to the eastern section of Yarmouth, but it was not until 1721 that a parish was established in what is now the village of Dennis. It was still pretty rough country and no suitable and willing pastor could be found to serve the new congregation. In 1725 the Reverend Josiah Dennis took on the challenge, served the town well for thirty-eight years, and joined the immortals by having all five villages of the town named in his honor. The Josiah Dennis Manse, the minister's home during most of his pastorate, is one of the fine historical landmarks preserved, restored, and open to the public, due in large measure to the efforts of the historical society.

Dennis men and women were among the earlier settlers of the Cape, but Dennis as a town was a late-bloomer. It was not until 1793, 154 years after the founding of Yarmouth, that the East Parish was incorporated as the Town of Dennis.

Each town has its favorite deepwater captains and Dennis is no exception. It had 379 of them and they are all favorites. On the list are 41 Howeses, 40 Crowells, 37 Nickersons, 33 Kelleys, 29 Bakers, 23 Searses, and a goodly representation of Halls, Chases, Thachers, Studleys, Baxters, and Wixons. The master mariners of the village of Dennis were named Crowell, Hall and Howes, with one fellow named Robbins thrown in to keep it honest.

My favorite Dennis sea captain is Captain Joseph Baxter of West Dennis. His story was related to his daughter, Miss Hattie M. Baxter, who passed the information on to Neva O'Neil for inclusion in the Dennis Historical Society's booklet *Master Mariners of Dennis*.

Captain Baxter was born in 1834 and spent fifty-five of his allotted eighty-two years as a mariner. He first went to sea at the age of ten as cook on his father's ship. At nineteen he was mate on the brig *Erie,* but was soon drawn to San Francisco by the gold rush. Sizing up his western prospects, or the lack of them, he signed on with various vessels out of San Francisco and was soon mate on the schooner *Harrison,* off to the Ladrone Islands for fruit and the Marshall Islands for turtle.

On Saipan in 1856, the ship's captain and Mate Baxter negotiated for fruit, loaded the vessel, and gave a farewell dinner for the pagan king and his royal family. Mr. Baxter recalled:

His marriageable daughter was among the guests who dined with us on board the vessel. I do not recall that I was especially attentive to the young lady, and I cannot imagine what quali-ties the king saw in me which might develop sufficiently to warrant my becoming a member of his royal family. But he wished me to remain on the island and marry his daughter. He said that he would appoint me the next king if I would consent to do this. (The king appoints his successor, and if the natives are not pleased with his choice they fight to drive him out.)

I told him that this was very unexpected, that I had started out a humble seaman, simply looking for fruit and other mer-chandise which might give me a reasonable return for my labor. To become a king had never been any part of my ambi-tion, and that I should want at least one night in which to think it over.

I surmise that the captain did not approve of this love affair, for bright and early next morning he was off for the Marshall Islands to get a deck load of turtles, and I lost the only opportunity that ever presented itself to me of becoming a monarch.

Shortly after returning to California, Captain Baxter signed on the clipper *Golden West* for a voyage to China.

South China was in turmoil at the time, and much of Canton was in flames as British warships bombarded the city in retaliation for the killing of the English consul. Captain Baxter recalled:

A soldier ordered us to halt, right about and march back. He said that a white man's head was worth about five hundred dollars in that part of the city at that time. We thought best not to sell at that figure but wait for a better market.

* * *

On our way from Macao to Hong Kong we had a new and exciting experience. After getting well under way we saw coming for us a very peculiar looking boat. It was considerably over one hundred feet long, very narrow, had a mast at either end, and was rowed by one hundred and fifty oars. We soon learned that there was trouble in store for us and that we must prepare ourselves for a battle with Chinese pirates.

We knew that should these pirates succeed in getting near enough, they would throw from the mast heads, where men were posted, upon the deck of our boat a peculiar kind of weapon, looking somewhat like a bombshell, made of earthenware and charged with powder and other materials of an offensive and suffocating odor. When these strike, they explode and throw off an odor which disables those near it, giving the wretches an opportunity to murder and rob. We saw them in time, however, and having the advantage of being in a steamer and well provided with guns, we kept them at bay and escaped without injury.

By 1863 the Captain had returned to West Dennis and married Miss Harriet Stanton. The captain was twenty-eight, and his bride nineteen. The Civil War was on and a year later the captain went to Norfolk, Virginia, and was immediately called on to act as a pilotmaster for the Union forces. He saw considerable action, describing one engagement as follows:

A little incident which occurred here will show how close was our range. The head gunner, a man from Ohio, said, "Look boys. I'm going to knock that flag master off that tree." (He was on a branch waving his flag.) He then fired and down came limb, man, flag and all.

But we were not the only crack shots for during this time the gunners at the forts had been training their guns on us. They had riddled our boat to such an extent that she was now rapidly sinking.

When the Ohio man saw this, he jumped overboard. Being unable to swim, he soon sank. I was the last man to leave the boat which took with it to the bottom all I had including $125.

Three men who were swimming near me were shot by the sharpshooters, but I succeeded in reaching the bank of the river.

In a later incident the captain recalled:

I was seized by a detective who mistook me for the murderer of President Lincoln. Capt. Brown and the Brigadier General heard the commotion and came to my assistance. They asked the detective what he was trying to do. He said, "Look at this picture, it will tell for itself," but the Brigadier General answered "He is no Booth, for he has been on this boat two months to my knowledge!" This seemed to satisfy the detective who then went elsewhere to look for the assassin.

After ten months' service Captain Baxter returned to the north and engaged in trade along the Atlantic seaboard, in the West Indies and South America.

In about 1883 Captain Baxter bought in on the barkentine *Ralph M. Hayward* and resumed long voyaging. His son Obed made several voyages with his father with the clear understanding that no favors would be shown. Obed Baxter later said that his father did not speak to him after they stepped aboard at New York until their arrival at Sydney, Australia, except as he would to any sailor, to give an order.

Captain Joseph Baxter sailed the seven seas in the *Ralph M. Hayward* for many more years before he rolled up his charts, packed his sea chest, and retired to West Dennis in 1899. He died in 1916, one of the last of the old sailing masters of Dennis.

Dennis today is a charming town of five villages, Dennis, East Dennis, South Dennis, West Dennis, and Dennis Port, with one village at each corner and South Dennis, of all places, in the center. The town stretches from the Bay to the Sound with more miles of town-owned saltwater beach than any other town on the Cape.

Most of the Cape towns are frankly worried about the current real estate boom in their villages. True to the muted rhetoric and demure traditions so characteristic of

Cape Cod, the following advertisement appeared in a recent edition of the *Dennis-Yarmouth Register:*

OBITUARY
NOTICE

DENNIS, VILLAGE OF
at the age of 179 after a lingering illness of NO PLANNING. Laid to rest Monday, April 24, at the Dennis Planning Board meeting. The fatal blow was a 116 lot subdivision on 36 acres on Scargo Lake. It is reliably reported that her sister village of East Dennis is afflicted with the same fatal disease and that the latest attack is a 270 lot subdivision on 123 acres. She is survived by 14 other towns on Cape Cod. Services should be conducted in every village of every town for our deceased brethren.

I think it's safe to say that the 6,500 citizens of this 20-square-mile town will not be an easy prize for buccaneers of any description.

ANTIQUE HOMES DRIVING TOUR

The Dennis Historical Society has researched and marked close to a hundred antique homes in the five villages. Another score or so have been closely dated, but the work is not yet complete enough to issue an emblem. At this stage in their research, the society has concentrated on structures of 1830 and earlier.

Most of the homes in the pre-1830 period are unpretentious Capes, half-Capes, salt boxes, and colonials. The larger, more pretentious so-called captains houses, often of rather makeshift architecture, generally came later. For those of you who enjoy the traditional Cape architecture, there is a concentrated grouping of these old homes in the north side village of Dennis. With the exception of the Josiah Dennis Manse, they are all privately owned and therefore not open to inspection.

Coming from Yarmouth on Route 6A, you will pass Black Ball Hill Road on your right. About a hundred yards farther on your left is the Captain Jabez Howes House, built near Bass Hole in Yarmouth in 1800 and moved to its present location sometime before 1900. It is easily identifiable by the house number 472 and the "1800" emblem. The house is a traditional half-Cape, two front windows with the door to one side. Half-Capes were usually tiny homes consisting only of a parlor, keeping room, pantry and borning room. When more space was needed in a half house, the addition was sometimes extended to the side to make a three-quarter or full Cape, but more often the ells were added to the rear. Many of the front windowpanes on this house are obviously very old; the early crude glass is apparent from the street.

A short distance farther on behind a stone wall at number 496 is the David Howes House (1795). It was originally a full Cape cottage and faces south in the old manner. The enclosed porch is of course a much more recent addition.

The next house on the left and set well back is the John Howes House (1735). It's difficult to see behind the trees in summer, but it is a fine example of an early eighteenth-century Cape cottage. The front of the house faces south (yes, south is to your left as you face the house). The earlier homes almost always faced south to alleviate the heating problem in the front parlor. This home still retains the original fireplaces, wide board floors, and other interior features. The ells were added in about 1800.

Just past Signal Hill Road on your left is the Captain Uriah Howes House (1820). Now occupied by the Grose Galleries, Captain Uriah's home reflects his obvious prosperity. It is a hip-roof colonial, or "square rigger," built in the half-Cape style. The extension to the right is of later vintage. The captain owned the sloop *Salty* built by the Bray brothers at Bass Hole. His son was lost at sea in the infamous October gale of 1841.

About a hundred yards before the next intersection on your left is the 1787 Nathan Stone House. Nathan Stone, son of the Reverend Nathan Stone (the successor to Josiah Dennis), was the first trained builder in the area and this was the first house he built. It is a fine full Cape, close to the road, with a short hoist and a long peak. Nathan learned his trade in Boston and returned to build many fine homes on the Cape.

Drive a few yards further on to the intersection of New Boston and Nobscusset roads and turn left. At the corner on your left is the recently reshingled John Howes House facing New Boston Road. This half-Cape, built in 1775 and moved to its present location in about 1890, is on the site of the first schoolhouse in the area.

Down New Boston Road a short distance on your right you will see the 1700 Ebenezer Howes House, one of the oldest still standing on the north side. The building began as a two-story half house and was soon expanded on the other side of the front door, resulting in a typical early colonial. The house served for many years as a stagecoach stop and tavern and is still owned by descendants of Ebenezer Howes.

Considering the house names encountered so far, it's not surprising that the Howes family burying ground is located nearby. The Howes cemetery is discussed in the next section of this chapter.

To reach the Josiah Dennis Manse, turn in Beach Street and turn right on Whig Street; the Manse is on your right at the corner of Nobscusset Road.

Dennis is said to be the only town in the United States that owns the house of the eighteenth-century man for whom the town was named. The manse was built in 1736, a two-story salt box on three acres of land bordered by a brook and old stone walls. Plans are being made to furnish the house and open it to the public on a regular basis. The interior is truly representative of a fine early eighteeth-century home, with the original five fireplaces, old wide floorboards, paneling, wainscoting and beams intact.

Josiah Dennis was the first minister of the East Parish and served the community for thirty-eight years. He endeared himself to his people by his kindness and cheerful disposition.

The Reverend Dennis stored grain and staples in a small room of his house. Rats gnawed a hole through the floor and the simple-hearted old divine placed a bag of shot over the hole, resulting in the loss of his shot down the hole. When Dennis saw how his efforts worked he good-naturedly exclaimed, "Good heavens, I have shot a rat!"

Another time, returning from the marriage of a Mr. Robbins and a Miss Crowell, he met a friend who asked him where he'd been. "Oh," he said, "to marry a Robin to a Crow."

He once gave a neighbor going to Boston a list of articles to be purchased. When the neighbor consulted the list he couldn't make head nor tail of it. He brought it back to the reverend, who could not read it either. "Well," he said, "I did not write it to read myself. I wrote it for you to read."

Returning to Route 6A, a left turn will take you to the Zaccheus Howes house just before the Cape Playhouse. This house began its career as a half-Cape but has seen many changes and additions over the years, including a large dormer and sheds and ells of various descriptions.

Farther on at the corner of Corporation Road is the old Masonic Hall and schoolhouse built in 1802. The building originally stood on the site of the present Dennis Union Church and was moved to its present location in 1858. A two-story hip-roof, the house is now a private residence.

Continuing on Route 6A you will find the 1803 Aaron Crowell House on your right. It is a fine half-Cape with the interior largely unspoiled. This Aaron was the third in a direct line of five Aaron Crowells. The home is still owned by a direct descendant.

The second house after Elm Street on your left, set well back behind a stone wall and angled south as befits its age, is the Captain Daniel Howes House (1725). It is a fine full Cape or "double house" and is still owned by a direct descendant of Daniel Howes.

A little farther on your left across from the town landing is the Captain Laban Howes House. It does not carry a date marker as only the second story is pre-1830; the original full Cape was raised and the first floor built underneath in the 1850s or 1860s. It's a large white house, number 954, set close to the road. The columned entranceway is obviously from a post-1830 period.

Last, a bit farther on your left, is the John Gorham House (1768). The home is a fine three-quarter Cape with ells added to the rear in later years. Captain Walter Hall owned the house in the mid-1800s and was later lost at sea. If you look closely you will note that a tree is growing directly through the roof of the ell behind the main house.

We have covered less than two miles by road but many years in early Cape architecture. There are many more antique homes in the village and scores more in the other Dennis villages. The Dennis Historical Society will be pleased to answer any questions you may have.

HOWES FAMILY CEMETERY

Old cemeteries have a charm for many people, particularly when they are as picturesque as this one. Well off the main roads in a wooded glen, old stone walls with iron gates enclose a unique graveyard. There are over 150 headstones, and all but one are members of the same family: seven or eight generations of the Howes family of Dennis lie buried here.

Thomas Howes sailed from England in 1637 with his wife, Mary Burr, and two sons, Thomas and Joseph. A third son, Jeremiah, was born on the voyage. Thomas chose the family burial plot and directed that he and his family should take their final rest here. The founder's headstone has long since crumbled, and not much is known about when he and Mary died. Legible headstones date from 1712 to the late 1800s, with recent burials of 1918, 1953, and 1971 also represented. At least nine out of each ten are named Howes; the others but one are blood relations.

Many were the Captains Howes of the seagoing history

of Dennis. One, in command of the clipper *Lubra,* was a trader in the South Seas. In 1846 he was murdered in his cabin by Chinese pirates, but his wife, with him on the voyage, was not harmed. Another Captain Howes died on the passage from Liverpool to Boston and yet another went west in the 1849 gold rush and died in San Francisco. All are remembered in their home plot in Dennis.

Among the legible epitaphs, I enjoyed that of the redoubtable Mrs. Susanna Howes who died at the age of seventy-five in 1828 and advised the world: "Friend,/ Mourn not for me,/But prepare to follow."

The Howes Family Cemetery is not easy to reach. From Route 6A at Dennis take New Boston Road to its junction with Hall Street. Directly across from Hall Street is what appears to be a private driveway; it is also a public right of way to the cemetery. The house with the driveway was owned and occupied by the most recent addition to the Howes family plot. He was Dan Chase, Dennis historian and owner of the land surrounding the Howes graveyard. He wanted to be buried in the center of his land, and the Howes family was glad to welcome him aboard.

CAPE PLAYHOUSE AND CINEMA

America's most famous summer theater began its career in 1870 as the Nobscusset Meeting House. Moved three times in Dennis and used over the years as a church, schoolhouse, tinshop, slaughterhouse, blacksmith's shop, stable, and garage, the old building was purchased by producer Raymond Moore in 1926.

Moore had been drawn to the Provincetown art colony in the 1920s. He wrote several plays and in 1926 formed his own producing company in a Provincetown barn theater. Scouting for a more satisfactory and central location he purchased the old church in Dennis and, with the assistance of Cleon Throckmorton, theater architect, converted it into the "cradle of the stars" we know today.

Many of America's most famous stars have appeared at the Cape Playhouse. Bette Davis began as an usher, Lee

Remick was an apprentice, Mel Ferrer a stage manager and James Franciscus both house manager and stage manager. Robert Montgomery, Henry Fonda and Anne Baxter made their first professional appearances here. Ethel Barrymore was a regular, but perhaps the Cape Playhouse's most popular star was Gertrude Lawrence. From 1939 to 1950 the beloved "Mrs. A.," a part-time Dennis resident, appeared many times on the Playhouse boards and brought a glamorous glow to Cape theater that has never been equaled.

From the first Fourth of July 1927 production of *The Guardsman* starring Basil Rathbone, the Cape Playhouse has lived up to its reputation as a "star house." Its present policy is to concentrate on light comedies featuring current stage and television stars. Recent appearances by Shirley Booth, Jessica Tandy, Arlene Francis, Robert Stack, George Gobel and Joan Fontaine carry on the Cape Playhouse tradition.

The Cape Playhouse opens its summer program about the first of July and runs to Labor Day. Performances are generally at 8:30 P.M. except Sunday, with matinees at 2:30 each Wednesday and Thursday.

The Cape Cinema is a more recent but interesting addition to the property. The building was designed by Alfred Easton Poor, who patterned the façade after the old Congregational church in Centerville. The theater boasts upholstered armchair seats and the largest ceiling mural in the world. The 6,400-square-foot mural designed by Rockwell Kent and Jo Mielziner is a modernistic, artistically impressive conception of the heavens.

The Cinema is also air conditioned and features first run motion pictures during the summer season. Performances are generally at 7 P.M. with a later performance at 9:15 or 9:30. Reservations are generally not necessary.

HOKUM ROCKS

Legend has it that many years ago an old Indian lived alone in the woods of Dennis in a small cave formed by a large mound of cracked and eroded granite boulders. When anyone approached the hermit's lair he was said to call out "Ho kum?" (Who comes?) The old Indian became known as Hokum, and his home as Hokum Rocks.

From Route 6A in Dennis take Old Bass River Road to Hokum Rock Road. The pile of boulders is down this road about three quarters of a mile on your right. The last few hundred yards have not been paved as yet. There is a picnic area here and youngsters will enjoy the cave and climbing the rocks.

SCARGO LAKE AND TOWER

Indian folklore on the Cape is studded with legends, some with a wee kernel of fact, such as this one. Mashantampaine, also called Sagam, was indeed an ancient Sachem of the Nobscussets of Dennis. He had a beautiful daughter, Princess Scargo, whose mother had died in childbirth. Sagam vowed that his child would never know the pangs and sorrows of the death of a loved one.

Suitors from many tribes brought gifts to Princess Scargo. Her favorite brave, soon off on a long trip, presented her with a scooped-out pumpkin with "little perch and dainty trout" in the water inside. The legend says that the brave would live if the fish lived, and Princess Scargo took loving care of them. When they grew too old and large for the pumpkin, she dug a small pond by a fresh stream, but an unseasonable drought began to dry up their little home.

Sagam was heartbroken to see his daughter grieving for her dying fish. He called all his people from miles around and told them they must dig a pond as broad across as an arrow's flight. Princess Scargo chose the strongest brave to shoot the arrows as far as he could. Some say that she cheated a bit and placed one of the markers farther on; that's why the lake is longer than it is wide. Throughout the summer the squaws dug the pond with clam shells and piled the sand by the side. At last, in the fall it was finished, and the pile of sand, Scargo Hill, stood beside it. The rains of autumn filled the lake and the trout and perch put in by Princess Scargo, or at least their descendants, can be found there today.

The legend has been told with many variations, one of which was published as an anonymous poem in the January 1922 *Cape Cod Magazine*. The poem concludes:

> *Where the shadows lie the deepest*
> *Loving couples often pause.*
> *They are listening to the echoes*
> *'Tis the grumbling of the squaws.*

Alongside the lake is an old graveyard surrounded by a gateless stone-posted iron fence. Inside are tall trees and thick underbrush. There are no headstones, only an inscription on a carved slab of pink granite that reads: "Burial ground of the Nobscusset Tribe of Indians of which Tribe Mashantampaine was Chief."

Scargo Hill tower is easily reached from either direction is 160 feet high, the tower an additional 28 feet. It is the highest vantage point in the mid-Cape area and one can see 80 miles on a clear day. Bring a map to orient yourself to landmarks in Provincetown and Plymouth. The stone tower was erected in 1902 in memory of Thomas Tobey, an early settler of Sandwich who came to Dennis in 1678. The family gave the tower to the town in 1929.

Scargo Hill tower is easily reached from either direction on Route 6A. The Nobscusset burial ground is on the other side of the lake, behind the barn-garage on the private property of Charles Welles. The property is the fourth lot east of the town landing on Route 6A, house number 985. You can catch a glimpse of the graveyard from the road: look to the left rear of the barn.

SHIVERICK SHIPYARD

In 1815 Asa Shiverick came from Falmouth to establish a shipyard on what is now known as Sesuit Harbor. His business prospered in a small way and his sons grew up learning the trade.

Asa, Jr., had been to Maine and Boston and seen the new clippers that were setting the pace. He and his brothers, David and Paul, wanted to try their hands at the larger ships. They found an ally and benefactor in Captain Christopher Hall, shipmaster and ship owner, who was willing to provide the financial backing. In 1849 their first clipper, the *Revenue,* came off the ways and proved their ability. They went on to build seven more clippers and four schooners over the next fourteen years. Two of the larger clippers, over a thousand tons each, were among the most famous of their day: the *Wild Hunter* and the *Belle of the West.* These, and such ships as the *Kit Carson, Webfoot, Christopher Hall,* and the *Ellen Sears,* account for some of the unusual street names you see around Dennis and Yarmouth.

Another clipper they built was the *Hippogriffe,* a fine but slightly jinxed ship that ran aground in the China Seas. It managed to pull off safely at high tide, but the spot is still charted as Hippogriffe Shoals.

At its height the shipyard was a substantial operation for its time. There were ways and a dock, a main workshop, blacksmith shop, caulking yard and related activities. The large clippers could be launched only twice a year, on the highest spring tides. Most of the vessels were commanded by Dennis men sailing out of Boston and other East Coast ports. The Shiverick boys closed down in the 1860s and there is now little evidence, except for their homes, that they had ever been there.

A historical marker commemorates the shipyard site on Sesuit Neck Road just over the crest of the hill before the marinas and yacht club on Sesuit Harbor. The bronze plaque depicts the shipyard as it looked in the 1850s with a clipper ship hull on the ways. The Shiverick homes are a few hundred yards back on Sesuit Neck Road, three on the right and two on the left just past Shiverick Road. They were built in the 1820–1840 period; Asa, Sr., owned the hip-roof house number 270, his brother David was next door, and three of his sons in the others nearby.

SEARS'S FOLLY

Captain John Sears lived in the East Dennis area about fifty years earlier than the Shivericks. When the Revolution came, Captain Sears was left ashore, stewing and thinking. The British blockade was a nuisance and salt was scarce and expensive. "Sleepy John" Sears set his mind to do something about it.

In 1776 he built a long vat, 100 by 10 feet, with removable shutters that could be quickly adjusted to keep out the rain. He filled the vat with salt water, replaced it as fast as it leaked out, and let the sun go to work. The operation was crude and cumbersome and leaked like a sieve. Neighbors came from miles around to laugh at Sears's contraption and it was quickly dubbed Sears's Folly. The ship captain soon made the vats watertight and in his first season produced 8 bushels of salt. With hand pumps and other improvements, production went up to 30 bushels the next year, and people began to see that John Sears was on to something. A Harwich friend, Major Nathaniel Freeman, suggested using a windmill to pump the water, and production boomed. The solar evaporation method of producing salt was on its way on the Cape.

From 1777 to the 1850s, salt works were scattered up and down the coast, and by the 1830s they formed the most important land-based industry on the Cape. Salt was a key commodity, primarily for the preservation of fish, and brought as high as $8 a bushel in 1783. In the 1830s there were close to 500 salt works producing about a half million bushels of salt and millions more of Glauber salts, which were used by tanneries to prevent hides from stiffening. Another by-product was Epsom salts. The last "bitter water" after being refined and rerefined to remove all else of value was sold to the cement industry.

The finest salt works of the day were owned by Loring Crocker at the Common Fields in Barnstable. The crude trough of Captain Sears had evolved into an intricate system of reservoirs, falls, vats, and boiling rooms that extracted the last penny of value from the sea water. By the 1850s the development of new salt mines and the decline of the salt fish industry signaled the demise of the salt industry on the Cape. Loring Crocker's works were still in operation into the 1870s and one was in operation in Dennis as late as 1885.

Heavy salt works timbers were often used in home and barn construction as the old vats were dismantled. These boards and timbers were the dismay of carpenters, whose tools rusted in a few days from contact with the wood that had been pickled in brine for so many years. Structures of the period with salt works beams and boards are readily identifiable because they won't take paint. Salt works beams were used to build Stoney Brook Mill in Brewster. Visit the upstairs museum to inspect them.

John Sears's old home is located at 36 North Street off Cold Storage Road in East Dennis. The old full Cape, built in 1758, is still occupied by members of the Sears family. A full-size replica of a salt works may be seen at the Aptucxet Trading Post in Bourne.

JERICHO HOUSE (1801)

When Francis Baker's son Nathaniel purchased a large tract in South Dennis, he built a home in 1680 on land now occupied by the grounds of the Ezra Baker School. Succeeding generations of Bakers split the land and built their homes in the area. For many years this area of South Dennis was known as Baker Town, and most of the early homes can be traced back to members of the Baker family.

Jericho House was built for Theophilus Baker, a sixth-generation Baker on Cape Cod. He built the home in 1801 — the date was obtained from a coin found under the sill of the house. Baker was a sea captain in command of the schooner *Jane Brothers*. He died in his thirty-third year in 1805 and is buried in the South Dennis cemetery. The old home remained in the Baker family until 1955, when it was sold to Elizabeth Reynard, author of *The Narrow Land.*

Miss Reynard bought the property with the intention of restoring it and turning it over to the town as a historical center. It was about this time that the property received the name Jericho. The walls were indeed "tumbling down," despite the efforts of Miss Reynard and her friend, Dr. Virginia C. Gildersleeve. Miss Reynard willed the property to Dr. Gildersleeve, who in turn gave the old homestead to the Town of Dennis in 1962.

The town and its historical society have done well by the gift. The old full Cape, with a slightly bowed roof and beautiful doorway, is now fully restored and open to the public as a memorial museum for the Town of Dennis.

Jericho House is beautifully furnished with nineteenth-century antiques, many of them traced back to early Baker families. The three fireplaces, paneled walls, and wide board floors are authentic, and any damaged or missing architectural details were expertly restored.

The original barn behind Jericho has been expanded and is now a museum filled with early Cape Cod tools, exhibits, and artifacts. Dennis is justifiably proud of its role in the development of the cranberry industry, its master mariners, its inventor of the solar evaporation process of salt making, and its master shipbuilders, the Shivericks. Each of these contributions to progress and history is recognized by special exhibits here in the Barn Museum.

Jericho House is located at the corner of Main Street and Trotting Park Road in South Dennis, a few hundred yards north of Route 28. It is open every Wednesday and Friday from 2 to 4 P.M. from July 1 to Labor Day. There is no admission fee but donations are gratefully accepted.

Nathaniel Baker's 1680 home is now located at 54 Pine Street. A fine full Cape, it was completely remodeled in about 1830 and now bears little resemblance to a home of the seventeenth century.

SOUTH PARISH
CONGREGATIONAL CHURCH (*1835*)

When this meeting house was built, two tablets were placed on the west wall of the sanctuary to perpetuate the names of 102 sea captains, most of whom lived in the village. This "Captains Church" is representative of a fine period of American church architecture.

Services were held in the South Parish as early as 1765; however, it was not until 1795 that the first meeting house was constructed on the site of the present church.

The church possesses many rare mementos of its early history. A stately Sandwich glass chandelier hangs in the sanctuary. The old whale-oil lamps are electrified now, but retain the artistry and charm of a bygone era. On the east wall is a painting depicting the Adoration, done by the famous artist Edwin Howland Blashfield, a former Dennis summer residents, who painted this mural as an experiment on a new method he was introducing to his art. The old rosewood organ was brought to the church sometime before 1854. It was built in London in 1762 and is reputed to be the oldest pipe organ in actual use in America.

Located on Main Street in South Dennis, the church welcomes visitors to all services.

THE DRIFTWOOD ZOO

Have you ever looked at an oddly shaped stone or branch and visualized an animal, a bird, or maybe even old Uncle Eben? If so, you'll feel right at home at Sherman Woodward's Driftwood Zoo. Since 1940 he has been collecting and assembling driftwood, cork, shells, odd stones, and other flotsam and jetsam from the shore into models of real and imaginary members of the animal world.

Captain Nickerson is majordomo here, and any resemblance to a coconut washed ashore is purely coincidental. The good Captain commands quite an Ark. A windswept pheasant, dapper penguin, shy Bambi, the Loch Ness monster, and 150 others make up his crew.

Woodward looks for shapes that suggest actual or mythical birds, fish, animals, or people. He is happiest to find pieces complete by themselves, such as a driftwood northern pike that is exactly like the real one in the photograph nearby. Another prize is Gargantua, totally natural except for a bit of plastic wood to bolster his face. His Balinese dancer is as graceful as the Indonesian original. Wind, sand, and weather can perform wonders and Woodward has captured some of their secrets.

The members of the zoo are not for sale; they are their creator's avocation. Woodward lectures and writes, and his zoo has been featured on television shows and in motion picture shorts. One visitor commented, "Every time I'm on the beach and I see something queer, I'll think of you." Captain Nickerson didn't appreciate it at all!

The zoo is quite informal; a collection box is marked "Four bits per person to help feed 'em. Children free." It is located on a small lane off Main Street in South Dennis on the right side between the town offices and Route 28. It's open every day in the summer from 10 A.M. to 5 P.M.

WEST DENNIS COMMUNITY CHURCH

In the early 1800s the Methodists began to gain footholds on the predominately Congregationalist Cape. Truro and Provincetown had Methodist churches by the turn of the century, Barnstable by 1813, and Chatham by 1819. The Dennis Methodist Society was holding meetings in Carleton Hall by 1820, and shortly thereafter moved to Christian Hill, to the west of the present West Dennis Free Public Library.

By 1835, funds were raised to build their church. The cost of the project was reported as $1,188, a large sum considering that many of the forty-five families in the village earned less than $300 per year.

In 1848 the church was sawn in half and enlarged and in 1856 the clock and bell were installed in the steeple.

The minister at this time was the Reverend James M. Stanton, father of Harriet, the bride of Captain Joseph Baxter referred to in the history of Dennis.

Located on Route 28 at the corner of Church Street in the center of the village of West Dennis, the church welcomes visitors to its services.

BASS RIVER BRIDGE

The bridge connecting South Yarmouth and West Dennis on Route 28 is an innocent-looking crossing, great for lazy fishing and watching the boats go in and out — but it wasn't always so.

In the early 1800s Eleazar Kelly of West Dennis ran the ferry boat here, and it was quite a trip. Bass River, unlike almost any other, flows both ways: in on the flow tide and out on the ebb. Many a man in a hurry at crosstide found himself headed out to the Sound instead. Eleazar was a Cape skipper, however, and at two cents a man he always delivered the goods, sooner or later.

CAMPSITES AND TRAILER PARK

There is one family camping area and trailer park in Dennis. Airline Trailer Park is located on Old Chatham Road, just off Airline Road a little north of Exit 9 on the Mid-Cape Highway in South Dennis. Airline offers 250 sites in its 20-acre wooded campground. The park operates seasonally from June 1 to October 1 and advance reservations are strongly recommended. Three-way and two-way hookup sites are available, but the three-way sites are usually fully booked by the middle of spring. Airline Trailer Park provides hot and cold showers, modern rest rooms, a general store for light groceries, swimming and wading pools, playground, sports field, bicycle rentals and a recreation hall for the youngsters. Pets and single persons are not admitted.

For further information, write to Box J, South Dennis, Mass. 02660.

PUBLIC GOLF COURSES

There is one 18-hole golf course in Dennis open to the public.

Dennis Pines Golf Course is located off Route 134 in East Dennis. From Route 6A drive south on Route 134 about ⅔ mile. From Exit 9 on the Mid-Cape Highway (Route 6) go north about 3 miles.

Dennis Pines is a 7,029-yard, par 72 course, and electric golf carts may be rented.

PUBLIC SWIMMING BEACHES

Dennis visitors may purchase a beach parking sticker from the Ezra Baker School, Route 28, South Dennis, or Carleton Hall, Old Bass River Road, Dennis, during the summer season.

The major Dennis saltwater beaches on the south side are West Dennis Beach and South Village Road Beach, West Dennis, and Sea Street, Glendon Road, Inman Road, and Raycroft Parkway beaches in Dennis Port. Major north side saltwater beaches are Cold Storage Road, Sea Street, and Harbor Road beaches in East Dennis; and Howes Street, Corporation Road, Bay View Road, Horsefoot Path, and Chapin Memorial beaches in the village of Dennis. The town also requires a beach sticker for parking at the freshwater beach on Scargo Lake.

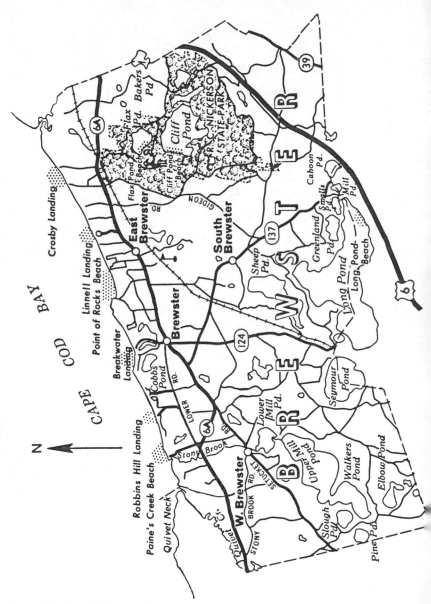

Copyright, THE NATIONAL SURVEY, 1973
Chester, Vermont

CHAPTER VI

Brewster

Named for Elder William Brewster "for fear he would be forgotten else" — so wrote Thoreau as he hurried through the town. We fear that Thoreau completely missed the considerable charm of Brewster; perhaps all its captains were at sea during his brief visit.

Until 1803 Brewster was the North Parish of Harwich. As early as 1752 the North and South Parishes were exchanging insult for insult. The Reverend Edward Pell expressed it well by his desire that he be buried in the North Parish because he feared the Lord would never think to look in the South Parish for a righteous man.

The division of Harwich and the incorporation of the Town of Brewster in 1803 was attended by hot debate and animosity on both sides. The North Parish had long contained a large share of the men of commerce and leadership and they were now determined to go their own way. Present-day Brewster, the original settlement of old Harwich, has been proud and opinionated ever since.

The pride of Brewster has been its special relationship with the sea. Plagued with some of the poorest harbors on the Cape but blessed with some of its saltiest men, Brewster was the home of more deepwater captains in proportion to its population than any other town in America.

In 1789 Captain David Nickerson brought back the infant widely believed to have been the lost Dauphin of

France. His story is told later with that of the First Parish Church. A few years later, in 1794, Captain Elijah Cobb of Brewster also visited Paris. He was determined that the French Revolution was not going to stand between him and his due. His ship captured and taken as a prize by a French frigate, he went to Paris and personally presented his grievance before Robespierre at the height of the Reign of Terror. He secured his papers, tarried long enough to witness the execution of Robespierre himself a few days later, and then raced for Hamburg to claim his money just before the French agent there attempted to stop payment. The fearless Yankee skipper was satisfied; his memoirs report that the prices he received were "a good beginning, being over 200 per cent on the invoice."

Captain Jeremiah Mayo of Brewster might have brought Napoleon to America, but for the efficiency of the British. In 1815 his vessel, the *Sally*, was anchored in the port of Le Havre. Agents of Napoleon made the deal, but the emperor was captured before he could reach the port, and the Cape was denied a retired corporal. As luck would have it, the *Sally* had an unmolested passage straight through to Boston.

In 1807 President Jefferson tried to protect American interests with an embargo on trade with the warring powers of Europe. Several Brewster captains defied the embargo and went to sea. The War of 1812 was no more popular in Brewster. When Captain Richard Raggett in the H.M.S. *Spencer* demanded $4,000 ransom from the town, Brewster paid. Brewster's shipmasters were in a state of rebellious idleness and brought no glory to the town in this unpopular war. Captain Cobb was captured by an armed British schooner early in the war, but with an exchange of prisoners Cobb made his way home. After the Reign of Terror, a British prison, and more than one rum-running assignment to the Irish coast, the captain retired to Brewster and died peacefully on his Cape Cod farm at the age of eighty in 1848.

When peace finally came in 1815, no group in the country was quicker to profit by it than the shipmasters of New England. Deepwater captains refitted their ships and returned to the four corners of the world; the packet masters entered their golden years.

Brewster's Packet Landing was located at the foot of Breakwater Road in Brewster village. A breakwater was constructed about a hundred yards from the high water mark and the Boston packets moored behind it. Southwest of the old packet landing is Cannon Hill. The cannon was fired when each packet arrived and an empty barrel was then hoisted to the top of a tall pole, to remain there until the packet sailed.

A Brewster man carried the first cargo of ice to the tropics in 1852. The same commander later brought over the first load of wild animals for P. T. Barnum's circus. A Brewster ship, the *Titan*, took French troops to the Crimea, cotton to Liverpool, colonists to Australia, and guano to London — all in a day's work for a Brewster captain.

The deepwater sailors were back where they belonged. Captain John Higgins of the brig *Morning Star* is noted for having put pants on the natives in the Caroline Islands. He also did his best to bring them religion as he followed his chosen vocation of trading gospel and goods throughout the South Pacific.

Captain Josiah Knowles of Brewster was marooned when his clipper *Wild Wave* was wrecked on a coral island. All forty hands and a small ship's boat reached shore, but the outlook was grim. Leaving most of the crew behind, Captain Knowles and six others set out in a dory for Pitcairn Island, about a hundred miles away. They reached Pitcairn only to find its inhabitants had moved to Norfolk Island. Knowles and his men dismantled homes for wood, nails, and iron and built a larger boat, a sailing craft this time, and, leaving three behind on Pitcairn, took to the sea again. Unfavorable winds took them away from Norfolk. Undaunted, Captain Knowles plotted a course to the Marquesas, 1,300 miles away. Twelve days later they reached their goal and found the first American ship in port in five years. The sloop *Vandalia* picked up the two marooned groups and Captain Knowles returned to Brewster to tell his tale.

Captain William Freeman of Brewster also visited Pitcairn many times. On one voyage in 1883 he brought his daughter Clara. She found a friend in Rosa Young, the granddaughter of one of the *Bounty* mutineers. The girls exchanged correspondence and a copy of a long letter from Rosa may be seen in the Brewster Public Library.

Another distinguished Brewster master was James Dillingham, Jr. Sailing from Penang, Malaya, for New York during the Civil War, his clipper *Snow Squall* was hailed in the Atlantic by an American bark, the *Tuscaloosa*, flying the Stars and Stripes. Laying close and to windward, the *Tuscaloosa* ran out her guns, ran up the Stars and Bars, and commanded Captain Dillingham to "Heave to!" Dillingham shouted "Aye, Aye," but kept working his ship. By the time the *Tuscaloosa* knew what was happening, the *Snow Squall* was in the wind and running. The *Tuscaloosa* hung on till dusk but couldn't catch the Brewster man.

Many of these Brewster shipmasters are buried in the old cemetery behind the First Parish Church. Captain Nickerson's memorial stone is there along with Captain Elkanah Crosby, whose seven daughters all married sea captains. Captain Tully Crosby whose clipper *Kingfisher* raced and beat the mighty McKay clipper *Bald Eagle* is there. Also there is the shopkeeper Irishman John Silk, whose widow married the postmaster, Edward O'Brien. In 1810 the selectmen and town clerk of Brewster remonstrated against O'Brien's appointment, "he being a foreigner, a catholik and, in the opinion of the town, an alien." Town meetings in Brewster are still lively affairs.

Brewster today is a beautiful old town, retaining much of the charm and character of its heyday in the 1850s. Thoreau's liver must have been acting up when he described Brewster houses as "little removed from lumber."

(It is just as well that he never aspired to the postmaster's position.)

Brewster's population of 1,800 covers 22½ square miles with all but a few yards of its coastline on Cape Cod Bay. The southern coast's few yards on Pleasant Bay are reportedly due to a Brewster man finishing second in a two-man drinking bout. Its villages are Brewster, East Brewster, West Brewster, and South Brewster.

SEALAND OF CAPE COD

An attractive marine park and aquarium are located on the north side of Route 6A in West Brewster. Sealand of Cape Cod features its dolphin family — but with a difference. The emphasis is on the informative and educational; authoritative commentary, interesting demonstrations, and question-and-answer sessions are included in the 35- to 45-minute dolphin show as well as the usual delightful bag of tricks. Of particular interest is the demonstration of the echo location ability of these mammals, a natural radar system that can transmit and receive sound impulses over six miles.

After each dolphin show visitors are escorted to the rock-lined seal pool and the penguin rookery next to lovely Quivet Creek. Commentaries and demonstrations are well done and the youngsters will enjoy seeing the creatures fed.

Other buildings and pools on the seven-acre property house North American otters, sea turtles, sharks, and many other varieties of tropical and local fish. A picnic area and nature trail are also available.

Sealand holds special graded lectures for school and organizational groups and will appreciate your inquiry. Group activities may range from simple group tours to lectures and demonstrations on the subject of marine and marsh environment. The management is now planning scheduled adult educational activities for their new auditorium in future seasons.

Functioning year round in a parklike setting, Sealand

is open from 10 A.M. to 8:30 P.M. daily in the summer.
Dolphin shows are held about every two hours. Off season,
Sealand closes at 4 P.M. and all day Wednesdays. One ad-
mission covers everything.

DRUMMER BOY MUSEUM

The American Revolution in review is the theme of this
most unusual museum, an official stop on the New England Heritage Trail.

Drummer Boy Museum is a new concept of historical
re-creation. There are twenty-one mural-sized original
oil paintings, 9 by 18 feet, some with three-dimensional
figures or other special effects. While each stands alone
as a dramatic scene, all together they depict an absorbing
story of the American Revolution from the Boston Massa-
cre to the climax at Yorktown. The commentary of the
guide makes you feel that you are actually witnessing
these stirring and critical moments of American history.

The museum is open from mid-May to Columbus Day
from 9:30 A.M. to 6 P.M. daily. Admission to the gift shop
is free and visitors are welcome without taking the tour.
Drummer Boy Museum is located on Route 6A in West
Brewster.

MUSEUM OF NATURAL HISTORY

One of the most important additions to Cape Cod in
recent years has been the Museum of Natural History, on
Route 6A in Brewster. Supported by its membership and
a small admission charge to the general public, the museum is a nonprofit institution founded to provide information about the natural environment on Cape Cod.

For the transient visitor, the museum offers exhibits,
wildlife, and nature trails for those who wish to know
more of the natural history of the Cape. It owns 50 acres
of marsh and upland in the Stoney Brook Valley and its
marked nature walks are among the best on the Cape.
Two trails are maintained by the museum and one, the
John Wing Trail, by the town. The museum provides trail

guide literature to help you to identify the marsh, meadow, and woodland plants that you will encounter on your walk.

The John Wing Trail is of particular interest because of the historic ground it covers. In 1656 John Wing, a Sandwich Quaker, built the first house and became the first settler within the limits of old Harwich, now Brewster. His home was located on what is now called Wing's Island, a beautiful 33-acre "island" surrounded by beach and salt marsh. The entrance to the trail is on Route 6A about a hundred feet west of the museum parking lot. The trail is well marked and a tablet on the island indicates the approximate location of Wing's homestead. From fall to spring exceptionally high tides occasionally cover the causeway to the island. Allow about an hour and a half for your walk.

Wing's Island and the surrounding marshes were important in the early history of Brewster. Salt hay was harvested here and for many years, to the 1850s, various windmills, sheds, and vats used to evaporate seawater to produce salt were located on the island and the southern edge of the salt marsh. These were some of the salt works for which the town of Brewster paid $4,000 to protect them from Captain Raggett in the War of 1812.

The Museum of Natural History is far more than a collection of animals, artifacts, and nature trails to Cape residents and others interested in the Cape's preservation as a place where the natural environment can be seen and appreciated. The museum conducts field classes for children and adults, maintains a library as a central reference point for all groups interested in natural history and conservation on Cape Cod, and sponsors film and lecture series, clubs, and other activities for children, members, and guests. Those interested in membership are encouraged to write or visit the museum. The Cape Cod Museum of Natural History is open daily in the summer; it is closed Mondays and Fridays from October to May.

NEW ENGLAND FIRE AND HISTORY MUSEUM

Fire fighting — from bucket brigades to horse-drawn steam pumpers — is the theme of this new museum in Brewster. Authentic old hand- and horse-drawn engines, splendid relics of the proud volunteer companies of the past, highlight this comprehensive collection of fire fighting memorabilia, a visual history of American fire fighters and their equipment to the turn of the twentieth century. The great Chicago Fire of 1871 is re-created in a carefully scaled and animated diorama, and youngsters will enjoy climbing aboard an old hand pumper of great-grandpa's day.

The scope of the museum is being expanded to demonstrate other aspects of early America. A nineteenth-century apothecary shop has been re-created intact and an old Brewster blacksmith shop of the same era will soon be operated as it was more than a hundred years ago.

The New England Fire and History Museum is located on Route 6A about a half mile west of Town Hall in Brewster. It's open from 10 A.M. to 7 P.M. seven days a week from about May to October, and to groups and by appointment year round. An admission fee is charged.

CRAFTSMEN'S FAIR

An event of increasing interest each year is the fair, sponsored by the Society of Cape Cod Craftsmen, that displays and sells the many handcrafts produced on the Cape. The fair is usually held on the second Wednesday and Thursday of August under the big tents on the elementary school grounds, Route 6A in Brewster.

Cape Cod has long been noted for its hand craftsmen. Early scrimshaw artists on the whaling ships and whittling Yankee sailors would be pleased to know that men and women with similar talents have carried on their traditions. The Cape now boasts a concentrated colony of craftsmen in many fields; pottery, jewelry work, weaving, metal smithing, and wood carving are particularly well represented. Demonstrations of the various crafts are usually presented at the fair. As dates and location may change, check with a member, such as the Lemon Tree Shop in West Brewster, before planning your visit.

JOE LINCOLN'S BIRTHPLACE

Cape Cod's most famous author and publicity man, Joseph C. Lincoln, was born in Brewster in 1870. Fittingly, he was the salty and homespun son of a sea captain, but the great days of sailing ships were over and he never went to sea.

Joe Lincoln left the Cape when he was thirteen, began writing in 1896, and sold a number of short stories to the *Saturday Evening Post* and other magazines around the turn of the century. His first novel, *Cap'n Eri,* was a best seller in 1904. From then on he kept up a pace of almost a novel a year, most of them best sellers, until his death in 1944. He lived off-Cape during the winters, but built a fine summer home in Chatham, where he did much of his writing.

It is said that Joe Lincoln helped to make the Cape, and there is no doubt that the Cape made him. Millions of his readers became familiar with Cape Cod through his mind's eye. His characters became household names, and the villages he described — Harniss, Ostable, Trumet and Orham — were thinly disguised copies of the boyhood villages he knew so well. He had a tremendous knowledge of Cape folklore and history, which he wove into the fabric of his novels.

Copies of old Lincoln books sell at a premium today and reading them is still a salty experience. His birthplace is a small clapboard 1½-story gable end home on the south side of Route 6A about 150 yards east of Route 137, identified by a historical marker on the right front. His former summer home is located on Shore Road in Chatham.

FIRST PARISH CHURCH (1834)

The rip-roaring Reverend Nathaniel Stone carried on his war with the devil at a small meeting house at the current location of the First Parish Church of Brewster. His 1700 structure was replaced first by a new structure in 1722, and in turn by the present building in 1834.

Known as the Captain's Church, the First Parish Church is a fine example of its period. A collection of antique flags and the old brass nametags on the pews are of special interest. Unitarian services are held each Sunday at 10:30 A.M. and visitors are welcome. The church is located in the center of the village on the corner of Route 6A and Breakwater Road.

Behind the church is an old cemetery that honors many a ship captain on its headstones, a large number of them lost at sea. One of those lost captains could well have been the famed lost Dauphin of France.

Captain David Nickerson of Brewster was in Paris in the autumn of 1789 during the fury of the French Revolution. Shortly before he was due to sail a veiled woman thrust an infant into his arms with a few words of pleading and instruction, then off she went. Captain Nickerson was requested to name the boy René Rousseau and to raise him in America as his own son.

As Kittredge says, "Captain Nickerson's idea of how to bring up a child was exactly like that of any other Cape Codder of his day; he let René do his teething on a belaying pin, swung his cradle from the spanker boom and turned him out to crawl the quarterdeck in a brisk no'theaster." René learned quickly. Highly intelligent and aristocratic in bearing, he became Captain Rousseau at twenty-three, as good a sailor and as close-mouthed a man as his foster father.

Captain Rousseau was lost at sea at the age of twenty-five and Captain Nickerson died at sea five years later in 1819. It was the custom to put the names of fathers and sons lost at sea on the same memorial headstone. If you look on a tall orange headstone in the center rear of the burying ground you will find Captain Nickerson's name with Captain René Rousseau in the usual place of honor below. Was this engaging young Frenchman the lost Dauphin? Brewster says so.

MIMSY PUPPETS

For several years now, the First Parish Church in Brewster has sponsored the Mimsy Puppets each Wednesday and Thursday during July and August from 4 to 5 P.M. Admission fees are nominal.

Traditional children's stories are charmingly re-created in the wonderful world of make-believe. The puppeteers involve the children in each program with characters such as Mr. Tizzy, who "goes to pieces" in a crisis; the animated Birthday Cake, whose wish comes true when the audience blows out his candle; and Yuk the whatzit, who dances with the children. Some performances include a demonstration on "How to Be a Puppeteer."

The Mimsy Puppet shows at the First Parish Church are delightful, happy entertainment for the lollipop set and a nostalgic reminder for their elders.

TOWN HALL MUSEUM

In April 1880 the town meeting voted "to build a new Town House." Brewster's taste at the time demanded a grand example of the ornate Queen Anne style of the day. The sizable sum of $6,000 was appropriated for the job, but it took two supplemental appropriations totaling $4,-500 to finish the job. The proud town invited the governor, hired a band, and gave a grand banquet to celebrate the dedication. Newspapers of the day said "the proportion and design of the exterior are elegant, well-balanced and harmonious, the coloring of shades of olive green and roof of shades of coral red are grateful to the eye." Brewster's new Town Hall was an eyecatcher in 1880, and it still is.

Many a lively meeting has been held in the proud old

building, but its time may be almost over. Brewster residents are torn between constructing a new one or restoring and preserving the old. The upstairs auditorium, scene of so many school graduations, dances, plays and club meetings over the years, is now devoted to a museum of old Brewster sponsored by the historical society. It is a particularly interesting museum, the result of great effort on the part of society members. Each year the society develops a central theme and examines it in depth. In 1970, the centennial of the birth of Brewster's favorite son and author, Joseph C. Lincoln, was celebrated by a fine exhibit depicting his life and times. In 1971 the museum featured the lives of Brewster's famed sea captains, some of whose stories are told elsewhere in this book.

The theme for 1972 was Brewster Architecture. Each style and period of architecture was illustrated by drawings, photographs, and explanatory material. The homes depicted were all Brewster houses still extant today. The individual styles—Cape Cod, salt box, Greek Revival, Georgian, federal, Empire, Queen Anne, Victorian and contemporary — are equally applicable to other Cape towns; it is hoped the Brewster Historical Society will repeat this exhibit in later years.

Town Hall is on Main Street, just about opposite Depot Road. Stop in some afternoon in the summer.

STONEY BROOK HERRING RUN

Perhaps the most interesting and certainly the most scenic herring run on the Cape is located alongside the Stoney Brook mill in Brewster. Follow Stoney Brook Road from either of its two junctions with Route 6A and you can't miss it. The brook runs under the road and both sides are worth exploring. The mill side leads to the pond, the other side to the mouth of the brook on Cape Cod Bay.

Many people think of a herring run as a month or two of excitement each April and May, to be forgotten until the next spring. That's not so; there is action in the brook for more than six months each year. The brook, ponds, fish ladders and seining pool are all in constant activity from late March to November. Stoney Brook is fed from three ponds and covers more than two miles on its run to Cape Cod Bay.

The herring that come from the sea to spawn in freshwater ponds are not really herring at all — herring cousins perhaps, but more properly called alewives. They have a number of local names up and down the northern Atlantic coastline, but sea herring is not one of them. True sea herring spawn in salt water. The alewife, like salmon and shad, is born in fresh water, grows up in salt water, but leaves the sea as a three- or four-year-old adult to spawn in his old freshwater home. Unlike the salmon, the alewife lives to return to the sea and continues the cycle until age, accident, predator, or nature calls a halt; two or three spawnings constitute a rather exceptional career as alewives go, for the obstacles are formidable. A year's cycle in the alewife migration really consists of three mass movements in our pleasant little Stoney Brook: the run of the alewives to the ponds to spawn, the return of the spent alewives to the sea, and the exodus of the fingerlings to salt water.

In early spring the earth and water begin to grow warmer. At the same time, for reasons known only to nature, schools of alewives are moving through the ocean toward the outlets of rivers and streams that empty into the sea. It has been pretty well established that these individual schools were spawned and grew up together, and in some way are able to identify and return to the same stream they swam down three or four years before. The schools mill in the brackish mixture of salt and fresh water offshore until the fresh water of the stream is a bit warmer than the sea water. Late in March an occasional bold fish will decide that his time is right and enter the stream, but the main schools will wait until the temperature is more favorable, generally from mid-April through May. The particular dates may be earlier or later depending on how long and cold the winter has been.

The spawning alewives will range from 10 to 13 inches and weigh from about 8 to 10 ounces. A small proportion are three-year-olds; most are four or five with a few older veterans. The change from salt water to fresh etches marks into their scales that can be analyzed to determine the number of times a particular fish has spawned.

At the height of the run there are times when the stream is almost choked with fish; at other times very few are seen. Tides, sunlight, and temperature all play a part in attracting the alewives upstream. Their instinct is not infallible, some are sidetracked off into small creeks and ditches and others beat themselves to death trying to climb insurmountable obstacles. The herring gulls harry them all the way, but on they come. Most stay in groups, undulating like seaweed in the current, resting and facing upstream until the time and energy come to take on the next hurdle. The continual chewing motion of their jaws is merely breathing. With mouth open and gill covers closed, water is drawn in; with mouth closed, water is forced out of the gills, removing the oxygen in the process.

Unlike salmon, alewives don't leap. They swim hard and fast into the cascades pouring over the fish ladders; it's a fascinating sight to see them tunnel through these spouts of water. They have been known to climb more than two feet in this way, but most ladders call for much less.

After the alewives have navigated the first series of ladders on the north side of Stoney Brook Road, they cross under the road and enter the seining pool next to the grist mill. The pool is large enough to reduce the force of the water and give the fish a chance to rest for the final series of ladders to the pond. Some years ago, it was also a convenient place to herd the alewives for the annual harvest.

The herring rights at Stoney Brook were sold to the highest bidder until five or ten years ago. At times they brought several thousand dollars, in more recent years only a few hundred. The successful bidder used commercial nets to trap the alewives in the seining pool on four specified days each week. The fish were allowed free passage on the other days to assure proper stocking for coming seasons. Residents are still permitted to take their own requirements on designated days. Most individuals today are after the roe, which are delicious baked or fried in butter. Children love to catch alewives by hand or net, often dumping them back in a few ladders closer to their goal. It's a great sport for children and no one seems to mind if they don't get too rough.

Salted and smoked alewives were once popular, but are considered too bony for current tastes. Alewives were so plentiful in the early years of the Cape that they were primarily used as fertilizer, a trick learned from the Indians. A few alewives in each hole, covered with earth and then seeded, produced three times as much corn in poor soil. In recent years alewives have shown up in supermarkets, mainly in the pet food department.

From the seining pool there are several more ladders to the head of the run where it enters Lower Mill Pond. The wooden dam at this spot is perhaps the most important on the run. It must be adjusted so that the force of the flow is correct all down the line. When the alewives wiggle through the final barrier to Lower Mill Pond they may go on to Upper Mill Pond or Walkers Pond to spawn, but the struggle is temporarily over.

In a spawning season, more than half a million alewives complete the two-mile migration up Stoney Brook. Each female deposits 60,000 to 100,000 sticky eggs, which sucker fish and other predators gobble up before many have a chance to touch bottom. Male alewives follow the females and cover the eggs with milt. Those that survive hatch in two to six days, depending on the water temperature. The fry that do manage to hatch are even more tasty to predators in the ponds. Perch, pickerel, frogs, herons, kingfishers, and water snakes all have a good feed on millions — but there are millions more.

By mid-May some of the early spawners are already

going down the brook, but most are still coming upstream to spawn. By early June there are few still coming up and progressively more going down. Both face the current until they make their break in either direction. You may see white fungus patches on the sides and backs of some. These are wounds on returning spent fish. Their stay in fresh water produced the fungus, which disappears after they return to the sea.

The longer an alewife is in fresh water, the less edible he is. Years ago spent fish were harvested on their return trip and shipped to the West Indies to feed the slaves. They were called "poison fish" by the slaves and the practice soon stopped.

Alewives may spend from a few days to a few weeks in the ponds after spawning. In June most of the fish you see will be these spent alewives returning to the sea. By early July some of the fingerlings will be joining them. These early birds will be only a little over an inch long, like a big-eyed minnow pretty well out of control in the rushing current. By August the fingerling schools begin to head for salt water in earnest. They are mostly 2 inches by now, and the schools to November are progressively larger, up to 4 and 5 inches, and better equipped for the trip.

Assuming 250,000 to 300,000 spawning females, over 15 billion eggs are deposited from which perhaps 150 million fry are hatched. About 5 million of these must reach salt water to insure a normal run at Stoney Brook in three or four years' time. Predators are all around and it's a wonder they make it. Birds, eels, saltwater fish, and the tides take a tremendous toll after the pond predators have eaten their fill. The fingerlings come out of the ponds by the millions and reach the sea due only to the sheer magnitude of their numbers.

Little is known about where they go and what they do at sea. Alewives at sea have reportedly been taken at all depths and all distances from home. The consensus of opinion seems to be that most do not stray too far. They are plankton eaters and are common from the Carolinas to Newfoundland.

Today's runs are not what they were many years ago. Natural old runs have been blocked by mills, dams, and rubbish, and of course water pollution has taken its share. Runs can be renewed, however, as ponds can be seeded with eggs spawned in other ponds. The alewives will return to the home of their birth and childhood in increasing numbers if conditions are made favorable.

For those interested in a more detailed analysis of the migration of the alewife, I suggest John Hay's exceptional book *The Run*. Hay, a noted naturalist and author, is president of the Cape Cod Museum of Natural History in Brewster.

STONEY BROOK MILL

The "Old Mill" by Stoney Brook is the last remaining relic of several mills and businesses in the area known as Factory Village.

The first mill was built in 1663 by Thomas Prence on the north side of Stoney Brook Road. It was located about thirty yards off the road, straddling the righthand spur of the brook. The miller took his pay in kind, in this case his "pottle" or toll was three quarts to the bushel. This was a water-powered grist mill, and it operated until it burned down in 1871.

A few years later, also in the 1660s, a fulling mill was constructed at the site of the present mill. The loosely woven homemade cloth was fulled: paddled, and squeezed until it became close, firm, thick, smooth, and suitable for manufacture into clothing. Fuller's Earth, a clay imported from England, was used to remove any oil still in the homespun cloth. In 1760 the old fulling mill burned and was not rebuilt.

In 1814 a woolen mill was built on this site. This mill is said to have produced the first factory-made woolen cloth in America. The same mill later became a cotton mill and, still later, a carding mill.

In about 1819, Freeman Winslow opened a cobbler's shop a few yards down Stoney Brook Road. The business was later taken over by Sidney Winslow, who went on to found the future industrial giant, the United Shoe Machinery Company.

In about 1830 a tannery was constructed across from the grist mill on the north side of Stoney Brook Road. Leather was tanned by a soaking process in a hemlock bark mixture. The 1871 fire that took the grist mill also razed the tannery.

The old wool, cotton, and carding mill on the site of the present mill had evidently burned some years before, for by 1873, a new grist mill was constructed on the old foundation. This is the mill that exists today. The mill has had a checkered career: from grist mill to overalls factory to ice cream plant to private home. In 1940 the town purchased the mill and the old sites and opened the area to the public.

During the summer a miller is on hand to grind corn for visitors and a small museum is open on the second floor. Of particular interest are the salt works beams used in the construction of the mill. A map of the old mill sites is usually available in the museum or posted by the brook on the north side of the road.

BASSETT WILD ANIMAL FARM

If you want the children to entertain themselves for a few hours, try the Wild Animal Farm on Tubman Road in Brewster. Scores of wild and domestic animals and birds in pleasant, natural surroundings provide a fine setting for a family outing and picnic.

The farm covers 18 acres of the Brewster countryside. Hayrides around the meadow are fun for everyone, and pony rides are available for children of all ages. There are unusual animals, such as llamas, buffalo, monkeys, ostriches, peacocks, a leopard, and a lion cub, in addition to the more usual raccoons, foxes, deer, bobcats, and bears. Farm animals are also well represented and the children are allowed to play with many of them. The wildlife community on the farm changes a bit each year, so there is always something new. It's my guess that the playful lion cub of this year will be a rather large young lion by next year and may well have to give way to something more manageable.

Just off Route 137, Bassett Wild Animal Farm opens in late May and closes after Labor Day. Admission fees are charged. Picnic tables and light refreshments are available on the premises.

NICKERSON STATE PARK

The first state park in the Commonwealth of Massachusetts, Nickerson is a naturalist's and sportsman's paradise, beautiful and unspoiled. Camping, picnicking, hiking, bathing, boating, and fishing are all available here.

Roland Nickerson was a Brewster boy who went west and made good. He was a pioneer in the building of the Atchison, Topeka and Santa Fe Railroad, a dry-land sailor, they called it. His boyhood home was too small, so he proceeded to build his idea of a summer place on the Cape, one with a bit of elbow room. The "summer place" he built is the mansion now known as La Salette, and his "elbow room" the 1,750-acre Nickerson State Park. The park was given to the state by Mrs. Nickerson in 1934 after the death of her husband and opened to public use in the summer of 1937. The park entrance is to the right on Route 6A in East Brewster as one approaches the Orleans line.

Nickerson chose his summer estate well and the Cape is fortunate that such a beautiful forest has been maintained intact. The natural jewels of the park are its 204-acre lake and three sizable ponds, all now stocked with trout by the Massachusetts Division of Fisheries. Cliff Lake provides brown and rainbow trout, Flax Pond has brook and rainbow and Little Cliff and Higgins Ponds are stocked with brookies. Boat launching ramps are available. The park is well operated, the setting natural, and the beauties of nature unspoiled.

There are 418 type II campsites on a first-come, first-served basis. Day use of the picnic and recreational facilities is also welcomed. Community sanitary facilities and hot and cold showers are available for each group of campsites. Each site has its own fireplace and picnic table and is limited to one family with a maximum of two tents or one recreational vehicle.

The regular campgrounds are open from mid-April to the end of October. One area is kept open in the off-season for self-contained recreational vehicles only. Should the campgrounds be full when you arrive, the supervisor will give you a numbered ticket representing your place on the waiting list. Available sites are awarded to ticketholders at specified times. A new series of tickets are issued daily and you must be present to claim the site. Campsites are $3 per day, with a maximum stay of two weeks in season.

CAMPSITES AND TRAILER PARKS

Brewster offers five commercial camping and trailer parks in addition to the facilities at Nickerson State Park. They are of widely varying types and quality. Advance reservations are strongly recommended during the summer season; many camping and trailer enthusiasts are disappointed each year because the limited Cape facilities are full when they arrive. All towns are very strict concerning camping or the parking of camping vehicles on beaches or highway rest areas.

Sweetwater Forest is an excellent year round family camping and trailer park located off Route 124 in Brewster. Sweetwater provides 164 sites of which most have electrical and water hookups and a smaller number sewerage as well. The forest covers 60 acres and includes 600-foot frontage and a nice sandy beach on a fine pond. Small skiffs are available, swimming is excellent, and the youngsters will enjoy the fishing. Hot and cold showers, clean rest rooms and a dumping station are all provided.

Playgrounds and a teen-age clubhouse are available for the younger generations but there are no planned activities. A limited number of sleeper campers are rented on a weekly basis. All facilities are winterized and heated and suitable for camping in any season. Well-behaved pets are welcome.

Dave and Ann Klein are the owner-operators; for full information write to them at Sweetwater Forest, Brewster, Mass. 02631. Reservations for each summer season open January 1 each year.

On Route 6A opposite Route 137 is the Shady Knoll Family Camping area, owned and operated by Bob Thomas. Shady Knoll is a fine operation for family tent camping and smaller camping vehicles not requiring hookups. The camp now consists of 60 sites but plans are underway to increase this to 100, including about 20 with electrical and water hookups. Shady Knoll provides hot and cold showers, clean rest rooms, a playground, and a sports field on its wooded 9½ acres. Dogs kept on leashes are permitted. Shady Knoll is just off the main highway in the center of Brewster, but you don't realize it is so close to the mainstream once inside the campground. It is sufficiently private so that many town residents don't even know it's there. The season runs from mid-May to mid-October, and there are seasonal as well as weekly and daily rates. A brochure may be secured by writing to Shady Knoll, Brewster, Mass. 02631.

Between the Harwich and Orleans lines on Route 39 in South Brewster is Henry's Camp Ground. Norman Anderson offers 34 tent and tent trailer sites in a very nice wooded setting. Hot and cold showers, clean rest rooms, and a playground are provided in the 10-acre camp. Well-behaved, leashed pets are permitted. Henry's is located in Brewster; the mailing address is Box 169, South Orleans, Mass. 02662. Brochures are available.

The Jolly Whaler Trailer Park on Route 6A is a small operation for trailers only. The park is on the main highway with little privacy. Trailer sales and rentals are also offered and a brochure is available.

Arrowhead Park is a large campsite and trailer park located off Tubman Road in Brewster. In 1972 it came under the new management of the Newmans. A brochure will be sent on request.

During the summer season a camp or recreational vehicle site is almost impossible to secure on the Cape. Many are fully booked for the summer by late spring, so be sure to make reservations as soon as you know your plans.

PUBLIC GOLF COURSE

There is one 9-hole golf course in Brewster open to the public. Brewster Country Club is located on Thad Ellis Road off Route 6A in East Brewster. The course is a 3,130-yard par 35. Electric golf carts, pull carts, light snacks, and cocktails are available at the clubhouse.

PUBLIC SWIMMING BEACHES

Brewster residents and the general public may use all Brewster town beaches without charge. Beach stickers are not issued in Brewster.

All of the Brewster beaches are on the north side off Route 6A. Proceeding east from the Dennis line you will find public beaches at the end of Paine Creek Road, Robin Hill Road, Breakwater Road, Ellis Landing Road, Linnell Landing Road, and Crosby Lane.

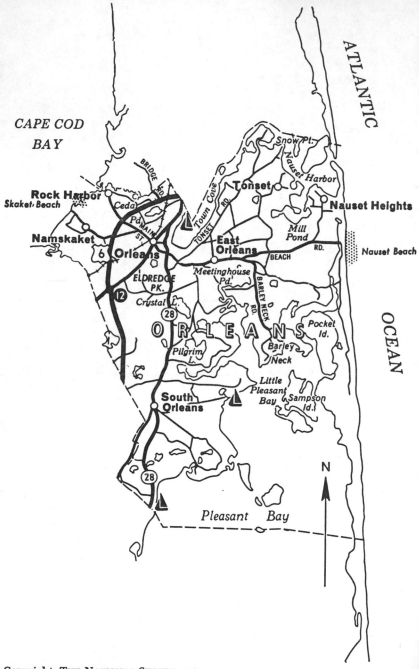

ATLANTIC

CAPE COD
BAY

Snow Pt.

Nauset Harbor

Tonset

Rock Harbor
Skaket Beach

Nauset Heights

BRIDGE RD.

Cedar

Pd. MAIN

Town Cove

TONSET RD.

Mill
Pond

Namskaket

6

Orleans

East
Orleans

BEACH RD.

Nauset Beach

ELDREDGE
PK.

Meetinghouse
Pd.

BARLEY NECK RD.

12

Crystal L.

28

O R L E A N S

Pocket
Id.

Barley
Neck

Pilgrim
L.

Little
Pleasant
Bay

Sampson
Id.

OCEAN

South
Orleans

N

28

Pleasant   Bay

Copyright, THE NATIONAL SURVEY, 1973
Chester, Vermont

CHAPTER VII

Orleans

Orleans, with its French name and Yankee pronunciation, adds a touch of salty sophistication and continental savoir faire to Cape Cod. Orleans is a charming town; its graceful streets and winding lanes lend an unplanned and easygoing air that complements the studied natural landscaping of its attractive homes.

In Orleans, nothing is more pleasant than taking a lonely road to see where it will lead. The tree-lined lanes seem to open up on cue as bends in the road bring the water in view. William Blake wrote, "Improvement makes straight roads, but the crooked roads without improvement are roads of genius." Orleans has made the best of both worlds. Whether by accident or design, Orleans has maintained a feeling of spaciousness and grace while fashionably tailored, and in only a few places tattered and torn. Some of the fringes of the town are like fringes anywhere, rather ragged. Orleans is where Route 6A loses some of its charm and Route 28 regains it. But forget highways for Orleans is a town of village and country roads and until you discover them you will be unable to uncork the considerable charm of Orleans.

The old part of town radiating out from Main and Tonset streets is a good place to start. As you travel the byways there is a distinct air of the gentleman farmer mingled in with the unpretentious homes in the country-side.

Orleans is blessed with a rare landscape for Cape Cod — soft and gentle, and a bit foreign to those used to the Yankee villages along the Bay, the suburban South Shore, or the rugged and sandy moors of the lower Cape. At times it seems that each Cape town breeds its own weather to suit its character; Orleans usually appears sunny and cool. Cape Cod Bay on the west and the sands of Nauset and the Atlantic on the east leave no doubt you're still on the Cape, but the long fingers of inlets and coves probing the town help to make the lanes of Orleans different in character.

The second smallest town on the Cape, Orleans has much more than its fair share of waterfront. The great barrier beach of Nauset encloses the ragged coast left by the glaciers, leaving beautiful Pleasant Bay with all its nooks and crannies intact. The one break in the great beach, Nauset Harbor, extends its arm two-thirds of the way across the town. The many protected coves and inlets of Orleans are calm and quiet, perfect for mooring power or sailboats and pretty as a postcard. Sixteen freshwater ponds help to compensate the few Orleans residents who find themselves more than a stone's throw from water.

The town has done well by its natural advantages. About a dozen town landings await the visitor who wants to launch a boat or merely admire the picturesque settings. Sailboats dance at their moorings in the Pleasant Bay coves until late fall, but the landings are worth a visit in any season. Wander down most any of the lanes in East or South Orleans and you'll end up on an attractive cove of Pleasant Bay. Barley Neck Road, River Road, Herring Brook Way, Arey's Lane, Namequoit Road, Portanimicut Road, and Quanset Road will all open up sights you can't see from the highways. Pau Wah Pond Landing, at the end of Portanimicut Road was named for a chief of the Potonamiquoits who drowned himself here after Chief Quanset refused the hand of his daughter, Wild Dove. Legend has it that Pau Wah will put a fish on your hook if you bribe him with a pinch of tobacco cast on the water.

Lanes in the village and Tonset areas lead to Town Cove and Nauset Harbor landings. Asa's Landing is a short way up the cove off Gibson Road, and Mill Pond and Snow Shore landings are right on the harbor off Champlain Road for those looking for a launching site close to the ocean. A landing is also available at picturesque Rock Harbor for those who wish to cruise Cape Cod Bay.

Orleans is the shopping center of the lower Cape. The old downtown section is very pleasant in a small-town way; modern banks and supermarkets blend in, with their "banker's colonial" architecture. The town must have a fine cupola salesman, for Orleans is dotted with them. Newer commercial areas on the outskirts with their neon-treed asphalt lawns are some of those ragged fringes I mentioned.

The land of the Pochet has as long and varied a history as any town on the Cape. In fact, if you subscribe to the theories of one historian of the Viking sagas, Orleans was the site of the discovery of America. Edward F. Gray maintains that Leif Eriksson and a crew of thirty-five sailed into Nauset Bay in 1003, his first landfall in the United States. The winds and tides had not yet smoothed the coastline as we now know it, and the island Leif reportedly set foot on is now many fathoms under water. Gosnold anchored off Nauset in 1602 shortly after naming Cape Cod, and Champlain dropped anchor in Nauset Harbor in 1605. The Chamber of Commerce pinpoints the spot as being at the foot of Snow Shore Road, on the Orleans side of the harbor, of course, leaving Eastham without a claim.

When the first settlers came to Eastham in 1644, the present area of Orleans was included in their grant. Orleans, then largely known as Pochet, had been purchased from Mattaquason, Sachem of the Monomoyick. A small settlement had sprouted up by 1710, prompting the Eastham fathers to set aside ten acres of woodland for a future ministry. By 1718 a meeting house was built and the South Parish of Eastham created, with Samuel Osborn as their minister. This first Orleans meeting house was replaced in 1829 by the present Federated Church. The graveyard next door dates back to 1719.

The origin of Orleans's French name has always been a mystery. When Orleans became a town in 1797 we were between two British wars and far from friendly with France — quite the contrary, for insolent French cruisers taunted our captains and plucked cargoes and men from our ships on any pretext, and talk of war was in the air. Orleans is the only Cape town without an English name other than the later Indian name given to Mashpee. Wherever the name came from, it's evident that even the founding fathers of Orleans were searching for something different, something with a sophisticated flair to set them apart from the rest.

In 1890 the *Compagnie Française des Cables Telegraphiques,* or French Cable Company as Orleans called it, came over from Eastham and set up shop at the corner of Cove Road. The new cable from Brest came in to Nauset Harbor in 1898 just about where Champlain had landed almost three hundred years before. The company's French and Belgian employees undoubtedly account for some of the continental atmosphere in Orleans today. Many of their descendants are still here, dyed in the wool "Or-leens" Cape Codders by now.

An irrelevant but interesting footnote of history appears in the town records of 1831, when there were twenty-two individuals on welfare in this town of about 1,500. Orleans built a poorhouse and sustained its needy on a budget of 62 cents per week.

Orleans includes the villages of Orleans, East Orleans, and South Orleans.

JEREMIAH'S GUTTER

The first known crossing of Cape Cod entirely by water is that of Captain Cyprian Southack in a whaleboat in 1717. Captain Southack was the king's representative, sent to secure the riches of Black Bellamy's wrecked flagship, the *Whidah*, for the Crown. The captain was too late — the "mooncussers" beat him to it — but his route across the Cape on the highest spring tides was later improved and enlarged to become the first commercial Cape Cod Canal.

At the boundary of Orleans and Eastham the Cape is only 3½ miles wide. From Boatmeadow River on the Bay side to the Town Cove the unnavigable portion narrows down to about three quarters of a mile of low land and salt marsh. This area often flooded on high tides in years past; Gosnold in 1602 recorded that the northern part of Cape Cod was an island. He was probably misled by one of our higher spring tides.

In 1804 the Eastham and Orleans proprietors dug a small canal following the route of the wandering tides through the marsh. It was never much more than a one-lane ditch and came to be known as Jeremiah's Gutter in honor of a one-time owner, Jeremiah Smith.

Over succeeding years, both Orleans and Eastham suffered occasional fits of canal fever; companies were formed and grand plans prepared, but cooler heads always prevailed. The land was perfect for the purpose, but of what use is a highway to nowhere? Outside Nauset Harbor awaited the Monomoy Shoals and Peaked Hill Bars — and with them went the major benefit to be derived from a commercial canal. During the War of 1812 the canal served its purpose; salt boats and supply vessels evaded the British blockade by transshipping cargoes across the Cape at Jeremiah's Gutter.

Other than its service in the War of 1812, Jeremiah's Gutter was never a successful commercial operation. Maintenance soon ceased and the ditch gradually filled and became overgrown. High tides occasionally opened the passage for short periods; Henry Thoreau noted the brook when he passed by in 1849. Some years later the state built a dike to prevent further encroachments of the tides for all time.

The remains of Jeremiah's Gutter may still be seen in Orleans and Eastham today. About 50 feet after the Entering Eastham sign and just before the rotary on Route 6A, Canal Road is on your left. About a hundred feet in on the right is a historic marker in front of a surviving bit of the old ditch. You'll notice it winds off through the Route 6 rotary and beyond. You can roughly trace the old route off through the marsh toward Cape Cod Bay by the line of plume grass waving in the breeze.

MARK SNOW HOUSE (1723)

The oldest home still standing in Orleans is the Mark Snow House, built in 1723. The oak frames for the old structure were taken from Eastham's first meeting house and fort. Originally a small "half house," the front door was enclosed when the front ell was added on in later years. Occupied by six generations of the Snow family from 1723 to 1956, the home is still privately owned and is not open for inspection.

Mark Snow House is located on Canal Road less than a quarter mile in from Route 6A on the left. A historic marker identifies the property.

THE BATTLE OF ROCK HARBOR

The Orleans port of Rock Harbor was the scene of one of the few battles on Cape soil in the War of 1812. British warships under Admiral Lord Howe and Captain Richard Raggett patrolled the Cape Cod Bay ports, demanding ransom from the towns to spare their ships and salt works. Eastham was bullied into paying $1,200 and Brewster came up with $4,000, but the war was more popular in Orleans and they elected to fight. The militia was reorganized and the British demand for $2,000 was bluntly refused. The demand turned out to be largely a bluff. A small shore party was landed up Skaket Creek, but as soon as the Orleans militia opened fire the British made haste to withdraw. A cast-iron shell from the British bombardment is now in the possession of the Orleans Historical Society.

In December 1814 the patrolling British frigate *Newcastle* went aground on the flats outside the harbor. Catcalls and jeers from shore raised the English dander; a boat was sent in and two Orleans sloops burned; a schooner and another sloop were captured. The British prize crew on the captured schooner *Betsy* impressed an Orleans man as pilot and he promptly ran her aground at Yarmouth, resulting in the capture of the British crew.

The *Newcastle,* minus some spars and rigging, finally heaved off the flats and took her remaining prize to Provincetown, but the day belonged to Orleans. Sixty years later Congress awarded land grants to the participants and their heirs for services rendered in what came to be known as the Battle of Rock Harbor.

From the end of the war to the 1850s, Rock Harbor increased in importance as the town center of Orleans. Packet boats to Boston and the fishing and marine trades flourished, and shops, small factories, and homes lined the harbor. With the decline of the marine trades from the 1860s, the town center gradually shifted inland to its present site.

Rock Harbor is bustling again today as the center of deep sea charterboat fishing on the lower Cape.

JOSHUA CROSBY HOMESTEAD

Orleans distinguished itself in the War of 1812 at home and at sea. Perhaps the town's resolve was stiffened at Rock Harbor by the exploits of one of its men on Old Ironsides early in the war.

Joshua Crosby ran away to sea at an early age, served with Commodore Perry at the Battle of Lake Erie, and commanded a quarterdeck gun on the 44-gun frigate *Constitution* in the famous battle with the H.M.S. *Guerriere* on August 19, 1812. Joshua was an Orleans man and his old home is about two miles from Main Street down Tonset Road on the right. A historical plaque marks the house. It is a humble little home, close by the road, and was old even when Crosby lived there.

A Hardwich boy served with Joshua on Old Ironsides, and his version of the battle gave credit for the victory to "a bar'l o' merlarses." The booklet *Cape Cod Legends* reports:

So sure was the *Guerriere* that the fight was theirs, that they placed a barrel of molasses on deck to be made into "switchel" (a mixing of molasses, ginger, rum and water) with which to "treat" the Yankees whom they expected to defeat. "Switchel" was what was known as a "landlubbers" drink and to be offered it was a supreme insult to the manhood of a tough jack tar in 1812.

But good markmanship raked the deck of the *Guerriere* early in the engagement. By good fortune one of these shots smashed the barrel of molasses. Over the deck the sticky mess ran, and, mixed with blood and water, it made the deck so slippery, it was almost impossible to obtain a foothold and man the ropes of the *Guerriere*. This was a serious handicap in maneuvering the ship, and so *Old Ironsides* won the fight "by a bar'l o' merlarses."

Joshua Crosby returned home to Orleans, was keeper of the Nauset Light for a time, and died in 1861. He lies buried in the Orleans cemetery.

On your way back on Tonset Road is a historical marker on the right about a hundred yards before Main Street, marking the site of the Giles Hopkins homestead. Giles Hopkins was born in England, came as a boy to Plymouth on the *Mayflower* in 1620, and settled in Orleans in 1648. He is buried in Eastham's Old Cove burial ground.

FRENCH CABLE STATION MUSEUM

The first cable station was established on Cape Cod just south of Nauset Light in 1879. The undersea cable then ran from Brest, France, to St. Pierre Island off Newfoundland and then to Nauset Beach. In 1890 the station was moved to its present location on Route 28 at the foot of Cove Road, and in 1898 a direct cable was laid from Brest to the nearby Town Cove. Another cable connected the station directly with New York.

From 1880 to 1940 the station was a primary source of important international news and communications. Some of the events first reported by this station were the sinking of the steamer *Portland* off Truro, with the loss of 176 lives, on November 27, 1898; the sinking of the *Lusitania;* Lindbergh's safe arrival in Paris; and the attack of the German submarine off Nauset Inlet in 1918. When the Cape was cut off from the mainland in the 1938 hurricane, the French Cable Station was the only means of contact with the outside world.

When France was overrun by the German armies in the spring of 1940, the message came over from Brest, "Don't say anything more. The Boche are coming. Good-bye and bless you."

The cable station reopened in 1952, but the increased speed and efficiency of other means of communication brought the final closing of the station on November 24, 1959, with the words, "Happy Thanksgiving. Station closed." In 1971 a group of public-spirited citizens formed a nonprofit corporation and purchased the property from the French government for the purpose of preserving the only cable station in the United States to be saved as a museum.

A trans-Atlantic cable station of the early 1900s communicated by the Morse code. The highly skilled operators read the dots and dashes from a narrow strip of tape which came off the "siphon recorder." The distance was too great for sound transcription, so the sound impulses were transformed into minute strokes on the tape and read by sight rather than sound.

The museum is filled with equipment from the days when technical apparatus was largely handmade. Beautifully cast brass instruments mounted on mahogany bases were generally made to order for each cable company.

Just about everything in the station dates from 1900 to 1920. The operations room, the heart of the station, is set up just as it was when the facility was a key link in the international communications chain.

FIRST UNIVERSALIST MEETING HOUSE (1834)

The Orleans Historical Society has recently acquired the old meeting house of the First Universalist Society, constructed in 1834. The building, on Main Street near the corner of River Road, is the beginning of an Orleans Historical Museum, we hope; it is open to the public on Tuesdays and Thursdays from 1 to 4 P.M. during the summer season.

Built in classical Greek Revival style, the graceful proportions and simple lines of the old meeting house provide an excellent example of the architecture of the period.

PACKET LANDING

The byways of Orleans lead to some of the most attractive bays and coves on the Cape. The fingers of Pleasant Bay, Nauset Harbor, and Town Cove wind through the town to such an extent that quaint moorings flecked with sailboats and power cruisers crop up in the most unexpected, delightful places.

One such picturesque harbor is the old Pochet Pond packet landing at the end of River Road, just a few minutes from the center of town. The Orleans packets to Rhode Island and New York sailed from this landing during much of the last century. This old landing is one of the few that still looks much like it must have looked in its prime.

ORLEANS ARENA THEATRE (1873)

The old Orleans Town Hall on Main Street has been the home of one of Cape Cod's most interesting summer theatre companies for over twenty years. High on a knoll, the stately old square-rigged Town Hall of 1873 now hosts a modern theater-in-the-round that has launched many new actors, actresses, and playwrights into professional careers.

Orleans Arena Theatre presents a varied program from late June to Labor Day. Broadway hits, pre-Broadway tryouts, new plays by new playwrights, and experimental plays by noted authors all get their chance. *Waiting for Godot* by Beckett was first seen in summer theater at the Orleans Arena and several of Barnstable author Kurt Vonnegut's new plays received their baptism here.

Orleans Arena Theatre has always involved itself with community service; this interest has been reflected in the pride and loyal support of the townspeople of Orleans. Curtain time is 8:30 P.M. from Tuesday through Saturday, with preview performances at a reduced price each Monday evening. Season subscriptions are available.

CAPTAIN LINNELL HOUSE

Captain Eben Linnell was one of the foremost sailing masters of his time. He learned his trade in the trans-Atlantic cotton business, commanding stout ships on a tight schedule. In 1847 he was ordered to the Orient, and immediately bought a pair of brass four-pounders in the event he met any of those Chinese pirates he'd heard so much about.

Leaving San Francisco in the full-bodied *Buena Vista* on a later voyage, Captain Linnell found the clipper *Southern Cross* sailing for the same destination. Captain Stevens's *Southern Cross* made the run to Calcutta in 56 days, with the *Buena Vista* only four days behind. It was a fine performance with an ordinary vessel, and Captain Linnell's reputation soared.

After 31 years at sea in 1853, the captain was given command of the new clipper *Eagle Wing*. On one voyage in 1855 he made the crossing from London to Hong Kong in 83½ days, a record for a sailing vessel that still stands today.

The captain was a connoisseur of grand and gracious living, and during one of his many visits to Europe he was taken by a large French villa and decided to build one like it in Orleans. When in command of the lean and lovely clipper *Flying Mist* in Hong Kong on Thanksgiving Day 1859, the Orleans skipper gave a grand ball on board. Captain Joshua Sears of the *Wild Hunter* wrote his wife in East Dennis,

Invitations were sent to all, from the Governor down to the shipmaster. It was really a grand affair. I should like to have had you and Lulu there, for crinoline was very much in demand, as there is only about fifteen ladies in port, and some of them have got such damned jealous husbands that they cannot let them dance with anyone else.

On a later voyage to New Zealand, his ship guided to a mooring by two pilots and double-anchored, the *Flying Mist* dragged both anchors and went on the rocks, a total loss. Captain Linnell went back to the *Eagle Wing* after this tragedy, but his luck had turned. Caught by a loose boom and smashed against the wheel in a squall in 1864, he died a few days later, never to enjoy retirement in the beautiful French villa waiting for him in Orleans.

Henry Kittredge says of Captain Linnell, "For native ability, energy and shrewdness, few American shipmasters were his equal; his record from London to China remains a thorn in the side of the historians of British sail."

The Captain Linnell House, with its enclosed Captain's Walk and beautiful Ionic columns, is located on Namskaket Road shortly before Skaket Beach. It is open to the public in a way that the grand captain would appreciate, as one of the finest restaurants on the Cape, open all year.

CAPTAIN KENRICK HOUSE (c. 1780)

Captain John Kenrick had a chance for fame and fortune and muffed it.

One of the early deepwater captains, John Kenrick was born in Harwich in 1740. He commanded privateers in the Revolution and was one of the most respected skippers of the day. British markets closed to American ships after the war, so speculators determined to open a Northwest fur trade. It was proposed that the first voyage circumnavigate the globe, going around Cape Horn to the Oregon coast for skins, to China to trade for silks, then west through the China Sea, around the Cape of Good Hope, and across the Atlantic to Boston.

Captain Kenrick was chosen to command and sailed from Boston in 1787 in the 83-foot *Columbia* with the sloop *Lady Washington* as tender. Despite wasted time, lack of provisions and a scurvy-riddled crew, the vessels arrived at the fur grounds and prepared for the winter. Captain Kendrick discovered and named the Columbia River on this voyage in 1788.

When enough furs had been purchased, Captain Kenrick turned command of the *Columbia* over to his lieutenant, Robert Gray of Boston, and remained behind with the *Lady Washington*.

Over the next several years the once-proud seaman degenerated into little more than an itinerant trader, pausing for months wherever he found life most agreeable. He wintered in the Hawaiian Islands and summered on the Northwest coast, with an occasional voyage to China when it suited his fancy.

In the fall of 1795 Captain Kenrick met a British naval vessel near the port of Oahu. In the tradition of the sea, salutes were exchanged. By some horrible mischance, the Engishman's gun was loaded and Captain Kenrick was blown to bits.

The captain's old home in Orleans was built in his palmier days, probably in about 1780. It's a fine center chimney full Cape set off by a beautiful low antique fence. It is on Route 28 about 200 yards north of the South Orleans post office on the other side of the street. It is privately owned and not open for inspection.

NAUSET BEACH

The Cape is just about surrounded by salt water and each area of its coastline has its own character, tempera-

ment and charm. The Cape Cod Bay beaches are quiet
and cool, as befits the more staid, historic north side; the
Nantucket Sound beaches are hot and noisy, in tune with
the effervescent south shore.

Then there are the beaches directly on the Atlantic
Ocean, the Back Side as it's called, from the Cape's elbow
to Provincetown — almost 40 miles of rolling dunes and
wide sandy beach, unbroken except at Nauset Inlet. Beautiful and relatively cold, this great Atlantic beach has
been the scene of much of the Cape's history of shipwrecks, pirates, mooncussing and lifesaving stations. Nauset Beach is that part of the great beach extending from
North Eastham to Chatham, protecting Nauset Harbor,
Pleasant Bay and the towns of Orleans and Chatham from
the fury of the Atlantic. Nauset is largely a barrier beach
formed over thousands of years by drifting sands washed
down the exposed coastline. Today it is a mecca for sur-
fers, swimmers and strollers; but one should see it in a
raging no'theaster to fully appreciate its reputation.

Nauset and her sister beaches on this lee shore are
bracketed by Peaked Hill Bars on the north and Monomoy
Shoals on the south. A northeast gale accompanied by a
flow tide acts like a magnet that few sailing vessels can
resist. No anchor can hold against the pull; even light-
ships have been dragged from their moorings in a northeast storm. Once within its clutches, very few sailing ships
escape.

Hundreds of vessels have come to grief off Nauset. One
of the earliest recorded was the *Sparrowhawk* in the winter of 1626–1627, which was off course "either by ye in-
sufficiencie of ye maister, or his ilnes; for he was sick
and lame of ye scurvie, so that he could be lye in ye cabin
dore, and give direction." Friendly Indians cared for the
ship's company and guided two to Plymouth to summon
aid from Governor Bradford.

The wrecked hulk of the *Sparrowhawk* disappeared
over the years, covered by the shifting sands. In 1782,
155 years later, a fierce storm swept the wreck clean

again. People paid little attention, and mother nature covered her up again. In 1863 she reappeared after another gale and it was reported she was "well built of oak, still wholly undecayed, the corners of her timbers being sharp as when new."

Parts of the vessel are now on display at Pilgrim Hall Museum in Plymouth. The dune on Nauset Beach under which the *Sparrowhawk* rested for so many years is known as Old Ship.

In 1717 Black Sam Bellamy invaded Cape waters. The notorious pirate captured two vessels and manned them with prize crews. One, the *Mary Anne,* her crew under the influence of Madeira wine and the urging of a gale, soon went aground off Nauset. Two Orleans men went to the rescue, not realizing that their seven guests were pirates until all were safely ashore. Still feeling no pain, the pirates tottered off down the road but were quickly rounded up and packed off to Barnstable jail for safekeeping. All were later marched to Boston, tried for piracy, and hanged.

In 1918 Orleans and Nauset Beach earned the distinction of being the only area in America to receive enemy shellfire in the First World War. The kaiser wanted to impress us with the range and power of his U-boat fleet and chose a tugboat and four coal barges off Nauset to do it. On a tranquil Sunday morning in July, the submarine surfaced for an hour and a half and fired more than a hundred rounds, at least one of which landed ashore. The barges were sunk, the tug damaged, and the crowd on the beach dumbfounded. The Naval Air Station at Chatham was called, but most of the pilots were at a ball game in Provincetown. Three planes finally got off the ground and one pilot reportedly attacked with the only weapon he had, a monkey wrench. A direct hit was scored and the submarine sank. Little credit is given to the yarn that the monkey wrench had anything to do with it.

Just behind Nauset Beach in Pleasant Bay is Hog Island. The northwestern point of the island is known as

Money Head, and for good reason. It has long been known that Captain Kidd frequented Cape waters, and it is reported that Kidd's gold "put into a box, lockt and nailed, corded about and sealed" was buried on Money Head. They say that "one must dig only at midnight on the seventh day of the seventh month; the moon must be full; and a sheep must be freshly slain on the spot so that it's blood may flow from the cut to the place where the treasure is buried." Good hunting!

PUBLIC SWIMMING BEACHES

Beautiful Nauset Beach is the only one in Orleans requiring a parking sticker or the payment of a parking fee. Visitors should purchase their sticker from the Town Offices a short way in on School Road off Main Street. Nauset is a fine surfing beach and also has several dune buggy trails.

Orleans also has a fine bayside beach at the end of West and Namskaket roads. Skaket Beach is warmer and without surf; at low tide the exposed flats and sand bars stretch well into the Bay. Parking and beach use is free to all.

The town maintains freshwater beaches on both Pilgrim and Crystal lakes. The Crystal Lake swimming area on Monument Road is a tiny beach, little more than an access to the water. Pilgrim Lake Beach, on the other hand, is one of those rare jewels that grace so many of the byways of Orleans. From Monument Road take Herring Brook Road past a delightful little cove and follow the road to the right about a mile. It's a fine sandy beach with picnic tables, swimming floats and fine fishing for the youngsters in a picturebook setting. Parking stickers are not required at the freshwater beaches.

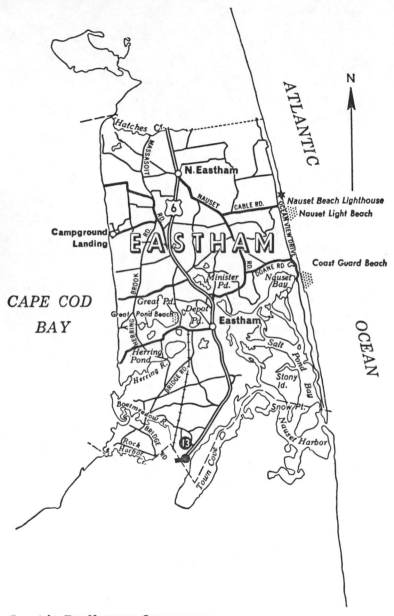

N

ATLANTIC

N. Eastham

CABLE RD.

★ Nauset Beach Lighthouse
Nauset Light Beach

Campground
Landing

E A S T H A M

DOANE RD.

Coast Guard Beach

Minister
Pd.

Nauset
Bay

CAPE COD

Great Pd.

Great Pond Beach

Depot
Pd.

Eastham

BAY

Salt

Pond Bay

OCEAN

Herring
Pond

Herring R.

Stony
Id.

Snow Pt.

Boatmeadow R.

Nauset Harbor

Rock
Harbor
Cr.

⓭

Town Cove

Copyright, THE NATIONAL SURVEY, 1973
Chester, Vermont

CHAPTER VIII

Eastham

One of the four original towns on Cape Cod, Eastham has had an illustrious history. At one time it was on an almost equal political footing with Plymouth, but new towns evolved so frequently over the years that Eastham's resting now, content to let its offspring assume the major share of its old responsibilities.

In making over to the Colony the patent he had received from the Earl of Warwick in 1630, Governor Bradford reserved "Nawsett" for the use of the "Purchasers" and "Old Comers." In 1640 this area from "the bounds of Yarmouth three miles eastward of Namskaket and across the neck from sea to sea," was put under the jurisdiction of the Plymouth Court. This vast area included the present towns of Brewster, Harwich, Chatham, Orleans, and Eastham.

Plymouth was, after twenty-three years, losing its attractiveness. Business was poor, the land not up to expectations, and Plymouth men felt crowded and cramped, itching for the fertile lands and open spaces they had seen on the lower Cape. There was talk of moving the Plymouth Colony intact to Nauset, the promised land of the Proprietors, and a small committee was sent in 1643 to investigate the possibility. Their report was hedged and incomplete and a larger group set out to settle the matter. Among them were Thomas Prence, John Doane, Nicholas

Snow, Josias Cook, Richard Higgins, John Smalley and
Edward Bangs — all of whom eventually became settlers.
Suitable arrangements were made with the court and the
Old Comers, those who came over on the first three vessels, the *Mayflower*, the *Fortune* and the *Anne*. The committee was authorized to buy the land from the Indians if
they deemed it advisable.

The second committee concurred with the first that the
area would not support all of the Plymouth settlement,
but they purchased large tracts anyway. From Mattaquason, Sachem of the Monomoyick, they bought Pochet,
much of present-day Orleans, and from George, Sachem
of the Nauset, what we now know as Eastham. When they
asked the Indians, "Who lays claim to Billingsgate?" — a
vague area including everything north of Eastham — the
Indians replied, "It belongs to no one." "Then that land
also is ours," replied the Plymouth men, and thus acquired Wellfleet, Truro and Provincetown. About 1666 a
lower Cape Indian named Lieutenant Anthony did show
up to stake his claim to Billingsgate, and Eastham paid
him off if only not to tarnish Governor Winslow's boast
that "The English do not possess one foot of land in the
colony but was fairly obtained by honest purchase from
the Indian proprietors." At a price of perhaps one hatchet
per square mile, the English undoubtedly complained
bitterly about the high cost of hatchets.

When the committee reported back to Plymouth, the
older colonists tried to discourage a move. They had lost
few of their own to the earlier settlements at Sandwich,
Barnstable and Yarmouth, and wanted to keep the Plymouth group together. The younger and more vigorous
half of the population was determined to emigrate, however, and left for Nauset in the spring of 1644. Large
areas of Orleans, Eastham and Wellfleet were included in
their grant, but the vague authority of the Nauset expedition actually extended from the bounds of Old Yarmouth
to the tip of the Cape.

Led by Thomas Prence, the settlement quickly prospered and was awarded township status in 1646, although it did not assume the name of Eastham until 1651. In 1654 the town was shorn of its first land when its western bounds were adjusted to exclude jurisdiction over the lands on which the proprietors and Old Comers still had a claim. The settlement of Old Harwich began, closely followed by the Nickerson escapade in Chatham. While these areas were never more than a theoretical part of Eastham, the partition of the grand old lady had begun.

Thomas Prence, who had already served two years as governor, was elected again in 1657. Prence refused to return to Plymouth, and to the delight of the Cape, the court relented and permitted him to serve and commute as necessary from Eastham. He was reelected every year for the next seventeen years and died in office in 1673.

In 1663 the selectman system of local government came to the Cape. Subsequent town meeting reports give a good insight into problems of the day. In the 1665 town meeting it was voted that "all persons standing outside of the meeting-house during the time of public worship shall be set in the stocks." This was the temper of the times that faced the Quakers, Baptists, and the Methodists of a later day. In 1667 the town ordered that "every housekeeper shall kill or cause to be killed, twelve blackbirds, or three crows" each year. This was reinforced in 1695 by decreeing that single men could not take a wife until they killed their quota. In 1685 the town offered a bounty of £10 per wolf or £5 for wolves' whelps to any Indian hunter — and doubled the bounty the next year. Eastham was by then a prosperous farming community and the safety of its crops and livestock took first priority.

By 1685 Eastham's population had boomed past 900 and the famed Reverend Samuel Treat was in the thirteenth year of his ministry. The genial and sociable Sam Treat was a Calvinist terror in his pulpit; it was said that his voice "could be heard at a great distance from the meeting house, even amidst the shrieks of hysterical women and the winds that howled over the plains of

Nauset." Treat ranged far and wide and claimed all the Indians below Yarmouth as his wards. His hellfire and damnation exhortations kindled the savage imaginations of his red men and they loved him like a father. Off the pulpit he was warm and sympathetic and gave much more than lip service to the Indians' welfare. He had five hundred "praying Indians" in his flock by 1693, with four native preachers, and Indian schools were established to educate the Nausets in their own tongue. He knew their language as well as they, devised an alphabet, and wrote sermons and lessons in the only written language most of them ever knew. Samuel Treat died in his sleep during the Great Snow of 1717 and the townspeople and Indians had to tunnel through the drifts to carry their beloved "little father" to his grave.

Treat's forty-five-year ministry marked the second phase of the Nauset Indian saga in Eastham. In little more than a hundred years the Nausets cycled from pagan savages to naïve Christians to extinction. Treat's praying Indians were down to four in 1765 and had almost disappeared by the turn of the century.

The Indians were not alone on their slide downhill. By 1700 Eastham was scattered all over the landscape with sizable settlements in what we now know as Orleans, Wellfleet, and Truro in addition to the mother settlement at Eastham. In 1709 Truro was incorporated and soon had unruly Provincetown under her wing. This development had little practical affect on Eastham, as it had never been more than remotely concerned with these two outlying districts. A decade later its southern citizens asked for and received permission to establish a South Parish at Orleans, followed in 1723 by the North Parish at Wellfleet. In each instance Eastham was fully cooperative and, unlike some other towns, almost encouraged her precincts toward town status. The incorporation of Wellfleet in 1763 dropped Eastham from first to fifth in population and political importance, and the inception of Orleans in 1797 reduced it to the bottom ranks. Eastham apparently never aspired to political glory; the town reports indicate more relief than regret as each of its wards went on its own.

When the Methodists came in 1820, the old order in Eastham was on its last legs. After a forty-year ministry under the Reverend Philander Shaw, the Congregational Church in Eastham virtually died with its old and infirm pastor in 1841. Peter Walker, Eastham's bard of the blacksmiths, recorded the event with his mocking:

> *A learned Treat, a pious Webb,*
> *And Cheever — all no more;*
> *Mr. Shaw then took the helm*
> *And run the ship ashore.*

The rich soil and lush forests that attracted Thomas Prence and his friends had long since disappeared from the Eastham landscape of the 1800s. After the settlers cleared the trees to plant their farms, the winds gradually swept the black crust from the land, replacing corn fields with scrub pines, beach grass and sand. Eastham turned to the sea; fishing and saltmaking took over and Eastham prospered as before.

Many of Eastham's sons stood in the front ranks of Cape Cod shipmasters. Captain Matthew Mayo was captured by the British in the War of 1812 and assigned to pilot a captured schooner patrolling the Bay. The yarn that followed his escape reads like a dime novel, but there is no doubt that Captain Mayo hoodwinked the crew and ran them aground off his home shore. With the schooner recaptured and the crew under guard, the cautious burghers of Eastham began to undo his good work. The crew was released to appease the British but Captain Raggett wanted more. Threatening to burn and loot, he demanded $1,200 for protection. Lacking Captain Mayo's strong will and cool nerve, the town damned the southern administration in Washington and paid.

Eastham's most famous skipper of the glory years was Captain Freeman Hatch. At the age of thirty-two he was master of one of the most nimble racehorses of the sea,

the rakish clipper *Northern Light*. In 1852 he made the
passage from San Francisco to Boston in 76 days, 6 hours,
"an Achievement Won By No Other Mortal Before Or
Since," as it says on his headstone. Three clippers were in
this particular race; one known speedster, the *Contest*,
was expected to win, but the owners of the *Northern
Light* offered Hatch a new suit of clothes if he could beat
the other. He came in 2½ days ahead of his nearest rival
and a new champion was crowned. Some credit is due the
designer, Samuel Pook, whose *Red Jacket* still holds the
record from New York to Liverpool.

When the land ran out in Eastham there was nothing
to do but let it grow over and go to sea. When the sea
industries ran out, Eastham came back to the land. Scrub
forests had overgrown much of the old farm land and
landholders found they could burn it off and develop a
passable soil again. The sandy soil was not rich enough
for the old bumper crops of corn, wheat, rye and flax, but
it was fine for "Truro grass," as asparagus was called, with
a few carrots and turnips to provide a fall and winter crop.
The plains of Nauset grew a fair grass and this, together
with salt hay from the marshes, was enough for some
good-sized dairy herds. The new trains carried Eastham
milk up and down the Cape. Eastham, greatly reduced in
size, was about back where it started; a small farming
town, stable and solid, now old enough to ignore the
taunts of its bumptious offspring as they chanted:

> *Provincetown for beauty,*
> *Wellfleet for pride,*
> *If it wasn't for milk cans*
> *Eastham 'd a' died.*

The milk cans are long gone and only a few home asparagus patches survive, but mother Eastham is improving with age. In 1961 the National Seashore took control
of a third of Eastham and the prophets of doom figured
the town might follow the milk cans after all. With a
population of 1,200 and an assessed valuation of $6.5

million there wasn't much leeway. A look at Eastham in 1972 shows it's very much alive. The population has almost doubled and valuation has gone up 800 percent to $42 million — not bad for a relaxed and resting old lady.

Eastham is where the outer Cape begins, the gateway to the National Seashore, and still keeping up with the younger towns "down Cape." Eastham is particularly summer-oriented; its roads and lanes still host a multitude of small private summer cottages of the type that used to pepper the Cape. Year by year more are converted to year-round residences, but the trend seems slower in Eastham. It's a quiet town; you can pass through the village centers of Eastham and North Eastham and never know you've been there. There is plenty to see and do, however, and a good place to start is right across the street from Town Hall.

EASTHAM GRIST MILL

In an area where windmills were once more common than supermarkets are today, it is increasingly difficult to find one in mint condition. Eastham has one of the few that remain and it's open to the public in the summer season.

The exact age of the old windmill is lost in the strands of time; the best guess is that it was built in Plymouth around 1688, dismantled and shipped across the Bay to Truro about a hundred years later, and moved to Eastham in 1793. It is one of a type that Eastham's millwright Tom Paine designed and built in the late 1600s. He constructed two in Eastham in 1683 at a cost of about £75 each; they were bought and sold, dismasted and moved many times over the years and long lost in history.

Eastham Grist Mill is a fine example of its type. All of the old hand-hewn machinery is still in operation — a massive octagonal shaft, seven-foot peg wheel, wooden gears, and a full set of sails that can still catch a breeze and send it through its paces as it did in the days when corn was king. Every once in a while they head it into the wind, release the brakes and off it goes. The selectmen turned out to show how it was done, not too long ago, snapping a shaft in the process.

The last miller was, appropriately enough, Thomas Paine, a descendant of the early craftsman. The windmill was closed down in about 1900 and for many years lay idle and abused — a convenient local dump, one oldtimer tells me. The Village Improvement Society recognized it as the historic treasure it is and turned it over to the town. First opened to the public in 1936, the windmill was fully restored in 1964 and is now capable of showing "off-Capers" how they did it in the old days.

The old gentlemen who operate the mill for the town are quite willing to spin a yarn or two along with the free admission. Eastham Grist Mill is on the Route 6 village green at the corner of Samoset Road. It is open from 10 A.M. to 5 P.M. weekdays and from 1 to 5 P.M. Sundays from early May to October.

FIRST ENCOUNTER

After the initial *Mayflower* landing at Provincetown, the weary Pilgrims, fearing the shoals and breakers to the east, set out to explore Cape Cod Bay. Their third excursion was made by a party of eighteen, led by Captain Myles Standish on December 6, 1620. In freezing temperatures, the group made their first night's camp on the beach at Eastham.

The next day passed with some men exploring inland, the others coasting the Bay. Indian burying grounds and shelters were found but no trace of the red man himself. The party camped again on the beach, determined to move on in the morning.

As dawn broke the first encounter came. In William Bradford's words, "one of their company being ahead came running in, and cried, 'Men, Indeans, Indeans,' and withall, their arrowes came flying amongst them. Their men rane with all speed to recover their armes, as by ye good providence of God they did . . . let flye amongst them and quickly stopped their violence."

The Nausets had a grudge to settle with the white man. Six years before, Captain Thomas Hunt had lured a score of Indians on board, some of them Nausets, shanghaied them to Spain, and "sold those silly savages for rials of eight."

One of the kidnapped Indians was a Wampanoag named Squanto. He escaped in Spain and "got away for England, and was entertained by a marchante in London, and imployed to Newfoundland and other parts." In early 1621, it was Squanto who befriended the Pilgrims at Plymouth, helped draw the peace treaty with the Sachem Massasoit, taught them to fish and plant corn, and gave freely of his assistance until his death from fever in 1622. Bradford saw in Squanto "a special instrument sent of God for their good beyond their expectation."

First Encounter Beach, at the foot of Samoset Road, is today one of the fine public beaches of Eastham. Few visitors recall the shower of arrows and flurry of musket fire of 350 years ago as they swim and sun on the lovely beach. For those who do there is a granite boulder and bronze tablet on a hill behind the beach marking the site of the incident the Pilgrims called First Encounter.

TARGET SHIP

About a mile out in the Bay to the right of First Encounter Beach is the target ship, *General James E. Longstreet*. It rests in a few feet of water on the bottom of the Bay and is used for target practice by U.S. Air Force planes stationed at nearby airfields. Light caliber ammunition as well as rockets and practice bombs are used to train the air crews, and the pyrotechnics are quite a sight from the beach, particularly at night. When towed into position early in World War II, the *Longstreet* was a new victory ship but incomplete and without engines.

Skaket Beach in Orleans also offers a good view of the

Longstreet, as do many points along the Bay shore of Eastham.

OLD COVE BURYING GROUND

A mile north of the Eastham-Orleans rotary on the right is Eastham's oldest burying ground. Three *Mayflower* passengers rest here, the first meeting house was located adjacent to the cemetery, and Governor Thomas Prence lived nearby. The governor's home and the meeting house are gone now, as are many of the oldest headstones in the graveyard.

The three *Mayflower* passengers known to lie here are Lieutenant Joseph Rogers (1608–1678), Constance Hopkins (1605–1677) and Giles Hopkins (1607–1690). Their headstones are gone but descendants have dedicated memorial tablets in their place. Legible headstones date from the early to mid-1700s. The most interesting ones historically are those of Major John (1719) and Mercy Freeman (1711). John and Edmund Freeman were sons of the leading founding father of Sandwich. Edmund, Jr., wooed and won Rebecca Prence and came home and told his younger brother about Rebecca's lovely sister Mercy languishing on the plains of Nauset. John moved to Eastham, married pretty Mercy, became assistant to his father-in-law the governor, and went into business as the local tar tycoon. Political connections were no more of a hindrance then than they are now.

The first meeting house on this site went up soon after the first settlers arrived in 1644. It was 20 feet square with a thatched roof and gun ports to serve as a fort in the event of Indian attack. Some of its timbers were reportedly used in the construction of the Mark Snow House in Orleans. In 1676 a new meeting house was built on what is now Bridge Road and a new cemetery laid out beside it. Deacon Samuel Doane was buried there beside the "Old South Meeting House" in 1795; his headstone reads: "Death is a debt to Nature Due/As I have paid it, so must you."

SCHOOLHOUSE MUSEUM

The proverbial one-room schoolhouse is no more than a tale of the "olden days" to most of us. Here is one that has been preserved and restored to show us what it was really like.

Built in 1869, this little yellow schoolhouse served all grades in central Eastham for a time. As late as 1905 all eight primary grades learned their ABCs in this one room. By then North and South Eastham each also had a one-room school; these buildings were moved to the central site and joined to this one-room schoolhouse to form a grade school complex that served the town as Eastham Central School until 1936. These later additions were removed when the schoolhouse was restored to its original condition.

In the early years, the school year extended from the Monday after Thanksgiving to the first of September. By 1896 the town boasted the three one-room schools, a superintendent, three teachers and a school budget of $1,-500. We met one of the ladies who attended all eight grammar school grades in the little school and must admit that a one-room school certainly didn't deprive her of a fine education.

Eastham's early school now serves as the Historical Society Museum. The museum contains an exceptional collection of early Eastham mementos. Indian artifacts, farm tools, household utensils and relics of Eastham's seagoing history are combined with early school furnishings to provide a fine insight into the early life of the area.

The Schoolhouse Museum is located on the same side of Route 6 and directly opposite the Visitor Center of the National Seashore. It is open from 2 to 5 P.M. on Monday, Wednesday and Friday throughout July and August. A nominal admission fee is charged.

CAPE COD NATIONAL SEASHORE

Salt Pond in Eastham is the gateway to one of the most unique National Parks in the country, Cape Cod National

Seashore. Beach, heath, forests and ponds are no longer threatened here in one of the last expanses of uninterrupted natural land along the Atlantic. The National Seashore will ultimately embrace some 27,000 acres of land, and will keep intact the resources, charm and beauty of the old Cape for future generations.

National Seashore facilities in Eastham are concentrated at three points, the Salt Pond Visitor Center, Coast Guard Beach and Fort Hill. Each facility is well marked to the right on Route 6 going down Cape.

Salt Pond

Salt Pond Visitor Center looms up like a giant eagle's nest on the hill overlooking the pond. It is the focal point of many National Seashore facilities in Eastham, with an information desk, Cape and natural history book counter, an auditorium, and a museum. Outside are an amphitheater, bicycle trail, and the entrances to the three guide-yourself nature walks in the Salt Pond area.

The museum concentrates on the natural history of Cape Cod. Several exhibits are augmented by slides and recordings, covering such subjects as "How the Cape was formed," "Signs of glacial and sea action," and "The life cycle of a salt marsh." Other exhibits focus on early explorers, the Indians and Cape Cod industries. A fine exhibit illustrates the architecture of the Cape Cod house. If the terms full Cape and half-Cape are confusing, this display will help to clarify them.

A short film, "Here Is Cape Cod," more of a natural history story than a travelogue, is shown hourly each day in the summer season or when attendance warrants it or visitors ask for it during the off-season.

The Salt Pond Visitor Center is open daily in season, closed Wednesdays and Thursdays from mid-October to mid-May. When the center is closed, you can still use the many other facilities in the area.

The outdoor amphitheater has evening programs on a wide variety of Cape and natural history topics nightly during July and August. A brochure outlining the schedule of events is available each spring and throughout the summer here or at the Province Lands Visitor Center.

Beside the amphitheater is the beginning of the paved two-mile bicycle trail to Coast Guard Beach. The trail climbs the red cedar–dotted hillside to a locust grove. This grove was an apple orchard about a hundred years ago when this area was a working farm, and a few of the old apple trees remain. After another grove of red cedars, the trail breaks out onto an open field with a panoramic view of Nauset Marsh. As the trail winds through the forests, views of lily ponds and glimpses of the Atlantic open through the trees. The trail passes near Doane Rock, the largest boulder on the Cape, then drops to Nauset Marsh and goes up again to the old Nauset Coast Guard Station on the bluff overlooking the Atlantic. A trail guide for all National Seashore bicycle routes is available at the information desk. They are all exceptional and walkers enjoy them as much as cyclists.

Three guide-yourself nature trails have access points near the Salt Pond Visitor Center. The Buttonbush Trail has been especially designed for the blind and near-blind. This quarter-mile trail is marked with a guide rope that even alerts walkers to steps in the path. The descriptive stations along the trail offer their texts in both large print and Braille.

Salt Pond Loop Trail is a half-mile walk connecting two ponds, Salt Pond to the right and freshwater Buttonbush Pond over the hill nearby. Walk the trail and see two entirely different life communities, the saltwater marine life on the edges and in the shallows of Salt Pond and the freshwater wildlife and aquatic plants of Buttonbush. The trail winds through fields dotted with red cedars and returns to the Visitor Center.

Two-mile Nauset Marsh Trail begins at the same point as the Salt Pond Loop. A comprehensive trail guide is available at a nominal charge at the book counter. Numbered stakes along the trail correspond to the numbered

stops in the booklet. Plants and birds that you may encounter are sketched and identified, together with notes
on the history and ecology of the area. The trail ends at
the Coast Guard Station, so keep in mind that it's a four-
mile round trip.

Both the bicycle trail and the Nauset Marsh Trail pass
quite close to Doane Rock, its picnic area, and the marked
site of the Doane Homestead. Deacon John Doane, one of
the proprietors of Nauset, settled in this area in 1644. A
small monument on the road marks the approximate location of his homestead. A left turn off the trail will bring
you to Doane Rock, a tremendous boulder brought here by
a glacier. Like an iceberg, most of its mass is below the
surface. Deacon Doane's young son was known to play
around this rock and many still call it "Enos' Rock." The
deacon died at ninety-five, and legend has it that he spent
his last days as he began, rocking in a cradle; when he
died the family thought he might appreciate a change of
position so they buried him standing up. Doane Rock can
also be reached by road; it's about halfway between the
Visitor Center and Coast Guard Beach and is a fine picnic
area.

Coast Guard Beach

The road from the Visitor Center past Doane Rock leads
to Coast Guard Beach. High on a bluff to the rear of the
beach parking area is the Coast Guard Museum. The
former Coast Guard Station is now used to house National
Seashore employees and host grade school groups, but the
service building is open to the public as a memorial to the
Lifesaving Service on Cape Cod.

The museum displays the equipment used when the
members of the Lifesaving Service had to row their surf
boats through raging breakers to reach shipwrecked seamen or to fire a line across the deck and haul the survivors, one by one, to shore.

A lifesaving station was first built at Nauset Beach in
1872. Eight more stations were set up on the great beach

in that year, and a few years later four more were added, so that the stations were less than five miles apart. The Nauset Station was replaced in 1936 after a vacationing secretary of the treasury took shelter there in a summer thunderstorm. Erosion had nibbled away the bank to within thirty feet of the sixty-year-old structure, and an impressed secretary was not long in securing action.

The usual station crew consisted of eight: the keeper and seven crewmen. The keeper acted as steersman when manning the surfboat. An unpaid but important member of the staff was the station horse, who was used to haul the cart, breeches buoy equipment, and surfboat to the beach. The crew lived at the station and patrolled its section of the beach each night and, if foggy, by day as well the year round, no matter what the weather. Daily drills kept them at the ready and each station was prepared for disaster at any time. From 1873 to 1889 the Cape Cod Lifesaving District reported 46 shipwrecks — 3,407 people on board and only 42 lives lost. In 1936 Nauset Station reported four major emergencies with no loss of life. Many other emergencies were prevented by the men on patrol. Their warning flares kept many a wayward vessel from dangerous bars and shoals.

Most of the items in the museum were received from the Coast Guard in 1964. The exhibits include a surf cart, two Lyle cannon used to fire a line to a disabled ship so that the breeches buoy could be used, the breeches buoy rig itself, and two surf boats. The museum is open from 1 to 5 P.M. daily in the summer season.

Fort Hill

The entrance to Fort Hill is about a mile and a half before the Visitor Center, back toward Orleans. Across from the parking area is a large yellow house, Eastham's best example of nineteenth-century Victorian architecture. It was owned by Captain Edward Penniman, one of two deepwater whaling captains from Eastham (the other was his son). As master of the *Minerva* in the Civil War, he narrowly escaped capture by the Confederate cruiser *Shenandoah*. On a later voyage the captain anchored and went ashore, leaving his wife and a few sailors aboard. A storm blew up and his wife took command, sailed out of danger, and returned three days later to pick up her impressed husband. When looking for whales on the *Europa*, the captain took a place in one of the whaleboats, leaving his wife and small son on the ship. When he glanced back he saw the ensign flying upside down. Thinking a tragedy had befallen his son, the captain was relieved to find the signal was the only way to attract him back to a large whale cavorting around his ship. Dispatched quickly, the whale oil brought $10,000 and Mrs. Penniman was forgiven for the scare.

Captain Penniman brought his house plans from France and intended to have the fanciest house in town. He did — along with the highest tax bill to prove it. The exterior of the old home has been restored by the National Seashore; access to the interior may follow in time. The exterior painting is a reasonably accurate indication of the captain's taste and the whalebone gateway is an original part of his landscaping plan; these happen to be the third set of jawbones on the site.

Fort Hill also boasts a trail, but of a slightly different character. The human history of this walk entwines with the natural history to take you through a 365-year panorama of Eastham.

The two-mile guide-yourself walk begins by the house (trail guides are available from the trail box at the parking area). Allow an hour or two for your trip. The Fort Hill and Skiff Hill areas covered by the trail were farmland until relatively recent times. The trail guide points out old orchards, stone fences, and homesites along the way. As the views open up the guide will remind you of the historical events that took place in the waters offshore. As your walk progresses you are reminded of the thick forests, fertile farmland, and superb shell and nearby ocean fishing that almost disappeared from the area during 250 years of improper use. The old spikes and rings in oceanfront boulders formerly anchored pulleys and ropes for hauling loads ashore or harvesting salt hay. An old salt works location is identified, and though it all runs the interwoven threads of man and nature, the interdependency of the human being and his environment.

At the crest of Skiff Hill is an interpretative shelter over Indian Rock. There appears to be good evidence that this particular 20-ton boulder was a favorite meeting place of the Indians, who used it to sharpen their tools and weapons. It was originally located down the bank, but high marsh tides and erosion from Skiff Hill were threatening to bury it.

THE OUTERMOST HOUSE

In 1927 a young writer built a snug two-room cottage with windows on all sides on a sand dune near the end of Nauset Beach as it approaches Nauset Inlet. He called his cottage the "Fo'castle" and set about recording the varied nature of his lonely outpost through the seasons of the year. Henry Beston's *The Outermost House* tells the story with such rare skill that it has become a Cape Cod classic.

With only an occasional visit by a patrolling Coast Guardsman, Beston had a few good books for companionship and the Atlantic Ocean for a front lawn. He wrote, "The world today is sick to its thin blood for the lack of elemental things, for fire before the hands, for water welling from the earth, for the dear earth itself, underfoot." His world was warmed at his tiny hearth and sustained by the pageant of nature that he observed on the great beach.

His "Fo'castle" is still there, now owned by the Audubon Society, and provides shelter for researchers of today. It's no longer technically the outermost house, as another has been built a bit farther on. Feel free to walk the beach from the old Coast Guard Station if you would like to see it. It is now a National Literary Monument but is closed to the public. A distant view is available from the lookout

point past the Captain Penniman House at the end of Fort
Hill Road. The "Fo'castle" is the second cottage on the
dunes from the right. Perched on top of the dune when
Henry Beston lived there, the house has since been moved
to the more protected inland side of the dune.

NAUSET LIGHT

The business of "mooncussing" — attracting ships
aground by waving a lantern on a moonless night — has
haunted Cape legends for years. Certainly the "wrecking"
business — legitimate salvage at its best and outright
thievery at its worst — was highly profitable along the
great beach. A man named Collins, advocating a beacon
at Nauset, "found obstinate resistance to the project of
building a lighthouse on this coast, as it would injure the
wrecking business." His comment lends credence to the
dark shadows and misty tales of mooncussing, but it's
hard to believe that a seafaring community could wish
such a fate on her own sons and ships at sea.

The first set of three lights was established at Nauset
in 1838 with Collins as keeper. As storm-tossed seas
eroded the coast, the towers had to be replaced several
times as old ones were moved back or toppled into the sea.
The present light, a steel tower moved to Eastham in 1923,
was one of the twin sisters of Chatham. Years ago mariners identified lighthouses by the number of lights, hence
Chatham had two towers and Nauset three. Now, single
lights have distinctive flashes; the Nauset light winks its
three flashes every ten seconds and can be seen from as
far away as 17 miles at sea.

The old lighthouse keeper's cottage is privately owned
and the light, automated now, blinks away unattended.

MILLENNIUM GROVE

Perhaps the most famous Methodist camp meeting
ground on the Cape was the ten-acre grove off Campground Road in Eastham. Methodist camp meetings began
in Wellfleet in 1819 and ended in Yarmouth in the 1900s,

but the era at Eastham from 1828 to 1863 had much to do with the establishment of true religious freedom on Cape Cod.

The orthodox Congregationalists had been under siege for many years; early Quakers, Baptists and Methodists were persistent but no more determined than the established church. All faiths were required to contribute to the support of the orthodox ministry, and town meetings had been, for all practical purposes, Congregationalist parish meetings since their inception. Camp meetings dealt the old order its final and fatal blow.

Thousands of persons of all denominations attended the evangelical crusades at Eastham. Families came for the week, sat on rough plank benches, and listened to the stern and stentorian exhortations of their ministers for hours at a time. Camp meetings had their lighter side as well and served as a family camping-vacation for many. The religious pilgrims lived in tents divided by a curtain, one side for the men, the other for the women, with self-appointed vigilantes to maintain the status quo. Before long the Methodists outnumbered any other denomination in many Cape towns and the old religious order came tumbling down.

When Thoreau passed by in the fall of 1849, camp meetings were in their prime. His lighthearted evaluation was:

They select a time for their meetings when the moon is full. A man is appointed to clear out the pumps a week beforehand, while the ministers are clearing their throats; but, probably, the latter do not always deliver as pure a stream as the former. I saw the heaps of clam-shells left under the tables, where they had feasted in previous summers, and supposed, of course, that that was the work of the unconverted, or the back-sliders and scoffers. It looked as if a camp-meeting must be a singular combination of a prayer-meeting and a picnic.

FISHERMAN'S PLAYERS

Certainly the most controversial summer theater group on Cape Cod, the Fisherman's Players present some of the best experimental theater with a purpose to be found in the country.

The players are a nonprofit organization sponsored by the United Methodist Church. The company's director and producer, and sometimes writer and actor, is the Reverend Richard D. Waters. An exceptional background in the theater and a strong social consciousness have combined in the Reverend Waters to produce enlightened drama of exceptional relevance and power. The drama critic of the *Boston Glove* said about one production, "Dick Waters is totally unfair. He's written and produced a play that makes us think! That's a shock to the average play-goer's system."

Fisherman's Players features about nine plays a year in repertory. All of a season's productions are related in some way and all say something about our times or the overall predicament of man. The repertory schedule allows visitors with a limited vacation to enjoy many if not all of a season's offerings.

Unlike most "message" theater, the Fisherman's Players give the audience an opportunity to enter the debate. Often referred to as "the fourth Act," the players sponsor a Coffeehouse after each production at which audience, actors, and director share impressions and interpretations of the performance. It's always a brisk, and sometimes disorderly, discussion. One woman complained of the swearing, and under church auspices too! The Reverend Waters replied, "When the man in the street stops swearing I promise there will not be one swear word in any of my plays."

Fisherman's Players are located on the right hand side of Route 6 in North Eastham about a mile before the Wellfleet town line.

CAMPSITES AND TRAILER PARK

Eastham Campground is located on Route 6 a half mile north of the entrance to the National Seashore in Eastham. There are 55 wooded sites in this eight-acre family campground; about half have electrical and water hook-ups. Rest room and hot shower facilities are available at two locations. Pets are permitted. Its season runs from April to November, with reservations required during the summer months. E. H. Putnam, the owner, is also the Cape's Lionel dealer and has an antique model railroad museum. Write to him at Box 452, Eastham, Mass. 02642, for a brochure and further information.

PUBLIC SWIMMING BEACHES

Sandy Eastham has long stretches of beautiful beaches on both the Atlantic and Cape Cod Bay shores, and on freshwater ponds inland. Eastham's bare backside is perhaps one of the most beautiful expanses of easily accessible ocean beach to be found in the country.

Coast Guard and Nauset Light beaches on the Atlantic are under the jurisdiction of the Cape Cod National Seashore and subject to their regulations. The road by the Visitor Center will take you to either one. (Be sure to visit the museum at Coast Guard Beach, and of course you can't miss Nauset Lighthouse at the other.) When entering Nauset Light Beach look to the right to see one of the retired lighthouses now doing duty as part of a summer residence.

The town beaches of Eastham are all on the Bay side and on freshwater ponds. An inexpensive parking sticker may be secured from the Town Hall on Route 6. Motel operators and landlords have supplies of the forms to be signed. Town beaches are scattered up and down the Bay; just drive along the shore roads and you can't miss them. First Encounter Beach at the end of Samoset Road is the site of the historical marker and also provides a fine view of the target ship *General James E. Longstreet.* Herring Brook Landing at the foot of Cole Road is also the location of the entrance to Eastham's herring run inland to Great Pond. Freshwater swimming is available at either Herring Pond or Great Pond.

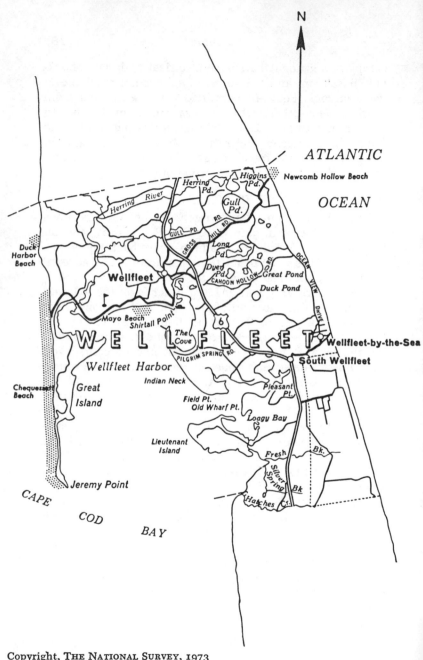

N

ATLANTIC

OCEAN

Newcomb Hollow Beach

Herring River
Herring Pd.
Higgins Pd.
Gull Pd.
GULL PD. RD.
GROSS HILL RD.
Long Pd.
Duck Harbor Beach
Dyer Pd.
CAHOON HOLLOW RD.
Great Pond
OCEAN VIEW DRIVE
Wellfleet
Duck Pond

Mayo Beach
Shirtall Point
The Cove
W E L L F L E E T
Wellfleet-by-the-Sea
South Wellfleet
PILGRIM SPRING RD.

Wellfleet Harbor
Indian Neck
Great Island
Pleasant Pt.

Chequesset Beach
Field Pt.
Old Wharf Pt.
Loagy Bay

Lieutenant Island
Fresh Bk.
Silver Spring Bk.
Jeremy Point
Hatches Ct.

CAPE COD BAY

Copyright, THE NATIONAL SURVEY, 1973
Chester, Vermont

CHAPTER IX

Wellfleet

With the sea, the beaches, and much of the landscape in common, one would think that the lower Cape towns from Eastham to Provincetown would be as alike as peas in a pod. Quite the contrary — each has a distinct personality, flavor, and charm of its own. Wellfleet went through the same wars and crises as its neighbors, but when the lean times came in about 1870, it pulled closer together rather than dispersing, established a self-sufficient town center, and defended its little village, come hell or high water. Wellfleeters defended it so well that the town center still looks more like an 1870 seacoast village than an active member of modern Cape Cod. Appearances are deceiving; Wellfleet is as modern as any town, so long as progress comes on Wellfleet's terms.

Wellfleet spent a long time before settling on its current village center, a bit like the family dog circling round and round before plumping down in the most comfortable spot. Today's Main Street, with its traditional byways of School and Bank streets and time-worn Commercial Street, is pure village America — vintage Cape Cod.

Settlers from Eastham began looking toward Billings gate, as Wellfleet was known, not too many years after Eastham was established. Its early attractions were its fine harbors and prolific oyster beds. As Cape Codders began to look to the sea in the late seventeenth century,

Billingsgate offered a passable soil for crops, fine shell and bay fishing, and some of the best shore whaling grounds on the Cape.

Early settlements were well scattered without recognizable village centers — self-sufficient homesteaders off on their own. Many chose to settle on the "islands" — Billingsgate, Great, Griffiths and Bound Brook islands. In those days these were true islands, but the last three have long since been joined by nature to the mainland. Billingsgate, the Atlantis of Wellfleet, has been reclaimed by the sea.

By the turn of the eighteenth century, Wellfleet began to achieve some sort of unity. Settlers on the islands and around Duck Creek began to realize a common identity and another smaller group with closer ties to Eastham evolved around Blackfish Creek in South Wellfleet. In 1710 Eastham acknowledged its growing northern outpost by setting aside ten acres for a future ministry, and in 1723 it authorized the North Parish Meeting House in the Chequesset Neck area to serve Wellfleet. The old Oakes Cemetery marks the site on a sand lane about 200 yards in off Kendrick Avenue just before it joins Chequesset Neck Road. A new meeting house was built in 1740 at the head of Duck Creek. The burying ground remains on Route 6 on the right just before the left turn to Main Street. The Duck Creek marshes across the highway were a fine anchorage in those days. Early Wellfleet is particularly hard to visualize because of the many changes in its landscape. Not only have the islands joined the mainland, but many of the old wharf areas of Wellfleet have been dammed up so that the coves that sheltered hundreds of sails are now small placid ponds and creeks gradually turning to salt marsh. The coming of the railroad in 1869 sealed off the upper half of Duck Creek to all but small boats. It's hard to believe, but deep-keeled schooners used to tie up off East Commercial Street where the wooden catwalk goes across the creek by Whit's Lane. That catwalk, by the way, is known as Uncle Tim's Bridge and occupies a sentimental niche in the hearts of all Well-fleeters.

The spiritual center of Wellfleet was at Duck Creek, but for many years the commercial centers continued to range wide over the islands and the countryside. In 1734 Wellfleet applied for town status, but it was not until 1763 that the old precinct of Billingsgate was incorporated as the Town of Wellfleet. The Boston Court christened the town Poole, but its citizens objected and the court agreed to their choice of a name. There seems little doubt that the name came from the Wallfleet oyster beds of England, despite the difference in spelling. At the time of incorporation Billingsgate oysters were a staple and distinctive commodity in Wellfleet and it seems quite natural they should take their name from a similar area in the mother country.

In 1606 Champlain was so impressed by Wellfleet oysters he named the harbor Port Aux Huitres, and the Indians had enjoyed oyster feasts here as long as they could remember. Wellfleet oysters were regulated by the colonists as early as 1680 and were an important factor in any Wellfleeter's diet from the first. In 1770 a mysterious epidemic killed the oyster beds, and with them went an important ingredient of Wellfleet's prosperity. Blame ranged from water pollution by blackfish carcasses to the act of an angry God. Apparently the oysters disappeared because the old oyster shells were removed to make lime and new oyster seed were left without their traditional home. After the Revolutionary War, transplant seed oysters were imported from the south and the oyster business boomed as never before. From the 1830s to 1900 the town supplied most of the oysters for Massachusetts, and Wellfleet oysters became an epicurian favorite throughout the world. Southern supply sources dried up early in this century and the industry began a gradual decline. A few commercial fishermen still plant and harvest them, with scallops and quahogs to fill in enough to make a living.

Wellfleet was one of the earliest and most successful whaling towns. Truro sent out the first deepwater whaler from the Cape but Wellfleet was not far behind. In the years before the Revolution, whaling was Wellfleet's only commercial business; those not at sea either serviced the ships or tended their homes and garden plots ashore. When the war came, nine-tenths of its townsmen were unemployed as the harbor was blockaded. During the war its twenty or thirty deepwater ships rotted from disuse and the industry never regained its feet in Wellfleet. A few deepwater ships went out each year over the next twenty years or so, but most carried fishing gear as well. Before long it was the whaling gear they chose to leave at home. Wellfleet whaling captains did earn their share of fame, however. Captain Jesse Holbrook was employed by the British to teach them the art of whaling, and Captain, later Colonel, Elisha Doane had the satisfaction of being buried as one of the richest men in Massachusetts.

Wellfleet found itself in an almost impossible position in the Revolutionary War. Its livelihood gone and its shores unprotected, there was little it could do but wait. The loss of the warship *America* in 1779, with twenty-three Wellfleet men aboard, didn't make the waiting any easier.

When peace came in 1783, oystering was dead of the plague and whaling almost dead for lack of capital. Commercial fishing was the only alternative and Wellfleet went back to sea. The turn of the century found Wellfleet prospering again, the fishing industry in stride and its homesteads taking on the appearance of villages. Clusters of twenty or thirty families now lived on each of the islands and at scattered points on the mainland, each with a store, ship chandlery, and perhaps a small school. Packets connected the town with Boston and the old Duck Creek Meeting House was enlarged as the population grew to over 1,400 by 1810. The War of 1812 interrupted progress for three years, but its end spurred Wellfleet on to the most vigorous period in its economic history.

Small industries came to Wellfleet, and of course salt making grew in importance here as elsewhere on the Cape. Thirty-nine salt works were in operation in 1837, producing 18,000 bushels a year. Fishing and related industries remained the mainstay of the economy and the famous wharves of Wellfleet began to appear.

As Wellfleet grew, the scattered settlements began to draw together around the new wharves. The old island harbors were filling in fast and by 1840 most of the island vessels had been drawn in to the deeper waters of Duck Creek Harbor. When a Cape Codder changed his mooring in those days it was no great problem to move his home as well. On they came, floated or "flaked," reassembled on new foundations around Duck Creek. The settlement on Billingsgate Island was the last to leave. Its protected anchorage was excellent and in no danger of filling with silt. To the contrary, Billingsgate was slowly becoming all harbor and no island.

From the 1830s, new wharves sprang up like mushrooms around Duck Creek. Harding's Wharf went up in 1830, Commercial Wharf in 1835, Enterprise Wharf in 1836, and dozens of others were built over the years culminating with Central Wharf in 1863 and Mercantile Wharf in 1870. The wharves circled Duck Creek and continued on around Shirttail Point along Mayo Beach. It is estimated that half the fish consumed in the country were caught by Cape Cod boats at this time, and Wellfleet's vessels were second only to Provincetown's. Mackerel and cod were the staples and more than a hundred schooners gave chase from Wellfleet. As the demand came for larger and more sophisticated ships, Wellfleet hung on with Provincetown for a time, but by the turn of the century the lack of capital and its shallow harbors had squeezed her out.

The prosperous fishing years of the mid-1800s saw the emergence of the village center we know today. Banks, groceries, hardware stores, and lumber yards went up on Main and Commercial streets. Many are there today as homes, rooming houses, and shops. One of the earliest, Simeon Atwood's hardware store, is still in operation after 140 years. Town Hall looks old, but it isn't. The original building was a Congregationalist Church built in South Wellfleet in 1829 and moved to Main Street some years later. It burned in 1960 and was faithfully reproduced on the same site in 1962. It's a beauty, and the next best thing to the original.

In 1850 the ten-year-old son of a Wellfleet whaling captain followed his father to sea. By the age of twenty-one he was Captain Lorenzo Dow Baker, in command of his own schooner and trading up and down the eastern seaboard. In 1870 Captain Baker made his first voyage to the tropics in his new schooner *Telegraph*, with a cargo of mining equipment for Venezuela.

On his return voyage he loaded bamboo in Jamaica and had his first taste of a native fruit, the banana. He brought a few bunches back home but they were hopelessly spoiled by the time he reached port. He went back to Jamaica in the *Telegraph* the next year, loaded a full cargo of green bananas and thereby took a giant stride toward fame and fortune. A relative, George Baker, had financed this profitable voyage, and was given a choice of repayment in cash or shares in the new venture. George chose cash to his and his descendants' everlasting regret.

Captain Baker knew a good thing when he saw it; he bought and chartered additional vessels and kept raising capital and expanding his banana fleet. He and his brother-in-law, Elisha Hopkins of Wellfleet, organized L. D. Baker and Co. in 1881, offered their stock for public sale as the Boston Fruit Company in 1885, and became the United Fruit Company in 1899.

Captain Baker lived in Jamaica for many years and is credited with the return of prosperity to the island. He saw advantages other than bananas in the tropics, and pioneered in the island's winter tourist trade. Spending his winters on the island and his summers in Wellfleet, the thought occurred to him that here was a natural opportunity to combine business with pleasure. In 1885 he purchased the Mercantile Wharf in Wellfleet and built his hotel, the Chequesset Inn, out over the water on pilings. It was a gracious establishment staffed by the Jamaican crew of his winter hotel on the island. For the first time Wellfleet became known as a summer resort and residential colony for the affluent leisure classes of the 1890s.

The Captain's palatial home on what is now Baker Avenue was for many years the center of the summer social life of the village. As a reminder of his good fortune perhaps, a large bunch of bananas always hung on the front porch, from which all might help themselves.

In 1905 all Jamaica honored the Yankee skipper on his sixty-fifth birthday. In a shower of gifts and tributes, Captain Baker was eulogized as having "In thirty years . . . done more for Jamaica than the British Empire in three hundred years." His services to his home town were less eloquently, but no less warmly appreciated. He promoted local tourist trade, worked to revive the oyster industry, and gave freely of his time, talents, and finances to a number of community charities. At the time of his death in 1908 he was the town's favorite son by far, and now rests peacefully in the Pleasant Hill Cemetery, home from his last voyage.

The declining years of the prosperity of Wellfleet, from about 1880, seemed to catch Main Street as a camera snaps a picture — nicely maintained but little changed through the years. Shellfishing kept it going until tourism could gradually fill the gap. The trains that cut off the moorings of upper Duck Creek not only opened the outside world to Wellfleet but also opened Wellfleet to the outside world. Wellfleet had moved with the tides for more than two hundred years; it was merely a matter of patiently awaiting the next incoming tide.

The "summer people" who arrived around the turn of the twentieth century were people of some wealth, the type Captain Lorenzo Baker expected when he opened his stylish Chequesset Inn in 1886. Wellfleet began to be known as a summer resort and visits of the leisure classes prompted more inns and hotels as weekenders began coming down Cape on the trains from Boston and New York. As the oyster business declined rapidly in the 1930s, Wellfleet was already well on its way to becoming a resort town — quietly, but none the less steadily.

Today's Wellfleet offers gas stations in place of livery stables, automobiles instead of horse-drawn wagons and fiber glass boats instead of schooners, but the character of the village is little changed. Some of its virgin country has been given over to ice cream stands, summer homes, and cottage colonies but this was to be expected. The most radical change over the past many years has been the new town pier and marina. The inner harbor had become so silted over the years that boating had been restricted to a small shellfishing fleet and a few pleasure craft, none of which could enter or leave the harbor except at high tide. The new facility provides one of the finest small harbors on the east coast, a summer home for yachts, sailboats and small craft from all over the eastern seaboard.

Many people can't stand fish, wouldn't touch an oyster, and don't want sand in their shoes — but even they owe a vote of thanks to Wellfleet. It was, after all, Wellfleet's own Luther Crowell who invented that indispensable of daily living, the square-bottomed paper bag.

The 1,800 residents of Wellfleet village and South Wellfleet cover a broad spectrum: fishermen and millionaires, retired couples and artists. They are alike in little but town spirit — and it's a strong one in Wellfleet.

JOSEPH'S GARDEN

Scattered around Wellfleet and elsewhere on the Cape are old dories converted into charming flower boxes. The best known of those remaining welcomes you to the village of Wellfleet at the corner of Main and East Commercial streets.

The flower dories gained their name from a gentle parson of Falmouth, the Reverend Joseph Metcalfe, whose limited worldly wishes included "a boat in which to take mine ease on the deep."

Good fortune smiled on the poor shepherd and an inheritance seemed to make his dream come true. After canceling a church debt for unpaid salary, the parson ordered his dory. The stern church elders were horrified; casting bread upon the waters was one thing, but a minister casting for fish was unthinkable. If it was fish he wanted, fish he would have, but the congregation deemed it unseemly for a man of God to be seen rowing a boat. His new boat rested in the parsonage yard as the gentle soul pondered his dilemma.

That night a wild storm swept the area. When Joseph ventured out the next morning he found the wind had uprooted his rosebushes and some were lying in his boat. Joseph's faith had pointed the way; with his dream fading in his mind, he carefully covered the roots with soil and his flowers and his flock flourished year after year. The original Joseph's Garden has long since disappeared, but retired dories around the Cape carry on his romantic tradition.

FIRST CONGREGATIONAL CHURCH (1850)

Reminiscent of the days when almost every Wellfleet lad went to sea, the clock in the steeple of this church is said to be the only one in the world that strikes ship's time. As every sailor knows, the custom originated when the sand glass used for marking time was turned every half hour and the turning was announced by a bell. In ship's time, the day is divided into six four-hour periods, and within the period each half hour is marked by an increased number of bell strokes; thus, 12:30, one bell; 1:00, two bells; and so on to 4:00, eight bells.

The church also features a rare stained-glass window depicting a ship of the *Mayflower* period and a Hook and Hastings organ of 1873 that is a delight to the eye and ear. Visitors to Wellfleet will also enjoy the chimes concerts during the summer months on Tuesday, Thursday, and Sunday evenings from six to seven bells — 7 to 7:30 for the benefit of us landlubbers.

Services are held each Sunday at 11 A.M. and a warm welcome awaits all visitors.

HISTORICAL SOCIETY MUSEUM

Coming down the hill on Main Street, the Wellfleet Historical Society Museum is on your right about a hundred yards before the turn. The Main Street of Wellfleet is one of the most picturesque on the Cape; its fishing village character and spirit have changed very little over the years.

The museum is very much a Wellfleet memorial, for most of the exhibits are directly connected with the life and times of the town. Early sailing relics, farm and household items from Wellfleet families, and a wealth of old photographs, documents, and newspaper clippings trace the individuality and independence that have always been dominant qualities of the town.

The old photographs and their detailed captions are of particular interest. We all hear about the sailing vessels, salt works, landmarks, and personalities of bygone days, and this museum has made a fine effort to illustrate just what it was all about. For instance, there is a photograph of the ten elderly Gross sisters of Wellfleet. Born in the late 1700s, they and their two brothers accounted for more than a thousand years of life.

Formerly a village shop, the museum and its old box window storefront are in keeping with the character of Main Street. The museum is open Wednesday, Friday, and Saturday from 2 to 5 P.M. in the summer season. A nominal admission fee is charged.

THE WELLFLEET OYSTERMAN

In 1849, 1850, and 1855 Henry David Thoreau wandered the back roads and beaches of the Cape. His chief interests were those of a naturalist, life in all its varied forms. Though he claims to "have got but little salted," his impressions resulted in that most famous of all books about the Cape, *Cape Cod,* published in 1864. On his first visit, Thoreau spent a night at the home of a Wellfleet oysterman, John Newcomb, and devoted what some consider to be the finest chapter in his book to the home and character of his delightful host and his family.

The old codger proved himself a genial host and picturesque raconteur, prime material for Thoreau's mind and pen. Materially poor but mentally rich, the grizzled eighty-eight-year-old "was the merriest old man" Thoreau had ever met, "and one of the best preserved." John Newcomb claimed to be "under petticoat government here," but his eighty-four-year-old wife Thankful and his elderly daughter were no match for the old Cape Codder who couldn't be pushed, for after all, he'd "lived too long to be hurried."

When approaching the Newcomb house, Thoreau noted the Cape architecture in the area: houses a story and a half high, "their garrets apparently so full of chambers, that their roofs could hardly lie down straight. . . . The great number of windows in the ends of the houses, and their irregularity in size and position . . . had thus as many muzzles as a revolver, and, if the inhabitants have the same habit of staring out the windows that some of our neighbors have, a traveller must stand a small chance with them."

John Newcomb's house is still there, a fine Cape with a profusion of the garret windows that so tickled Thoreau. Located on the east side of Williams Pond, about a half mile north of Gull Pond Road on a narrow sand lane, the home has recently acquired an ell and the landscaping and interior have given the place a modern, well-groomed appearance unknown to Thoreau and his oysterman more than a hundred years ago.

THE WRECK OF THE WHIDAH

They say there's pirate gold still to be found near Wellfleet, off the Back Side shore of South Wellfleet to be exact. But be careful, it's guarded by the Sea Witch of

Billingsgate, and the ghost of Black Bellamy himself is said to tread the beach on moonlit nights gathering gold coins and jewels flung from the surf by the skeleton hands of his murderous crew.

Tales of pirates, ghosts and witches pepper the early history of the Cape, and Wellfleet provides one with a vein of truth that stirred the imagination of many a Wellfleeter as he walked the lonely dunes in the eighteenth century.

The Sea Witch of Billingsgate was always nearby, liable to take over any unwary soul to serve her nefarious purposes. She was ready and waiting when the notorious Black Sam Bellamy met pretty little Maria Hallet of Eastham.

Black Sam was tall and handsome, at the time a romantic adventurer looking for lost treasure. Maria was a babe of fifteen, her heart and mind easy prey for the dreams and promises of the handsome stranger. Black Sam left for the treasure wrecks of the West Indies and in that same winter of 1715 Maria was found in the Knowles barn, a dead baby in her arms. Held up as a horrible example to the younger generation, Maria was publicly whipped and clapped into jail.

Languishing in jail without a friend in the world, Maria looked up to see the beckoning finger of a cold-eyed stranger at the bars. Beguiled by his wise ways and dulcet tones, she listened to his proposition and nodded. As she made her mark on the sale of her soul, she noticed that the ink ran scarlet.

The town soon found that locks and bars could no longer hold Maria Hallett and she was warned out of town. It is said she took up quarters in a whale, hung a lamp on his tail, and lured unwary ships on the bars and shoals. Others say she lived in a ramshackle hut on the Back Side of Wellfleet bewitching unwary men and riding them like horses up and down the beach. On one point all agreed: Maria was the current incarnation of the Sea Witch of Billingsgate.

In the meanwhile Sam Bellamy despaired of seeking

legitimate treasure and became a pirate, a notorious and most successful buccaneer. In 1717 he came north in his flagship *Whidah* to reclaim his love. On the twenty-sixth of April, the treasure-laden *Whidah*, with Black Bellamy on the quarterdeck, came to grief off the Back Side of Wellfleet. Of the 147 on board, only two survived. His treasure, including a chest of gold coins, has never been found. Some say that Maria lured her lover ashore and took the treasure in payment for her shattered dreams. Others insist that Bellamy also escaped and slit poor Maria's throat in a quarrel over the gold. No matter; both dropped from sight that day, but their ghosts still haunt the windswept dunes of Wellfleet.

When the *Whidah* came ashore, the governor sent Captain Cyprian Southack to claim her treasures for the Crown. Arriving in Provincetown, he needed a horse, but no such transportation was to be found. Instead he took a whaleboat and struck down the Bay, intending to secure a horse at Orleans. When he reached Boatmeadow River the tide was at its highest so he kept right on — and crossed the Cape in a whaleboat at what came to be known as Jeremiah's Gutter. Captain Southack showed admirable tenacity in the pursuit of his mission, but the Cape Codders were one step ahead of him. When he arrived at the wreck it was picked as clean as a Thanksgiving turkey. The old bones of the *Whidah*, after 250 years of wear and tear, can still be identified off the outer beach in South Wellfleet.

CAPE COD NATIONAL SEASHORE

The National Seashore facilities in Wellfleet include the site of Marconi's first trans-Atlantic wireless station, two fine guide-yourself trails, and beautiful Marconi Beach. All but the Great Island Trail are located off Route 6 in South Wellfleet.

Marconi Wireless Station

Guglielmo Marconi, an Italian physicist and the inventor of wireless telegraphy, had sent his strange signals more than a mile in 1895 and across the English Channel in 1899. By 1901 he was ready to establish a permanent radio station across the Atlantic. His station at Wellfleet opened up the modern age of travel and communications.

Marconi himself chose the desolate bluff in Wellfleet with its unobstructed path across the sea to England. But Marconi, the genius of the airwaves, miscalculated the airwaves of Wellfleet. His first circle of twenty wooden towers came crashing down in the first icy no'theaster and he was back in 1902 for a second try. Four new towers of crossed steel construction took the bite out of storms on the outer beach and wireless testing began in December of that year.

On January 19, 1903, communication was established with the Marconi station at Cornwall, England. The first formal message was an exchange of greetings between President Theodore Roosevelt and King Edward VII. Representatives of the world's news media waited breathlessly in Wellfleet for the 3,000-mile message carried on air waves alone — but there was no way to get it the four miles to town except by horse and wagon. Instructed to "drive like the wind," stationmaster Charlie Paine took it easy when out of sight for he "wasn't goin' to kill my horse for nobody."

In normal operation the station had a range of about 1,600 miles, extended at night under favorable conditions up to 3,500 miles. The station closed at the onset of U.S. participation in the First World War and was dismantled in 1920. Its commercial work was assumed by RCA's Chatham Station and the government work by the Naval Station at Truro. Little of the original structure is left to mark the site. The National Seashore has constructed an interpretative shelter with models and exhibits describing the station as it looked in operation. To reach the site follow the prominent "Marconi Area" signs to the right off Route 6 going down Cape.

Atlantic White Cedar Swamp Trail

This trail begins at the rear of the Marconi parking area. Trail guides are available from the the trail box or at the book counters in the Salt Pond and Province Lands Visitor Centers.

The Atlantic White Cedar Swamp Trail is a guided journey through many natural communities that exist in the fragile environment of seashore lands. Scanning the seashore landscape, one might assume that there's little difference between one acre out there and the next. This 1¼-mile trail will introduce you to eight different and easily recognizable communities of nature and their stage in the development cycle and to the plants and wildlife around you.

Communities of nature like communities of man change with the passage of time. From pioneer conditions evolve villages, towns and mature cities, sometimes retrogressing and at other times remaining fixed over long periods of time. The wide range of plant life that has developed within this well-defined series of nature's communities makes this trail one of the most unusual features of the National Seashore.

Great Island Trail

A long hiking trail with an interesting history has been laid out by the National Seashore in Wellfleet. The complete round trip is eight miles, but you can cut it down to two miles or so if you prefer.

The entrance to Great Island Trail is at the end of Chequesset Neck Road, Wellfleet. Trail guides are available free at a self-service dispenser alongside the National Seashore parking area. You will want to wear hiking shoes and carry some water if you plan on going the full route. Check the tides as the last half of the trail does become submerged under the higher tides.

Great Island, a barrier beach protecting Wellfleet Harbor on the Bay side, was inhabited by early settlers and by

Indians for a few thousand years before that. The island
boasted a tavern in its early settlement and the site has
recently been excavated by archeologists. An interpretative marker explains Smith's Tavern site and the archeological work done there. A more detailed explanation is
available at the Salt Pond Visitor Center Museum.

About three-quarters of a mile off Jeremy Point at the
end of Great Island was the island of Billingsgate. A hundred years ago Billingsgate supported a fishing community
of over thirty homes, a school and a lighthouse. A hundred
years or so before that it was connected by land to Great
Island. Changing ocean currents, shifting sands and possibly a rise in sea level steadily cut off and then "sank" the
island. By 1935 high tides began to cover the last remaining mud flats and now only a small portion of the once-
substantial island is visible at low tide. Most of the homes
from Billingsgate and Great Island were floated to the
mainland and many are still in use today. Your map will
show Great Island, Griffin Island and Bound Brook Island;
they are all a part of the peninsula extending a protecting
arm south on the Bay coast.

The trail is not a shady one — it's mostly sand, scrub
and marsh. The views are exceptional, however. On your
way out, stop in the large turnaround area immediately
outside the entrance to the trail. This overlook is locally
known as Sunset Hill and provides a fine panoramic view
of Cape Cod Bay at any time of day. A picnic table and
benches are located there.

AUDUBON WILDLIFE SANCTUARY

For those who enjoy life in the natural world and want
to know more about it, the Wellfleet Bay Wildlife Sanctuary provides a wide range of activities and services. Its
650 acres of upland, ponds and salt marsh are held in
trust by the Massachusetts Audubon Society for the wild
creatures living here and for the visitors who appreciate
them.

In 1958 the society purchased the 350-acre Austin Ornithological Research Station, then one of the largest private bird-banding stations in the world, and has since added an additional 300 acres of salt marsh. Conducted bird and flower walks, guide-yourself nature trails, beachbuggy wildlife tours, natural history day camps, and tent camping facilities are among the many activities available.

The Audubon Wildlife Sanctuary provides feeding, resting, wintering and breeding grounds for migratory waterfowl and nongame birds. It's a birdwatcher's and naturalist's paradise; over 250 species of birds have been identified at Wellfleet Bay and new sightings are still being reported. Two nature trails are open to the public during daylight hours all year. You can follow Goose Pond Trail yourself; numbered signs along the walk correspond to those in a trail guide that you can borrow or buy at the office. The trail covers about a mile and a half and you should allow about an hour for your walk. A pair of binoculars and a camera are recommended equipment. Of particular interest from mid-July through August are the concentrations of migrating shore birds along the beach. Whimbrels gather in groups of up to a hundred to feed on their favorite fiddler crabs. Their long down-curved sickle bills probe the sand and shallows for these tasty treats.

Bay View Trail is unmarked and winds through a more wooded terrain. This trail is about 2½ miles and offers an excellent opportunity to observe inland birds and woodland natural history. Each Monday morning in the summer season a staff member conducts a Bird and Flower Walk at no charge to the general public. These walks take about an hour and have been scheduled at 8:30 A.M. in recent years.

Natural history day camps for grade schools children are scheduled Monday through Friday in three two-week sessions during July and August. Each session is for campers in a different age group; a brochure is available from the office. Both members and nonmembers are welcome. Activities are centered around the study of plants and animals that inhabit the seashore and nearby land areas. Instruction on weather, soil, rocks and minerals, care of wild pets, and nature crafts are included in each session.

Beachbuggy wildlife tours are part of the society's program of interpreting the distinctive wildlife values of Cape Cod. A special oversand vehicle carries you to the remote land of salt marsh, sand dunes, and tide-scoured shore. An Audubon guide assists in observing the wildlife of the great outer beach, an area rich in natural beauty and ecological importance. A choice of tours is available. The Nauset Beach tour is a two-hour trip leaving the Wellfleet Bay Sanctuary daily throughout the summer shorebird migration. Times vary according to the tides, as rising water concentrates the flocks. Fares are moderate and binoculars may be rented at the office.

The Monomoy Island tour is a more rugged affair; a sand vehicle is used where possible, but the rest of the exploration is on foot with up to four miles of walking. The trip focuses on birds, plant communities, seashore life and the geologic and human history of the island. Participants meet in Chatham at 9 A.M. and return at about 5 P.M. Reservations are necessary. A schedule of tours to both Nauset and Monomoy is available from the sanctuary.

Members of the Massachusetts Audubon Society may reserve tent camping sites in the wildlife sanctuary. There are 29 prepared sites and early spring reservations are necessary if you plan on a visit in the summer season. For information on Audubon Society memberships or Wellfleet Bay Wildlife Sanctuary activities write to the sanctuary at South Wellfleet, Mass. Better still, drop in for a visit. You'll see their sign on Route 6 about a quarter mile past the Eastham town line on your left. It's a beautiful place to visit at anytime during the year.

WELLFLEET HARBOR

Often called the best harbor for cruising visitors on the Cape Cod Bay side, Wellfleet Harbor offers fine facilities.

The channel is kept clear to a 9-foot depth and 100-foot width at low tide to the anchorage basin, and to a 5-foot depth on in to the Town marina.

About a hundred years ago the railroad reached Wellfleet, built a dike across Duck Creek, and helped to hasten the decline of fishing as a commercial venture. Deep-draft vessels had berthed in the Duck Creek area where marsh and ponds now prevail. Until recently the remaining harbor sheltered only a small shellfishing fleet and a few pleasure boats, none of which could enter or leave except at high tide. Beginning in 1955, the channel was dredged, pilings were put down, bulkheads constructed, and sheltered basins built where before there had been only tidal flats. It is now a fine sheltered harbor, accessible at all tides. The marina provides space for more than a hundred boats and the complex now offers a launching ramp, ample parking, and all of the services to be expected at a modern marina.

A few commercial shellfishing boats still operate out of Wellfleet. Wellfleet is noted for its oysters and a limited crop is still harvested. Quahogs and scallops fill in at other times in the season. The broken shells that litter the parking area are due to nature's fishermen, the gulls. In the off-season when the area is quiet, it's interesting to watch them bombing any available hard surface to break open the shells protecting their dinner.

Today, summer finds yachts from all over berthed in Wellfleet, and the colorful array of commercial fishing boats, small craft, and sailboats swinging at their moorings in this beautiful harbor have become a major attraction to native and visitor alike. Wellfleet Harbor is detailed on Coast and Geodetic Survey Chart No. 581.

CAMPSITES AND TRAILER PARKS

There are two commercial camping areas in Wellfleet. Twenty-acre Maurice's Tent and Trailer Park on Route 6 across from the drive-in theater offers 220 wooded sites, about half with electrical, water and sewerage hookups. Rest rooms, metered hot showers, a dumping station and a general store are available. Pets are not permitted. Its season runs from late May to mid-October. Write to Maurice Gauthier at Box 456, South Wellfleet, for a brochure and further information.

Paine's Campground is a family tent camping facility down Old County Road about a mile past the entrance to the Marconi Area on Route 6. They have more than a hundred wooded sites but have no facilities for travel trailers. Leashed pets are permitted. Write to Bob Paine at Box 201, South Wellfleet, Mass. 02663, for further information. Reservations are required during their season from the end of May through September.

PUBLIC GOLF COURSE

There is one 9-hole golf course in Wellfleet open to the public. Chequesset Country Club, on the harbor by Chequesset Neck Road, is a 3,000-yard, par 35 course. Pull carts are available and guests are permitted to use the tennis courts at the club.

PUBLIC SWIMMING BEACHES

The narrow waist of Wellfleet, little more than a half mile wide at Blackfish Creek, is noted for its fine town beaches on the Atlantic shore. Wellfleeters say there's no better place to get a suntan than on the Back Side. Newcomb Hollow, Cahoon Hollow, White Crest, and Lecount Hollow beaches are all located off Ocean View Drive. The building to the right as you enter Cahoon Hollow Beach is the old Coast Guard Lifesaving Station, one of the thirteen that operated between Provincetown and Chatham. The remains of the wreck of Black Bellamy's ship *Whidah* are located offshore, about a mile south of Lecount Hollow Beach, halfway to the National Seashore's Marconi Beach.

Visitors may purchase a beach parking sticker from the Town Offices on Main Street or pay a daily parking fee. Expansive Wellfleet Harbor has two beaches: Indian

Neck off Pilgrim Spring Road and Mayo Beach just past the town piers. Freshwater beaches are available at Gull Pond, Great Pond and Long Pond. Picnics and clambakes are permitted on all town beaches but a permit must be obtained for any type of fire. Call Fire or Police headquarters to secure your permit at no charge.

I haven't tried it, but they tell me one can canoe from Gull Pond to Higgins to Williams to Herring Pond, starting from an easily accessible pond in northeast Wellfleet and ending up deep in the woods well out of the range of civilization. If you make the trip, keep an eye out for the Wellfleet Oysterman's house. It's up on the bank close by the eastern shore of Williams Pond. You will recognize it by its age and the profusion of garret windows aimed over the pond.

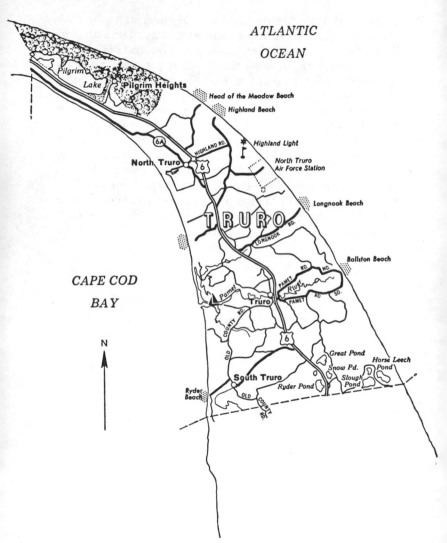

ATLANTIC

OCEAN

Pilgrim
Lake **Pilgrim Heights**

Head of the Meadow Beach

Highland Beach

6A

HIGHLAND RD.

North Truro 6

Highland Light

North Truro
Air Force Station

T R U R O

Longnook Beach

LONGNOOK RD.

Ballston Beach

PAMET RD. NO.

CAPE COD

BAY

Pamet   River   PAMET RD. SO.

Truro

N

COUNTY RD.

Great Pond

Horse Leech
Pond

OLD

Snow Pd.

Slough
Pond

South Truro

Ryder Pond

Ryder
Beach

OLD   COUNTY   RD.

6

Copyright, THE NATIONAL SURVEY, 1973
Chester, Vermont

CHAPTER X

Truro

The sharp cliffs, rolling hills, deep valleys, and wind-swept moors of Truro epitomize the storybook state of mind that is Cape Cod. When one enters the town on Route 6 it takes more than a mile before a solid sign of human habitation crops up. Truro is a town you have to search out; its modest homes are tucked into the nooks and crannies of its rolling landscape or perched like sentinels on its barren moors. The least densely populated of all Cape towns, Truro flirts briefly with history every century or so, and then reverts to its true character as the simplest and most unpretentious town on the Cape.

A few thousand years ago, North Truro at High Head marked the tail of Cape Cod. When the Cape Cod glacier receded, the rugged high land of Truro outlined the outer limit of its travels. The coastline, east and west, was rough and ragged and extended a mile or two farther east into the Atlantic. The winds and waves have shaped the land into the graceful curve we have today, but the ice-carved plains remain to match the weatherbeaten nature of the town.

When the Pilgrims landed in Provincetown in November 1620, they were sea-weary and growing anxious. With the approaching winter well in mind, progress to their Virginia patent was unfeasible and the level-headed band determined to explore this region on the chance that it might be a good place to settle. In Truro they found lofty forests, fresh water, fish, game, and seed corn, inviting discoveries to tempt exhausted colonists. Many favored settling here rather than risking the unknown and possibly faring worse. After considerable debate the more adventurous won out and on December 6 a party of eighteen under Captain Myles Standish set out to explore the entire Bay shore. Their pilot, Robert Coppin, had visited the area around present-day Plymouth and it was decided that his "Thievish Harbor" should be the outer limit of their exploration. The rest is well-known history; Truro missed her chance for immortality and the gentle Pamet Indians received a fifty-year reprieve.

Truro next popped up in history when the land of the Pamet was vaguely included in the vast tract granted to Thomas Prence and the other proprietors of Nauset in 1644. By 1689 a group of Eastham men known as the Pamet Proprietors began negotiating the formal purchase of large tracts from the Indians, and by 1697 the bounds of Pamet were established and farms allocated to newcomers. In 1705 the flourishing community was granted municipal privileges under the name of Dangerfield, and in 1709 it officially separated from Eastham and incorporated under the more attractive and equally appropriate name of Truro.

The town records of Truro, England, and the early history of Pamet are both peppered with the family names of Paine, Rich, Dyer, Atkins, and Higgins. Other similarities also point to the Truro of the Cornish coast as its namesake. Cornwall, a low-lying peninsula of rolling hills and moors, tapers to the rugged promontory of Lands End. The unknown Cornishman who named Cape Cod's Truro must have stood on High Head, looked over (or overlooked) Provincetown, and dreamed of home.

Farming was good in early Truro, but most of the townspeople made their living from the surrounding sea. Truro was in the forefront of the shore whaling industry, reserving common whaling grounds for the use of all.

Drift whales were a steady source of income — and dispute — one incident immortalized by the rhyme:

> *Down on East Harbor bar there lays a calf;*
> *Provincetowners swear they'll have the whole,*
> *Truroers swear they shan't have but half.*

As the shore whalers chased the leviathans from the Bay, Truro men led in pursuit. The first recorded deepwater vessel from Truro was the *Whale,* with Captain Henry Atkins on the quarterdeck, which hunted off Greenland in 1758. Others went south along the coast of Africa, around Cape Horn and on into the Pacific. But Truro's leadership in whaling was short-lived; shallow Pamet Harbor and the ravages of the Revolutionary War brought a quick end to Truro's dreams of whaling glory.

The next forty years were a struggle for the hardy sailors of Truro. Restricted to smaller vessels and with little capital behind them, the shipmasters of Truro no sooner began to gather headway when a war or natural disaster would rock them on their heels. There were a few brighter moments. The wreck of the British man-of-war *Somerset* in a November gale in 1778 bolstered the Yankee pride and lined the larders of Truro for a time. And in 1812 the blockaded fleet of Truro took some satisfaction in the exploits of Captain Nathaniel Snow in his privateering brig *Reindeer.* The captain and his crew were among the few in the town to see the end of the War of 1812 with money in the bank.

Peace ushered in the golden era of the Cape, and Truro prospered with the rest. Pamet River Harbor became a bustling center of energy. Wharves were improved, the old fishing and trading craft made seaworthy again, and the men and boys of Truro went back to sea. In 1829 they built the Union Wharf; the fifty shareholders hauled the sand themselves while one of their members stood by "to see that there was no shirking." About 1830 Henry Rogers and Nathaniel Hopkins established their shipyard at Pamet Harbor and turned out new brigs and schooners at a fast clip; two or three were on the ways more often than not.

At about the same time the elegant ship chandlering and general merchandise establishment appeared, the Union Company Store, along with sail lofts, salt works, a fish packing house, banks, and insurance companies. The Boston packets also sailed from busy Pamet Harbor and one, the *Postboy*, was considered by some to be the "finest specimen of naval architecture afloat in Bay waters." She had solid mahogany furnishings and silk draperies graced her ports. She also had Captain Zoheth Rich at her helm. Shebnah Rich, the Truro historian, offers the following vignette of one of his more colorful relations:

The first day from Boston was always a busy one, and the captain was on the alert. People would soon begin to enquire, "Captain Zoheth, when do you go to Boston again?"

"I think we'll go Wens'dy, wind and weather permit'n; yes, go to Bost'n about Wens'dy."

They knew well enough that the *Postboy* never went to Boston on that declaration; none expected it. The next day the same question would be asked, with this answer.

"Goin' to-morrer, if I can get out of the harbor; go to-morrer." "To-morrer" was sure to bring a scant tide, and scant wind, and the packet would not move.

Somebody was now sure to say, "Why, Cap'n, you didn't go to Boston today."

"No, didn't get out, divilish low tide, and head wind."

"Well, when are you going?" the last said, perhaps with a slight impatience.

"The *Piz-by* will go to Bost'n to-morrer; yes, sir, the *Piz-by* will go Bost'n to-morrer, wind or no wind, tide or no tide, by gracious!"

Now it was well understood the packet would go to Boston tomorrow. Early the next morning the Captain would be seen coming with his little black-leather trunk that always meant business; long before highwater the colors floated at the top-mast head, the signal for Boston; and the *Postboy* went to Boston, just about the time the captain intended, and when from the first it was understood she would go.

By 1840 the population of Truro had boomed to over 1,900 and Pamet Harbor was the commercial and industrial center of the thriving community. Fishing, trading, and the shore industries were at their peak when a major blow fell.

Great storms have been like wars to Truro, points from which each generation dates events. On October 2, 1841, a large fishing fleet was working the Georges Bank, 90 miles southeast of Truro. A violent gale broke the next morning and all vessels made a run for shelter at Provincetown — and very few made it. Truro alone lost seven of its eight vessels on the Banks and 57 of its men and boys — more than 10 percent of its mariners at the time. One survivor, Captain Matthias Rich, spent 12 hours lashed to the wheel as his schooner *Water Witch* ran the gauntlet to Race Point in the face of seas so heavy they swept the decks from stem to stern. Captain Joshua Knowles lost his vessel, the *Garnet,* but saved his crew. Almost torn apart by the raging seas, his ship was a drifting, half-submerged hulk when the winds abated. Rescued soon after, it took only one or two blows of Captain Knowles's ax to send the worthless wreck to the bottom.

The October Gale was a blow to Truro, but it was neither the first nor the last. Truro picked up the pieces as best it could, and its sons went back to sea. By 1855 the boom in Truro, as elsewhere on the Cape, began to lose its momentum, but few were willing to believe it. The backbone of commerce in Truro was the Union Company, merchant and banker to the town. Most of the townspeople owned shares and it paid a handsome 10 percent dividend year after year. About 1860 the final blow fell: the Union Company of Truro was bankrupt! Commercial Truro collapsed like a house of cards.

By 1880 the population of the town was down by half, and by half again to 500 residents in 1930. Today there isn't a trace of the extensive commercial area that once surrounded Pamet Harbor. Of the short span of years in

the commercial heyday of Truro, Shebnah Rich writes,
"In loss of life and property they were the most calamitous
that ever befell a community not blotted out." The cost to
Truro was amply illustrated in a brief conversation recorded by Thoreau on his visit in 1855:

> "Who lives in that house?" I inquired.
> "Three widows," was the reply.

Truro's most recent flirtation with history appears to
have resulted in an enduring marriage. The establishment
of the Cape Cod National Seashore in 1961 has assured
the protection and preservation of three quarters of the
land area of the town. The natural beauty of the rugged
old Cape town of Truro is no longer threatened by the
march of progress. The resulting simplicity and privacy
are the rare gifts that Truro offers.

Several years ago Mrs. Lyndon Johnson launched her
beautification program, a noble idea. In their infinite wisdom, the powers in Boston chose Truro as Massachusetts'
first beneficiary and appropriated $72,399 to cover the
scars of shad bush and bayberry, beach plum and wild
roses, Scotch broom and cranberries. What colossal nerve!

To see and appreciate Truro, by all means get off the
main road. There are three villages, Truro Center, North
Truro, and South Truro, but if you wink you may miss the
first two and I defy you to find the third. The 1,200 residents of these 20 square miles don't mind. They're proud
of what they have and equally proud of what they don't
have.

CORN HILL

Two days after landing at Provincetown, sixteen men
under Captain Myles Standish and William Bradford set
out to explore the region. *Mourt's Relation,* the Pilgrim
chronicle, records the fascinating conflict of conscience
and necessity that dogged them on their travels.

Hoping to find friendly natives, but armed to the teeth
just in case, the expedition did sight two who fled at the
sight of their small army. Following them as best they

could, they found a spring behind High Head; refreshed, they turned across the Cape toward the mouth of the Pamet River. They came across Indian fields and graves but piously took nothing, as "it would be odious to them to ransack their sepulchres." A bit farther on they came upon a hill "wher latly a house had been, wher some planks and a great kettle was remaining, and heaps of sand newly padled with their hands, which they, digging up, found in them diverse faire Indean baskets filled with corne, and some in eares, faire and good, of diverce collours, which seemed to them a very goodly sight." They filled the kettle and their pockets and came back for ten bushels more a week or two later.

Without the seed corn to plant the next spring, it is quite possible they would have starved. On the second expedition, however, they again found graves, which they dug up, and recently abandoned houses and utensils of which *Mourt's* relates, "Some of the best things we took away with us and left the houses standing still as they were." All this by the impetuous Myles Standish who rose in such righteous wrath a little later in response to the theft of a few trinkets by the Indians.

The next year the sins of the settlers caught up with them when they met the owner of the corn while retrieving a runaway boy. With the help of the friendly Squanto all was forgiven and restitution promised, and delivered, the following spring.

To reach Corn Hill take Castle and Corn Hill roads down the winding way through a beautiful little valley to the beach. Alongside the beach stands Corn Hill, with a paved road to the parking area on its crest. There's a cottage colony on the hill but a small area is fenced off and the site of the discovery is marked by a bronze tablet in the sand.

SECOND ENCAMPMENT

On their way back from Corn Hill, Captain Standish and his companions rested and camped on the shore of a pond, "making a great fire, and a barricade to windward of us; and kept good watch, with three sentinels all night." The next morning they sank the iron ship's kettle in the pond as it proved too heavy to carry. The kettle, safely hidden lest the Indians should steal it, then became lost to history.

Pond Village in North Truro was the site of the second night's encampment and a bronze tablet in a small park along the pond shore now marks the general area. You will find the encampment site about a half mile down Pond Road on your left.

HILL OF STORMS

Within a year or two after receiving town status in 1709, the first settlers built their meeting house on one of the many aptly named hills of Truro, the Hill of Storms. For almost a hundred years before the first lighthouse came to the Cape, the sturdy church on the windswept hill served as the major landmark of Cape Cod to those approaching from the sea. The ancient meeting house was torn down in 1840 and its time-tested white oak beams used elsewhere, but the churchyard burial ground remains.

The North Cemetery, as it is known now, is located on the crest of the Hill of Storms, on the right bracketed by Cemetery and Aldrich roads as you approach North Truro. The meeting house stood in the right front corner across Cemetery Road, facing south as was customary. Truro's first settled minister was the Reverend John Avery, enticed to the pulpit by the offer of 10 acres of land, £20 for a parsonage, and £60 yearly salary. He served the town well and was pleased to receive a £10 raise a dozen years later.

For more than a hundred years the church prospered under the ministry of only three pastors, the Reverends Avery, Caleb Upham, and Jude Damon. They were moderate men, wise in the ways of their seafaring congregation. The Reverend Damon solved one of his problems with the

wisdom of Solomon when, keeping in mind both inward-
and outward-bound fishermen, he prayed "O Lord, that
thou wilt watch over our mariners that go down to do
business upon the mighty deep, keep them in the hollow
of thy hand; and we pray thee that thou wilt send a *side
wind.*"

By the 1820s the old church on the Hill of Storms had
begun its decline. Inconveniently located for the majority
of the townspeople and rapidly losing members to the
Methodists, its remaining congregation gradually transferred to the new Congregational Church (1827) in Truro
Center and the Union Church (1840) in North Truro. For
tombstone buffs, however, the old graveyard is a treasure.
About four rows back, midway between Cemetery and
Aldrich roads, is the Reverend Avery's grave enclosed by
granite posts and iron rails. Eight markers to the left is
the oldest grave, that of Hannah Paine who died in 1712.
Her low gray slate headstone is almost as sharp and clear
as the day it was cut more than 260 years ago. Farther
on to her left is the stone of Deacon Hezeriah Purinton
(1717), with its crudely cut death's head, crossed bones,
and hourglass reminders of the stern faith of this pious
man. To the right and slightly to the rear of the Reverend
Avery's enclosure is a rarity; apparently homemade by a
grieving father is a crudely engraved little slate marker,
MARY, DR. TO IRA ATKINS, HAR 14 DAYS 1744. The Truro
historian Shebnah Rich rests over near the Cemetery Road
entrance.

HILL OF CHURCHES

As you approach Truro Center on Route 6 you will see
what appear to be two church buildings above the trees
on a hill to the left. One is the Town Hall, the other the
oldest remaining meeting house in Truro.

When Pamet Harbor entered its golden era in the 1820s,
the need quickly became apparent for a more convenient
church than the old meeting house on the Hill of Storms.
In 1827, one year after the Methodists built on the same

hill, the Congregationalists raised the so-called Bell Meeting House in Truro Center. With the architect and construction supervisor earning $1.50 a day and master carpenters $1.25, the cost mounted up to $3,116.64; it was expensive but worth it considering the detail and craftsmanship involved. Ten percent of the extravagance went toward the beautiful bell wrought by Paul Revere. The windowpanes are of Sandwich glass and the window latches resemble miniature whales. The meeting house still holds services each Sunday at 9:30 A.M. from mid-June to mid-September.

The most memorable of the early ministers was perhaps the Reverend Charles Boyter, a Princeton man of undoubted intelligence but limited in his understanding of human nature. At the height of Truro's prosperity he chose to give a sermon on "Fisherman's Luck." Luck holds an almost magic power in the mind of any fisherman, even today, and the town buzzed in anticipation of the coming Sunday. The fleet was preparing to sail in late March 1843, and any talisman would be most welcome.

As Shebnah Rich said, "Unquestionably he gave much wise and practical advice which the fishermen might well have heeded." But he also declared emphatically that there was no such thing as luck. Three- to five-month voyages on the Georges Banks he compared to "trouting in the brooks of Vermont with a fly and pole." He advised them to bait their hooks with red flannel, because if they didn't catch fish it was that they didn't try. The Reverend Mr. Boyter shortly found good reason to transfer his calling to Orange, New Jersey.

The old burying ground next to the church is of particular interest for its profusion of epitaphs, with this gem in the center of the first row on the headstone of Josiah Snow:

> *Look on me as you pass by,*
> *As you are now so once was I,*
> *As I am now so you must be,*
> *Prepare for death to follow me.*

The cenotaph in honor of the 57 men and boys lost in the October Gale of 1841 is also here. It's farther back, one of the few markers enclosed by a fence. Most of those lost also have individual stones; the ominous date October 3, 1841, appears at every turn.

Town Hall, a few yards farther down the road, was never a church despite the similarity in architecture. It was constructed as a commercial venture about 1830 and known as Union Hall. The upstairs auditorium was rented to various groups such as the Sons of Temperance, and the ground floor leased as, of all things, a Panama hat factory. A few years later the hat factory gave way to a handmade shoe factory, but the building was never a particularly successful commercial venture. In about 1840 the town purchased the property and converted it to use as the Town Hall, the function it serves today.

The earliest church on the hill was that of the Methodists. Approaching Town Hall the dirt lane on the left leads to the Bell Meeting House and the paved road on the right to the Methodist cemetery, and beyond that to the Catholic cemetery. About 50 feet inside the Methodist cemetery is a granite marker explaining that the 1826 Methodist Meeting House was "flaked," dismantled and rebuilt elsewhere as a studio in 1925. It is now a private residence hidden in the trees off Castle Road.

The Methodists had come to Truro in the 1790s, making great inroads on orthodox Congregationalism with their singleminded pursuit of the faith. As Shebnah Rich wrote, "It cannot be denied that they were somewhat ignorant of books and schools, but the book that contained their divine commission, was learned and conned by rote." To argue with them was to be harpooned.

A typical early preacher took as his text, "The world, the flesh and the devil." In announcing it he remarked, "I shall touch lightly upon the world, hasten to the flesh, and pass on to the devil, when I will give it to you hot as you can sup it!"

At the base of the hill is the relatively modern Roman

Catholic church, a welcome addition to the Hill of Churches.

PINE GROVE CEMETERY

Itinerant Methodist preachers had come to Truro and Provincetown in the early 1790s and, despite the bitter opposition of the established church, had gained enough converts to build a small meeting house, their second in New England, in 1794. The site they chose was high on a hill in South Truro, somewhere within the old Pine Grove Cemetery that remains today. To reach the cemetery take Old County Road from Truro Center and branch left on the dirt lane marked Cemetery Road. The cemetery is located on the barren crest of the hill; the meeting house must have been a fine landmark for ships in the bay.

The Methodists brought their lumber from Provincetown, but "a mob destroyed the timber and tarred and feathered the preacher in effigy and threatened to serve him the same." The flock succeeded with a second shipment and within four months had completed their church, or at least as much as they intended to. There was no plastering or finish work and "the swallows flew in and out at pleasure, building their nests on the rough open beams and feeding their young during divine services."

The church was enlarged and rebuilt twice in succeeding years, each time moving farther west. The last church was located on the Bay side of Old County Road just about opposite the entrance to Cemetery Road, and it was near this church that another of the many Truro tragedies unfolded in 1844.

It was a sunny Sunday morning that September 15, when the churchgoers noted that the fishing schooner *Commerce* had returned in the night and anchored about three quarters of a mile offshore. This meant the return of husbands, sons and friends, always a welcome sight and a happy lift for the community. When the men did not come ashore for services it seemed a bit odd, but no matter, they'd be home shortly. When still they didn't appear, a boat was sent out to investigate. The schooner was properly anchored and all seemed shipshape — but there was no trace of the men. A search was begun and sometime later the ship's boat was found a quarter mile offshore, a thwart stove in and one of the garboard planks sprung and stuffed with coats.

One by one the bodies came ashore. The theory is that the last man off jumped in, went through the thwart and sprung the bottom. Good fishermen that they were, there wasn't a swimmer in the crew. Nine of the ten-man crew were Truro men, the other a neighbor from Wellfleet. They left five more widows and fourteen more fatherless children. When Captain Solomon Lombard's body was found his watch was stopped at the predawn hour of 4:30. You will find the graves of the Truro men in the old cemetery, most in the left rear section, and all with the terse comment, "Drowned in Cape Cod Bay, September 15, 1844."

HIGHLAND HOUSE MUSEUM

The bluffs of Truro were dotted with small hotels around the turn of the century, and one, Highland House, has been preserved as the Historical Society Museum. It's located near the site of an earlier inn where Thoreau stayed on his visits to the area, just a few yards before Highland Light on your left.

A nostalgic reminder of a less sophisticated era, the old hotel houses a fine collection of early Truro memorabilia. Early fishing and whaling gear, household utensils, farming implements, ship models, and shipwreck mementos are well displayed in the museum along with a host of early photographs of Truro scenes and people.

The founder and first president of the Truro Historical Society was the late Courtney Allen, nationally known artist and model maker. A special room is devoted to an exhibit of his works, including fine examples of his celebrated wood carvings, paintings, drawings, and models.

Other exhibits honor lithographer Edward Wilson with a collection of his scenes of Truro, and Captain John and E. K. Collins of the Collins Line.

Highland House Museum is open from 10 A.M. to 5 P.M. from late June to early September. A nominal admission fee is charged.

THE COLLINS LINE

Much has been made of the record voyages and exciting adventures of many deepwater mariners, but one of the most significant Cape contributions to merchant marine history was made by the Collinses of Truro. Had they been supported, both American marine history and the economy of Cape Cod might have steered a different course through the latter half of the nineteenth century.

John Collins first achieved a measure of fame as an eighteen-year-old blockade runner in the War of 1812. His whaleboat ran the gauntlet around the Bay to Scusset Creek at Sandwich, portaged overland, and sailed on to Providence and New York to swap salt fish for flour and other staples. Still too young to vote, Captain Collins soon switched to deepwater privateering with considerable initial success. An aggressive young man, he made the costly error of mistaking a sloop-of-war for an East India trading vessel and emerged from a British prison a few years later, wiser, but no less enthusiastic.

Captain Collins's young nephew, Edward K. Collins, was a brilliant man who did his sailing in his mind, an office his quarterdeck. In the late 1830s he founded the Dramatic Line of Liverpool sailing packets, the pinnacle of passenger service in their day. His Uncle John commanded his flagship and it was his *Rocius* that picked up the crew of Captain Knowles's *Garnet* after the infamous October Gale in 1841.

John and E. K. Collins foresaw the end of the days of sail and leapfrogged the clipper ship era to join the few promoting the paddlewheels and fire boxes of steam. In 1847 they formed a partnership, secured a lucrative mail subsidy, and founded the Collins Line. Their new steam-driven ships, the *Arctic, Atlantic, Baltic* and *Pacific,* soon put them in the lead in the trans-Atlantic packet trade.

All went well until the *Arctic* was rammed in a fog and went down in 1855. The next year the *Pacific,* under Captain Asa Eldredge, was lost without a trace in the North Atlantic and the fleet was halved. The Collins Line began rebuilding but the final disaster struck when the mail subsidy was withdrawn and the line folded. Great Britain regained supremacy at sea and the deepwater sailors of the Cape were slowly but surely left ashore for good.

POMP'S LOT

Slaves were a fact of life in New England in the early days and it was not thought unusual when a whaling captain brought one back to Truro from the Congo. This young man, Pomp by name, was sold to Jonathan Paine and soon gained the reputation of a docile, reliable young fellow, though withdrawn and ever dreaming of home.

One day Pomp disappeared, and after several days they found him in his master's woodlot. With a jug of water and a loaf of bread by his feet to sustain him on the journey, and a noose from a high branch to carry him home, Pomp had taken his departure for sunny Africa. The exact location of Pomp's Lot is unknown, but it was somewhere at the eastern end of Long Nook Valley, probably near the end of present-day Higgins Hollow Road.

HIGHLAND LIGHT

The blue clay pounds of Truro seemed to provide a ready-made foundation for the lighthouse so badly needed to protect mariners off the backside of the Cape. In 1797 the government bought 10 acres on the bluffs and constructed the first lighthouse on Cape Cod. Highland Light is there today, but less than four acres of the land remain.

Highland Light is the first beacon visible to vessels on this side of the Atlantic making for Boston Harbor from European ports. It's a tranquil sight on a calm day, but its exposed position feels the brunt of every storm. Lashing, gale-driven seas relentlessly carve into the banks below, and if the sound of surf appeals to you, try Highland Light in a storm. Be prepared for a battle, as an aroused nature at Highland is a formidable opponent. To stand on the bluffs is, as Thoreau said, "like being on the deck of a vessel, or rather at the masthead of a man-of-war, thirty miles at sea."

The first lighthouse was powered by twenty-four whale oil lamps set in two circles, one above the other, each with a silvered reflector behind it. The keeper's duty was to trim, fill, and light his lamps, and above all else, to keep them burning throughout the night. This first structure was replaced in 1857 by the present one. In 1901 the whale oil lamps were replaced by a single lamp magnified many times by a prism reflector to produce the required candlepower. It became a revolving light, powered by a gravity weight such as is found in a grandfather's clock. The keeper had to wind this clockwork system three times each night to maintain a steady flash every five seconds.

In 1932 the government finally decided electricity was here to stay and equipped the light with a single thousand-watt electric bulb and huge bulls-eye lenses to magnify this into the equivalent of 4,500,000 candlepower. It is now one of the most powerful lights on the Atlantic coast and can be seen for more than 20 miles at sea. The groaning foghorn at Highland can be heard up to 15 miles at sea and at times, depending on the weather, 5 or 10 miles ashore.

When on the bluffs by Highland Light, look to the northeast about a mile and you'll see curling bands of surf offshore. These are the famed Peaked Hill Bars that have claimed so many ships over the years. One of the most famous of the sailing vessels to come to grief here was the British man-of-war *Somerset* in a November gale in 1778. Her 480 survivors were marched to Boston and the sagging morale of Revolutionary War Cape Cod received a much-needed victory. Truro and Provincetown were too busy to celebrate; a wreck such as the *Somerset* was far too valuable to put off until tomorrow. Like the wreck of the *Sparrowhawk* off Nauset, the ship buried herself in the sand and emerged again more than a century later. The rush of townspeople for relics and souvenirs in 1886 was fully in keeping with their early traditions. It is reported the decendants of the ship's doctor, who had escaped arrest and married a Truro girl, were among the interested spectators.

As you stand on the Highland cliff you are directly opposite northern Spain, across 3,000 miles of the Atlantic without so much as an island to come between.

JENNY LIND TOWER

As you stand on the scarp by Highland Light, you will see off to the right what appears to be a battlement from an old Norman castle rising from the beach grass. What you are actually seeing is a granite tower from the old Fitchburg railroad station in Boston, a rich man's memorial to his father, or as some say, to the "Swedish Nightingale" Jenny Lind.

The story goes that Miss Lind, the greatest coloratura soprano of her time, was engaged by P. T. Barnum for a pair of concerts in Depot Hall, as the auditorium in the Boston station was known in 1850. The promotors capitalized on her adoring public by selling many more tickets than there were seats available. A near riot came about as the crush of ticket holders was turned away from the overflowing concert hall and milled about in an angry mood on Causeway Street. Rising to the occasion, Miss Lind mounted the tower and sang to the crowds in the street below.

When the famous old structure was razed in 1927, Harry Aldrich bought the tower, had it brought to Truro by rail and rebuilt on his land high on the bluffs overlooking the Atlantic. The tower is 55 feet high, long since gutted of its spiral staircase to the top.

To reach the Jenny Lind Tower, follow the signs to the North Truro Air Force Station. About a quarter mile from the gate is a sand lane angling off to the left. This trail comes out in a field (keep to the right) and reenters the woods as a footpath leading to the tower. It covers about a half mile and poses no problem for most walkers. It would be fine if the town or its historical society could secure the land and provide a safe access to the parapet. But this can't happen while the radar station is there, however, as the radar path now intersects the upper level of the tower. The tower is within a cable's length of the radar bubbles and the juxtaposition of fortifications, old and new, provides an interesting contrast.

AIR FORCE STATION

Standing on the bluffs at Highland Light a lady once asked her husband what those white domes were off to her right. Rather impatient at her foolish question he replied, "Why heck, Millie, those are the places they put the telescopes, observatories, they call them." To set the record straight the three domes, which might also be confused with golf balls teed up for the Jolly Green Giant, are radar bubbles of the North Truro Air Force Station.

Manned by the 762nd Air Defense Group, the radar bubbles and communications systems located here are part of the vast network that surrounds the United States and Canada, providing the eyes and ears for the defense of North America. Personnel maintain an around-the-clock surveillance of the radar picture to warn of any threat to the northeastern United States or Canada. North Truro Air Force Station has direct communications to all-weather jet interceptor squadrons located around the country and, in particular, to those in and around New England. When needed, these aircraft can be launched and guided by radar and radio contact to meet the presumed threat, identify it, and if necessary, destroy it.

EAST HARBOR

Truro had a second harbor many years ago, but exposed as it was in the scrubby sand hills leading to Provincetown it never took on much importance. However, it is of particular interest, for it illustrates the tremendous forces of nature still at work shaping the sands of Cape Cod.

What we now call Pilgrim Lake on the Provincetown border was once known as East Harbor and sheltered a number of vessels in its day. When the Pilgrims arrived, even the sand hills of Provincetown were anchored by a goodly growth of trees, shrubs and grass. Early laws protected the trees, but Provincetowners were never noted for graceful compliance. By 1825, wanton logging and cattle grazing had denuded the hills to the extent that the shifting sands began to advance on the town and the harbor. The planting of beach grass and scrub pines saved the town, but the blowing sand from East Harbor washed into Provincetown Harbor and posed a serious threat to the only deepwater harbor on the Cape. At that time the only land connection between North Truro and Provincetown was a narrow strip of beach on the Atlantic shore, less than a hundred feet wide at one point. Constant traffic destroyed any vegetation and the sand link grew narrower each year. Should the sea ever break through, and it had trickled across in the past, it would carry with it enough sand to spell the end of Provincetown Harbor.

Various solutions were proposed and many tried over the next thirty years, but none succeeded in removing the danger. In 1858 the responsible committee faced the facts and came up with the answer. It was a shock to the taxpayers and they took ten years to mull over the $130,000 price tag, but in 1868 work began on an earthen dike 1,400 feet long and 75 feet wide across the mouth of East Harbor. The dike, built up over the years, underlies the highway you now take to Provincetown.

Pilgrim Lake, long since turned to fresh water, is now a calm and placid pond, delightful for ice skating in the winter.

CAPE COD NATIONAL SEASHORE

One of the four major developed areas in the Cape Cod National Seashore, North Truro offers walking, bicycle, and dune buggy trails, a picnic area, an interpretative shelter, and the beautiful Head of the Meadow Beach. Guided nature walks are conducted in season and include the historical site of the Pilgrim Spring, believed to be the spot where the thirsty Standish and Bradford drank their first New England water. Entrances to National Seashore facilities in North Truro are prominently marked on Route 6. Look for the signs to Head of the Meadow Beach, Pilgrim Heights, and High Head on your right as you approach Provincetown.

Pilgrim Heights

The guide-yourself nature trails, Pilgrim Spring, the interpretative shelter and picnic area all emanate from the Pilgrim Heights parking area. The shelter provides a relief map of the area and informative displays in addition to being a fine lookout. All facilities are unmanned and free to visitors.

Pilgrim Spring Trail is a pleasant half-mile stroll through the pines to a view overlooking an extensive cattail marsh. It then descends to a brushy valley where a tablet marks the general vicinity in which the Pilgrims "found springs of fresh water of which we were heartily glad and sat us downe and dranke our first New England water with as much delight as ever we drunke drinke in all our lives." During the summer season guided walks are conducted several times each week by National Seashore staff well versed in the historical significance of the area. Allow about a half hour to an hour for the round trip.

Small's Swamp Nature Trail is a 1½-mile circuit of an old kettle hole formed by a retreating glacier. Each glacier left large blocks of ice that gradually melted over hundreds, perhaps thousands, of years. During this time they were largely or entirely covered by sediment. When they finally did melt the ground sagged forming "kettles" such as Small's Swamp. The trail descends into the kettle below and skirts a blueberry-azalea swamp. On the far side it ascends over bearberry heath to a spectacular overlook where you will see salt meadow, sand dunes, and the ocean beyond. The trail returns to the shelter through a pitch pine and oak forest. Markers along the trail describe the significant features. Guided tours are provided during the season. Allow one to two hours for the walk.

High Head

At the base of High Head is a parking area marking the entrance to the bicycle and oversand vehicle trails. Geologically, High Head is the glacial end of Cape Cod; the sandy soil from there on has been formed over the succeeding thousands of years by the wind and waves.

The paved bicycle trail follows the general route taken by the Pilgrims in November 1620 as they made the first of three short trips from Provincetown "up the Cape." The two-mile trail passes close to Pilgrim Spring and ends at Head of the Meadow Beach. It is also a fine nature walk, but remember, bicycles have the right of way.

From the parking area, signs indicate the dune buggy trail. Oversand vehicles must use only the designated sand routes; a permit is required. Indiscriminate dune driving is prohibited and visitors are warned not to attempt the trail in a conventional vehicle. Permits are available from the Visitor Centers at Province Lands in Provincetown and Salt Pond in Eastham or at National Seashore Headquarters in Wellfleet. Guided walking tours of the dunes are conducted by staff members in the summer season.

Head of the Meadow Beach

Besides being a fine swimming and surfing beach subject to the standard admission fee, Head of the Meadow also provides an access point for the High Head bicycle and dune trails and is the location of a daily guided seashore tour in season. The walk covers about two miles and takes about two hours.

The Visitor Centers will be pleased to provide you with brochures outlining the guide-yourself nature trails, oversand routes, and bicycle trails. An additional brochure is

published each spring that gives the schedules and arrangements for the guided walks and field trips available free
of charge during the summer season. Most of the guided
trips are continued into mid-October on a reduced schedule; check with one of the Visitor Centers for current information.

SAND DUNE TOURS

From High Head the National Seashore provides a trail
for oversand vehicles. For visitors without their own
vehicles, commercial operators conduct hourly tours from
9 A.M. through the sunset hours during the season. Contact Drifting Sands Dune Tours, Route 6A, North Truro,
Mass. 02652, for information and reservations.

CAMPSITES AND TRAILER PARKS

Truro offers three camping and trailer parks, all located
in North Truro close to the Atlantic Ocean beaches of the
National Seashore. Advance reservations are strongly recommended during the summer season.

Thirty-five-acre Horton's Park provides 210 sites of
which about a quarter (open sites only) have electrical
and water hookups; most of these have sewerage as well.
Metered hot showers and rest rooms are available at two
central locations. Either open or wooded sites may be
chosen; a number of the latter have fine views of Highland Light and the ocean beyond. A general store for
staples, ice facilities, a small laundromat, a dumping
station, and an open pavilion recreational hall are on the
premises. Pets are not permitted. Its season runs from the
first of May to mid-October, at times a bit earlier or later.
The office is on South Highland Road opposite South Hollow Road. Write to Bob Horton at Box 308, North Truro,
Mass. 02652, for a site map and brochure.

North Truro Camping Area is on Highland Road, about
a half mile in from Route 6 on the left. The 250 sites in
this 20-acre campground are all wooded with 85 electrical,
36 water, and 24 sewerage hookups. Excellent tiled rest

room and metered hot shower facilities are available at three locations. The central sanitary facilities are winterized as this campground is open all year. A fine general store, ice facilities, a small laundromat, and a dumping station are provided. Dogs are prohibited, but other pets are acceptable. The camp provides trailer storage at reasonable rates and a growing number of campers use this method to continue weekend camping around the calendar. For a site map and brochure write to Ed Francis, Box 365, North Truro, Mass. 02652.

North of Highland Camping Area is located on Head of the Meadow Road on the left about halfway to the beach. The 218 sites on its 60 acres are all wooded and without utility hookups. Rest rooms, metered hot showers, a general store for staples, ice facilities, and a recreational building are provided. Leashed dogs are permitted as are other pets. Their season runs from mid-June to Labor Day. Address off-season inquiries to Malcolm Currier, 426 North Ave., Weston, Mass. 02193.

PUBLIC GOLF COURSE

There is one 9-hole golf course in Truro open to the public. Highland Golf Course is located on the bluffs of Truro overlooking the Atlantic Ocean, a stone's throw from Highland Light. Owned by the National Seashore and operated by the town, the course is a 3,000-yard par 36. Highland, like Cummaquid, claims to be the oldest golf course on the Cape (1892).

PUBLIC SWIMMING BEACHES

Residents and visitors must secure a beach parking sticker in order to use Truro town beaches. They are available from the Chamber of Commerce Information Booth on Route 6, North Truro, during the summer season. Motel owners and other landlords also have the proper forms. Town parking stickers are not valid at the National Seashore beaches in Truro.

The major Truro town beaches on the Bay side are

Ryder, Fisher, Corn Hill, Great Hollow and Beach Point: all very easy to find as all roads in Truro seem to lead to a beach sooner or later. Town-operated Atlantic Ocean beaches are limited to Long Nook and Ballston beaches. Head of the Meadow Beach is part of the National Seashore and subject to its daily parking fee. There are no town-operated freshwater beaches in Truro.

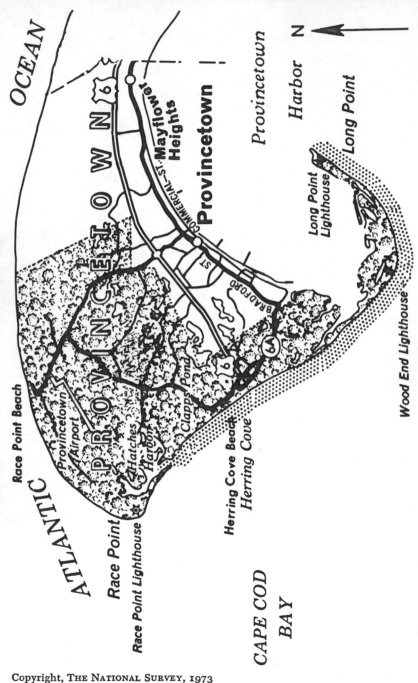

Copyright, THE NATIONAL SURVEY, 1973
Chester, Vermont

CHAPTER XI

Provincetown

Provincetown — the first and last frontier on the Cape — hasn't been tamed as yet! There is no place quite like it anywhere, an unending melodrama unfolding on the sunny sands of the town. Everyone awaits the next curtain to see what Provincetowners will do for an encore.

The first landing place of the Pilgrims was reported in *Mourt's Relation* as well wooded with deep, rich soil — sand was rarely mentioned. It must be that the beautiful seascapes of Provincetown bring out the rose-colored vision of most of us. Captain John Smith had passed by six years earlier, perhaps on a cloudy day, and reported the tip of the Cape for what it was: acres of beach grass, scrub pines, and sand dunes. There were a few stands of timber in the protected valleys, and a few survivors remain today, but the natural history of Provincetown, other than shifting its sandy feet, has changed little over the past 350 years.

In the earliest years of the Cape settlements, few colonists had any interest in the sand dunes at the tip. There were no commercial fishermen among them and the hardy Cape farmers had trouble enough catching a few fish for their own tables. During the 1600s phantom ships and crews were often reported at Provincetown; their shacks soon developed into a sand-dune Dodge City sheltering a "wild, undisciplined and unprincipled crew of traders and fishermen from nearly all parts of Europe. Drinking, gambling and bacchanalian carousals, were continued sometimes for weeks with unrestrained license." Pious Plymouth's reaction to these unruly, happy-go-lucky swingers may be imagined by the Puritan joke that made the rounds of seventeenth-century England, to the effect that "they objected to bear-baiting, not because of the pain to the bear, but because of the pleasure to the spectators."

As the settlers moved down the Cape, their newly acquired fishing skills and growing strength focused more attention on the tip. In those days only the sandy hook of Provincetown was called Cape Cod, and the Colony was determined to tame it. A minister was sent in the 1690s but he didn't last long. When Truro became a town in 1709, the "great resort" of Cape Cod was thrown in with it. A few English settlers arrived soon after, but the polyglot group of fishermen, smugglers, and privateers went on as before. Boston tried to crack down in 1714 by declaring Cape Cod a precinct of Truro, but Truro's practical authority was worth little more than the paper it was printed on. It was not until 1727 that enough English settlers had arrived to maintain a semblance of order and the unruly town was finally subdued, if not tamed, and incorporated in that year.

A fine example of the spirit of Provincetown under the frustrated stewardship of Truro was this account of a sea monster reported by typical sober-minded Provincetowners to Boston in 1719:

There appeared in Cape Cod harbour a strange creature, His head like a Lyons, with very large Teeth, Ears hanging down, a large Beard, a long beard, with curling hair on his head, his Body a bout 16 foot Long, a round buttock, with a short Tayle of a yellowish colour, the whale boats gave him chase, he was very fierce and gnashed his teeth with great rage when they attackt him. . . . None of the people ever saw his like befor.

But they have since!

Over the next quarter century Provincetown dwindled away, much to Truro's satisfaction, and was little more

than a ghost town at times. With the end of the French
and Indian Wars, however, deepwater whaling came of
age on the Cape and the fine harbor of Provincetown came
to life again. Twelve whalers worked out of Provincetown
by 1760, and after a pause for the Revolutionary War the
industry began to hit its stride. When the War of 1812
broke, Provincetown was a thriving town of a thousand
and had no intention of permitting this unpopular war to
be more than an inconvenience. For all practical purposes
a neutral port, Provincetown entertained its British visitors and patiently waited the chance to get back to sea.

The whaling ships of Provincetown brought back much
more than sperm oil and ambergris. Life on a whaler was
rough and crews hard to keep. As the 1800s progressed,
whaling captains found that the Azores and Cape Verdes
were fine ports to pick up replacements. Other Portuguese
had been fishing Provincetown waters for centuries and
their descendants began to return as immigrant settlers.
Toward the turn of the century Provincetown became
less of an old Cape whaling town and more of a Portuguese fishing village, and the Portuguese remain the
backbone of Provincetown to the present day.

At one time there were more than seventy-five wharves
along Commercial Street and their rotting piles can still
be seen at low tide. As a whaling center Provincetown
was second only to New Bedford and Nantucket. Whaling
was exciting and somewhat romantic, but commercial
fishing was soon the town's primary source of income. In
1849 Thoreau stood on the great beach and watched as
"the mackerel fleet continued to pour around the Cape
. . . in countless numbers, schooner after schooner, 'til
they made a city on the water." He later estimated that he
saw about four hundred ships pass into the harbor. Salt-
cured fish were in great demand and Provincetown was
ideally suited for the trade with its expansive beaches and
water of the highest saline content on the Cape. Its shores
were lined with salt works and fish flakes, low slatted
platforms to cure the fish in the sunny salt air. By 1840

Provincetown was a famous fishing port and boasted the largest fleet on the Cape.

By the Civil War, almost all Cape towns except Provincetown had been squeezed out of the commercial fishing business as the demand came for larger vessels and better harbors. Provincetown hung on, but capital was hard to come by and a slow decline set in. The independent Portuguese have never given up; stories of their record catches and colorful captains are passed down through the generations. The captain who continually brought in a full hold and negotiated a good price was known as a "killer." It took drive and hard work to become a killer but he had the respect of the town and the choice of the men for his crews. Just mention Captain Gaspar to one of the old Portuguese fishermen; he should be worth a good story or two.

The last whaler from Provincetown was the *Viola* under Captain John Cook. He took his wife on many of his lonely voyages in the early 1900s — two years at a time in the Arctic, at times locked in the ice for ten months at a stretch. It was generally agreed that Mrs. Cook returned from her last voyage "mentally ill." Her story was common knowledge in the town even as the Captain continued to the Arctic in pursuit of his whales and their "ile." In 1917 a young playwright, fresh from his success in Provincetown, opened a new play in a tiny theater in New York. Its theme was the creeping madness of a whaling captain's wife after the captain refused to turn back from his whale oil search in the frozen north. The author was of course Eugene O'Neill, the play *Ile*.

The Provincetown Players was established in 1915; O'Neill joined them the following year. He had worked as an able seaman and drew several of his early themes from his experiences ashore and afloat. A three-time winner of the Pulitzer Prize and a 1936 winner of the Nobel Prize, his was perhaps the greatest influence in establishing Provincetown as a summer theater colony. Many share the credit of course: Susan Glaspell, George Cram Cook and Mary Heaton Vorse were among the founders of the colony, and such as Sinclair Lewis and John Dos Passos appeared in later years. Although interrupted from time to time, the early theater-on-the-wharf tradition has come down through the years to keep Provincetown's claim to a place in the front rank of creative summer theater.

A fine arts colony was well underway in Provincetown before the theater people arrived. Charles Hawthorne established a school at the turn of the century and his subsequent battles in defense of "academic" art rocked the local art colony. He lost the battle but won the war. Provincetown continues to churn out artists, good and bad, just as it did in Hawthorne's day.

So here we have four waves of diverse character and temperament: stolid Yankee sailors, hardy Portuguese fishermen, imaginative artists, and serious writers — and they're all still here in force. In years past the adjectives "quaint," "picturesque," and "salty" would suffice as one watched the ships, admired the scenery, or peeked over the shoulder of an artist on the beach. Times have changed — the fifth wave has arrived!

A year or two ago a passing motorist asked directions to Providence. My friend, a fount of knowledge, quickly and expertly provided clear and concise information. "Naw," said the visitor, "you must be wrong. They tell me it's this way. You know, Providence, the place with all the hippies." Hippies, Yippies or what have you, Provincetown is loaded with what the gentleman had in mind.

As Cape Cod is reputedly a state of mind, so Provincetown is a happening. "A mosaic in character . . . it is many things to many people," to quote its Chamber of Commerce. Is it for show or for real? There's nothing phony about those fishing boats out there; they're working, and working hard. The artists and writers, for the most part, are hard in pursuit of their talent. But there is the feeling that the next act of the melodrama may not maintain the quality of its predecessors. Gone is the Chrysler Art Museum, and the town seems to be losing its pride in the old landmarks of its glorious past. The old cemetery is a rundown, uptidy tangle and the MacMillans, Gaspars, Hawthornes and O'Neills seem to be fading along with the early history buried in those neglected graves. Some can live quite a while on reputation alone, but as the man says, Provincetown is many things to many people.

Josef Berger caught the wide range of Provincetown when he overheard two Yankee sea captains while they watched an elderly woman pass by on a bicycle. "She had lived there for years, always wore pants, kept her hair to a crewcut, and talked in a rich bass-baritone." One captain "turned to the other and said in a calm, subdued tone, 'Obed, if there was any way of finding out, I'd give you three to one that craft carries a centerboard.'"

So much for the circus of Provincetown. Its three thousand year-round residents hate to be reminded that Route 6A into Provincetown is the ugliest approach on Cape Cod — though some say the fault lies not with the entrance to Provincetown but with the exit from Truro. Run the gauntlet anyway, I guarantee you'll find Provincetown of great interest.

COMMERCIAL STREET

About a mile after you enter Provincetown by the Shore Road (Route 6A) is a fork; bear left along the waterfront and you are on Commercial Street, the mainstream of Provincetown. A narrow one-way lane hugged by homes and shops, Commercial Street blends the many faces of Provincetown into one of the most interesting village thoroughfares in America.

For many years Commercial Street, or Front Street as it was then known, was merely a crooked track of ankle-deep sand meandering along the shore. Barber's Historical Collections mentions a Provincetown lad who, on seeing a horse-drawn wagon for the first time, "wondered how she could steer so straight without a rudder?" The very few vehicles in use had wide, wide wheels, and Thoreau noted a baby carriage with "tires six inches wide to keep it near the surface." Of the homes on Front Street, he noted, "The front-yard plots appeared like what indeed they were, portions of the beach fenced in, with beach-grass growing in them, as if they were sometimes covered by the tide." In 1838, with considerable local opposition, the crooked way was straightened and a plank sidewalk built beside the new sand road. They say that many of the opposition refused to use the plank walk, wading through the flowing sands to their dying day.

Today the first mile of Commercial Street is reminiscent of sturdy Cape fishermen, with echoes of the early theater colony in the background. At number 621, just past Allerton Street, on the left is the Bissel House where the Provincetown Players gave their first performance in 1915 and where Eugene O'Neill submitted his manuscript of *Bound East for Cardiff* the following summer.

Farther along on the same side at number 577 is the old John Francis apartment house in which O'Neill lived for a time, along with many other struggling artists and writers of the emerging colony. The building has recently been completely overhauled and is now a posh, skylighted apartment of artists' studios and psychiatrists' offices — a sign of the times in Provincetown.

A few hundred feet farther along the beach was the wharf owned by Mary Horton Vorse, the site of the production of *Bound East for Cardiff* and eighteen other new plays, five by O'Neill, in that magnificent summer of 1916. Many of the homes in this neighborhood were owned by the more solvent members of the colony and soon attracted others; John Dos Passos lived at number 571 until his death in 1970.

Farther on the right, just past Hancock Street at number 524, is the birthplace of the late Admiral Donald B. MacMillan, famed Arctic explorer and anthropologist. A comrade of Peary and Byrd, Admiral MacMillan made thirty-one voyages of exploration and was awarded a special Congressional Medal of Honor by a grateful country in 1944. Provincetown was always home base for the admiral — he lived most of his life ashore at number 473 a bit farther on.

Continuing, you'll find the Church of St. Mary of the Harbor (Episcopal) opposite Anthony Street. The little church attracts many visitors to view the artistic contributions of many well-known Provincetown craftsmen, painters and sculptors. The hand-hewn oaken cross in the beautiful front courtyard honors the men lost in the submarine S–4 off Wood End in 1927.

Just past the 1736 hip-roof home on the right at Howland Street is the old Eastern Schoolhouse at the site of the original town line in 1714. In those days the line began "at the jawbone of a whale set in the ground by the side of a red oak stump" and it's just as well they moved it.

At the top of the hill, number 476 on the right, is the mansard-roof "Figurehead House." Captain Ben Handy sighted a lady adrift in the Indian Ocean in 1867. His log records his catch as "A colossal full-length presentment of womankind, modeled with great beauty and vigor and measuring fully eight feet from the placid brow to the underside of the sandaled feet." The captain's enthusiasm may well have been kindled by his ten months at sea. Sawn amidships, her upper half now graces the porte cochere at the skipper's old home port.

On the right at number 460 is the Provincetown Art Association, the subject of another section of this chapter. The gallery is open daily in season and on a reduced schedule the rest of the year.

A hundred yards farther on the same side at number 418 is the former Christian Science Church, now a beautiful private home and, in season, the Church House Art Gallery. If you want large rooms and high ceilings, by all means convert a church. The next old church on the right has also been converted and served for many years as the Chrysler Art Museum; this old Methodist Church is for sale again — here's your chance for that conversion!

From here on things begin to get even more crowded and you are much better off on foot — if you can find a parking space! Fender to fender, elbow to elbow and often fender to elbow, you cannot be sure if it's Provincetown or you that's passing in review. It's a kaleidoscope of color, with the pervading perfume of incense overlaying the odor of fish, tides and popcorn. Psychedelic shops are cheek by jowl with hardware stores, craft shops, restaurants, fish piers, portrait artists, marine supplies, dune tours, antique homes, sidewalk cafés, and a little old lady promoting beach plum jelly. And above all is the wealth of humanity passing in review — including you — the in and out generations of every stripe with old Cape Codders and Portuguese fishermen going about their business with total unconcern.

MacMillan Wharf, the town pier, is the place for dune and harbor tours, deep sea fishing and sailing cruises, and is of course the anchorage of Provincetown's thriving fishing industry. Town Hall is up a block and across the way; behind it is a bas-relief of the signing of the Mayflower Compact flanked by memorial tablets. The Compact is considered by many to mark the birth of democratic government in America. Up Commercial Street past Winslow on the left is the present Provincetown Playhouse-on-the-Wharf, the front structure given over to a pleasant, arty little mall of craft shops. Across the street is the venerable Universalist Church (1847), rich in architectural detail and noted for its magnificent *trompe l'oeil* frescoes. Almost elbowed off the street by homes and shops on either side, the church was declared a National Historic Monument in 1972. Farther on the left is the Aquarium; the sea lions, penguins, sea horses, cannibalistic squid and piranha must recognize their land-based counterparts in the throngs parading by.

Once past Court Street you're moving rather abruptly back into life in an old Cape fishing village. Pick up your car again and press on, for the street has more charms to offer.

Past Pleasant Street, Commercial takes a sharp left. Instead, continue straight on Tremont to Cottage Street at the crest of Chip Hill. On the near left corner is the "Norse Wall Cottage." In 1805 Chip Hill was graded down 25 feet and in 1853 workmen excavating the cellar of the present home struck a stone wall a few feet below. Stones of the size found were never known in sandy Provincetown, and the depth, about 30 feet, gave rise to the theory that they were brought in as ballast, making the wall a Norse relic of a thousand years ago. It has never been examined by archaeologists, so the "Norse Wall" remains in the basement, the mystery unsolved.

Turn left and rejoin Commercial Street. On the left across from Nickerson Street is a grassy plot next to the West End Racing Club. Provincetown's second theater-on-a-wharf was located here in the twenties and thirties. Considerably less successful artistically than the first, its piles gave out and it collapsed on the beach in a 1941 storm.

A bit farther on is Provincetown's "oldest" house, number 72, on the corner of Soper Street. Having passed a "1736" hip-roof house earlier on our travels, this "1746" Cape obviously has a contender for the title. Its claim is supported by the Chamber of Commerce and its charms are open to the public, sufficient reasons to warrant a closer look.

At the western end of Commercial Street the traffic island contains a brick-fenced tablet commemorating the Pilgrims' first landing on November 11, 1620. The map in *Mourt's Relation* indicates that the Pilgrims first set foot on American soil in this immediate vicinity, a fact that Plymouth would prefer to forget. On the outer edge of the traffic circle begins the stone breakwater pointing its thin finger at Long Point with Wood End Light off to your right. You may wish to walk its mile of flat stones on a calm day. It provides a fine view of the village and harbor that will be worth the effort.

HEAR YE! HEAR YE!

The town crier on Commercial Street in the summertime is an engaging young fellow; colorfully dressed in

Pilgrim costume, he's always willing to pose with the children or answer questions with a smile. He's an ornament now, but it wasn't all that long ago when he was one of the most useful men in town.

Provincetown, far from the first to need the services of a town crier, was certainly one of the last. For well over a hundred years from the 1750s the town crier of Provincetown was the only consistent, and usually reliable, source of news for the man on the street. Isolated and without a local daily newspaper, the town crier's call was serious business in Provincetown until radios became commonplace in the 1920s. Telegraphy had come in 1855, the weekly *Provincetown Advocate* in 1869, the railroad in 1873, and telephones in 1882, but these media served and summarized for the town crier; they never replaced him. He carried a bell but wore no uniform then; a wide-brimmed hat and baggy pants were customary but no such rules were laid down for the individualistic criers.

There were many colorful criers, but all sources point to one man, George Washington Ready, as the reigning character. Called "The Professor," he once stated that he'd been all over the world "and a good many other places besides." Photos and news articles about the Professor are on display at the Museum. It seems that he not only disseminated the news — when it was scarce he wasn't above creating a bit himself. In 1886 he leaked one such report to the *Yarmouth Register* and the story was picked up across the nation. George had been down by Herring Cove when he saw a strange creature rise in the water and come ashore. The Professor jumped behind a beach plum bush to watch it pass.

Herman Jennings, a friend of Ready, recorded the apparition in the Professor's words:

about three hundred feet long . . . about twelve feet in diameter . . . covered with scales as large as the head of a fish barrel, and were colored alternatively green, red and blue . . . teeth at least two feet long . . . a tusk or horn at least eight feet in length . . . six eyes as large as good-sized dinner

plates and they were placed at the end of movable projections
. . . three of the eyes were red, three were green . . . a
strong sulphurous odor accompanied him, and intense heat
was emitted, so much that the bushes and grasses over which
he moved have the appearance of being scorched with fire.

The brave Professor followed the beast to Pasture Pond
and watched him disappear, leaving "a large hole in the
center some twenty feet in diameter, perfectly circular,
down which sounding leads have been lowered 250 fathoms and no bottom found."

Not one to back off under pressure, the Professor at-
tested his story as follows:

I, George Washington Ready, do testify that the foregoing
statement is correct. It is a true description of the serpent as
he appeared to me on that morning, and I was not unduly
excited by liquor or otherwise.

The sea monster reported in 1719 was obviously only a
pup and may have just been reaching maturity when the
Professor spotted him in 1886. If he keeps to his schedule
we should have another sighting any day now.

MACMILLAN WHARF

Provincetown's unrivaled harbor kept it in the fishing
business long after most Cape towns hauled in their lines
and nets for good. Lack of capital in the late 1800s took
her from the front rank as large-scale fishing centered in
Gloucester and Boston, but many of her hardy Portuguese
sons have continued in the boots of their fathers to the
present day.

More than ten million pounds of fish worth over $2
million were landed at MacMillan Wharf in 1971. Today's
fleet consists of about forty vessels, draggers and long line
hookers, plus a half dozen New Bedford boats that search
out the highest prices, and five or six local lobstermen.
The fishermen work a six-day week year round, taking a
pay-day break on Fridays in good weather and letting nature determine their days off during the rest of the year.

The boats leave at 3 or 4 A.M. and the best time to watch them return and unload is generally from about 4 to 6 P.M. Most have already iced and boxed their catch before they arrive, but others, particularly the New Bedford vessels out for several days, unload by hauling the fish in baskets from the hold. Within a very few hours the catch is delivered in refrigerated trucks to the Boston market.

In the summer the catch is predominantly cod, haddock and flounder, with seasonal spurts of mackerel and whiting. From November to May the emphasis is on flounder and cod. If your visit is timed for August or September check to see if one of several tuna tournaments is underway. The return of these sportfishing boats, with each fish weighing anywhere from two to eight hundred pounds, sometimes more, is a sight to behold.

MacMillan Wharf, or Town Pier as it's also called, is the place to go for harbor tours, deep sea fishing excursions, and sailing cruises, which are unique to Provincetown. To really appreciate the feeling of a windjammer under sail, try the moderately priced schooner *Hindu* from MacMillan Wharf. Two-hour cruises are scheduled three times daily in season, sunset and moonlight sails by arrangement.

BLESSING OF THE FLEET

What may appear to be an attraction staged for the benefit of visitors is, in fact, an earnest celebration by the fishermen of Provincetown. The traditional Blessing of the Fleet began in 1948, two years after Gloucester's, and is a day-long fiesta on the last Sunday in June.

Provincetown's fishing fleet is still predominantly manned by Portuguese descendants of the sailors who came to the town on the fishing schooners and whalers of the 1800s. Recent years have broadened the ethnic mixture as many young Portuguese look elsewhere for careers and are replaced by others from outside the community, but it is the older Portuguese captains and crews who keep the tradition alive. It costs them the loss of several days' income, but to the hard-working, fun-loving and deeply religious Portuguese the cost is unimportant.

The Friday before the Blessing finds almost all of the fishermen in the harbor, repainting and decorating their boats for the occasion. Around 10 A.M. on Sunday the fishermen gather at MacMillan Wharf and parade through the streets to St. Peter's Church for the Fisherman's Mass. The return parade is often joined by other organizations and highlighted by floats and symbols honoring "Our Lady of Good Voyage," "St. Peter," patron of fishermen, "St. Christopher," patron of voyagers, and "Our Lady of Fatima," a national religious symbol of the Portuguese.

As the fishermen board their boats the bishop boards a dory accompanied by a statue of St. Peter. The fleet slowly circles the harbor as the bishop blesses and sprinkles holy water on the bow of each boat in turn. Underlying the ceremony is the theme that Christ and his disciples were themselves but humble fishermen.

With banners flying, most of the boat crews and their guests then picnic in the outer harbor in anticipation of the evening's merrymaking. Street dancing and a Fisherman's Ball are highlights and a generally gay atmosphere enfolds the town.

SETH NICKERSON HOUSE (1746)

It may not be the oldest house in Provincetown, but the beautiful little Cape on Commercial Street is a well-restored architectural gem. Built by ship's carpenter Seth Nickerson in 1746, the home is owned by John Gregory, well-known artist and photographer, and open to the public from 10 A.M. to 5 P.M. daily in the summer season.

Nickerson House is in keeping with the sea-going history of Provincetown. Most of its interior wood was taken from abandoned or wrecked ships; the inside door frames and cabinet tops slant downward as they did in the ship's cabins. Wide random-width ships' planks were used as flooring and handmade ballast bricks form the massive center chimney. Gregory points out that such chimneys were called anchors, as they anchored these houses against severe storms. The main fireplace with its beehive oven is a particularly fine example of the period.

The simple fundamental charm of the Cape Cod cottage, graced by the Gregory's fine antiques and artwork, has been carefully retained in the nine rooms of the old home. Fine paneling, windowpanes of Sandwich glass and pegged, hand-hewn oak beams testify to the skill and pride of the ship's carpenter. The handwrought hardware is original; it is said that the H and L (Holy Lord) hinges were used in conjunction with Christian Cross doors to ward off witches from New England homes. The three bedrooms upstairs are reached by so called "Captain's stairs," a steep, narrow companionway reminiscent of a ship's ladder. The ells, side, and rear were of course of a later vintage, in keeping with the custom of expanding outward as space requirements dictated and affluence permitted. Homes of this size often sheltered families with up to a dozen youngsters.

Seth Nickerson House is located at 72 Commercial Street, on the corner of Soper Street, in the west end of town. The Gregorys also open the home on a reduced schedule in Indian Summer; pass by and check the sign when you are there.

PROVINCETOWN MUSEUM

One of the finest museums on the Cape is the historical museum in Provincetown. A nominal admission fee entitles you to visit both the museum and Pilgrim Monument — enter by Winslow Street from Bradford Street behind Town Hall.

The various wings of the museum offer collections highlighting both Cape and Provincetown history. Provincetown's favorite son, Admiral Donald B. MacMillan, contributed many artifacts and mementos of his 31 Arctic expeditions — a reminder of the worldwide influence of men and ships of the Cape in recent years. A mounted white wolf, found only within 12 degrees of the North Pole, is one of only two such specimens in the world. Other mounted specimens of polar bear, musk ox and walrus will keep the youngsters fully occupied as the older generations examine the life and times of the far north through MacMillan's eyes. His expeditions from 1908 to 1954, the last nine with Mrs. MacMillan aboard, span the golden years of the exploration of the Arctic.

The Pilgrim Wing does simple but effective justice to Provincetown's honor as the first landing place of the Pilgrims in 1620. Dioramas depict the events of those first few days in lifelike detail. A highlight is the large-scale model of the *Mayflower*, insofar as its true dimensions are known, fashioned by Courtney Allen in cooperation with other artists. Every schoolchild is familiar with the *Mayflower*, but this scene with its beautifully modeled figures and effective backdrop provides an exceptionally clear concept of life on the tiny vessel that carried the 102 Pilgrims on the two-month voyage from Plymouth, England. A section of the master cabin is cut away to reveal a diorama of the signing of the Compact in Provincetown Harbor. The sailing shallop that served the landing parties so well is at her accustomed place on deck.

Life in this early fishing and whaling center and the emergence of Provincetown as an art colony are well documented here. Of particular interest are the full-scale replica of a whaling captain's quarters, a display of Eugene O'Neill memorabilia, and a diorama of the Long Point Settlement, c. 1850. Long Point, that sandy spit at the end of the breakwater, was a thriving fishing community from about 1820 to 1860. Determined to be as close as possible to their source of income, as many as thirty-eight families built their homes, church and school on the very tip of the Cape. Fresh water brought from Provincetown supplemented the rainwater cisterns in the sand dunes. At its prime, six windmills powered extensive salt works and Long Point Light (1826) guided the fishermen home from the sea. The settlement was abandoned

in about 1860 and most of the homes floated across the
harbor on scows. Many settled in the west end and some
of their homes are still in use today. Long Point emerged
again briefly in the Civil War when two gun batteries were
erected there. Known locally as Fort Useless and Fort
Ridiculous, they were in fact well placed for the attack
that never came. The automatic light on Long Point blinks
today with only the electric utility poles to mar the sandy
landscape. The gun emplacements appear now as two
more humps among the dunes.

For those interested in Cape and Provincetown history,
the opportunities offered at the Provincetown Museum are
almost endless. Beautifully organized and displayed, the
exhibits are open daily year round and evenings in season.

PILGRIM MONUMENT

Directly behind the museum is the monument commemorating the first landing of the Pilgrims and their
activities in Provincetown. As Josef Berger (Jeremiah
Digges) noted in his *Cape Cod Pilot,* the Pilgrim Monument "is thoroughly American in its makeup. Although
the Pilgrims had never been to Italy, the designer is Italian; the plans were made by an army engineer of French
and Swiss descent; it was built by the Irish and is taken
care of by the Portuguese; and annually is climbed by
several thousand *Mayflower* descendants."

The cornerstone was laid in the presence of President
Theodore Roosevelt in 1907 and dedicated in the presence
of President William Howard Taft on August 5, 1910.
Constructed of Maine granite, 28 feet square at the base,
the tower rises 252 feet above its 100-foot hill. The climb
is a relatively easy combination of steps and inclined
planes — it's claimed that folks in their nineties have
made it without trouble. The interior walls are set with
many commemorative stones from Mayflower societies
and Massachusetts towns — even Plymouth is represented. It's the tallest granite structure in the United
States and hangs over Provincetown like the sword of

Damocles, bidding welcome and beware at this eastern outpost of America.

FIRST ART COLONY IN AMERICA

In 1899 Charles W. Hawthorne, famed portrait and genre painter, started the Cape Cod School of Art in Provincetown. He, his pupils, and others attracted largely through his influence established a colony of the highest professional level in the academic tradition. Early artists of national stature included Max Boehm, Richard Miller, John Noble and George Elmer Browne. The Hawthorne Memorial Gallery is still the focal point of serious art in Provincetown.

In the days of Hawthorne, visitors would see dozens of painters sitting on sketching stools along Commercial Street, the beaches and the wharves, painting portraits of grizzled Portuguese fishermen or merely the scenes before them. In time the colony attracted schools of modern artists: post-Impressionist, post-Cubist, woodblock printers, and many other of the less conventional forms. By 1925 the Hawthorne Gallery of the Art Association found it necessary to accommodate both factions, generally running separate exhibitions, one modern, one academic. In 1936, over the then-dead body of Charles Hawthorne, the association relented and decided both factions would hang together.

Since that time the academics have steadily lost ground to the moderns in Provincetown. From the picturesque recording of boats, dunes, tree-lined lanes, fishermen and children, the emphasis has shifted to art forms in which the inner organization, rather than the subject matter, is the vehicle for the artist's imagination and resourcefulness. The Provincetown art colony tolerates all manner, shape and form of art and artists. Charles W. Hawthorne is reportedly spinning in his grave.

The Art Association, founded in 1914, is still the backbone of the fine arts colony in Provincetown. Located at 460 Commercial Street, continuing exhibitions are staged during the season, open to the public daily and evenings for a modest admission fee. Periodic exhibitions in the off-season are held on a reduced schedule. The Church House Gallery at 418 Commercial Street and the Fine Arts Work Center on Pearl Street also operate galleries open to the public regularly in season. There are, of course, many more commercial galleries and art schools on the lower Cape; the advertisements in the exhibition program of the Art Association will lead you to most of them.

PLAYHOUSE-ON-THE-WHARF

Theater history in Provincetown has ebbed and flowed with the tide over the years, but it looks as if the next ebb tide may carry it all away. If so, it will be a great loss. There are many summer theaters on Cape Cod, but only one semblance of a theater colony, in Provincetown.

The Provincetown of 1915 was ideally suited to the young experimental artists of the era. Isolated, receptive and inexpensive, it was lively enough in the summer to provide an appreciative audience. The creative talent attracted under the leadership of George Cram Cook was certainly exceptional; many went on to national recognition in various phases of literature and the theatrical arts. The group took on the name of the Provincetown Players and, after presenting one or two plays in an old waterfront home, devised a makeshift theater on a Commercial Street fish wharf.

The next summer a shy young playwright appeared, offering his rejected manuscripts. Eugene O'Neill was quickly accepted; he wrote six of the nineteen new plays of that 1916 season. It was a memorable summer: the community shared in the project, box office and backers were relatively unimportant and artistic excellence reigned supreme. Creative summer theater had come to America.

The Players moved on to New York in the fall. Their productions in an old stable in Greenwich Village marked another milestone in theater history — the first important off-Broadway company. O'Neill's budding reputation blossomed in New York in 1916 and 1917. The rickety wharf on Commercial Street wouldn't support another season, however, and with war clouds approaching the Players disbanded and left Provincetown to the artists.

Several of the original group continued to summer in Provincetown and by the early twenties were ready to try again. In 1923 they opened as the "Barnstormers" in a refurbished barn on Bradford Street. Rifts quickly developed and half the company, under Mary Bickell and Raymond Moore, moved out and left Frank Shea and O'Neill to pursue art for art's sake. Within a year or two the Barnstormers dissolved in dissension and O'Neill left Provincetown for good.

Mary Bickell's new theater was a remodeled sail loft at 83 Commercial Street, quite professional for its day. Perched on pilings along the shore, it became the second playhouse-on-a-wharf. By concentrating on smart and sophisticated fare, the Wharf Theater managed to have a lot of fun and keep its head above water through the Depression years. It might be going still but for a northeast storm that swept its legs from under and dumped it on the beach in 1941.

A bit before this time, artist Heinrich Pfeiffer had built an avant-garde motion picture theater on a wharf at the end of Gosnold Street. But he was ahead of his time — Hollywood was in its prime and the public wanted stars, not art, in their films. Having experienced and appreciated the O'Neill era, Pfeiffer approached Miss Catherine Huntington of the New England Repertory Company, which decided to give Provincetown a try. In June 1940, shortly before the lighthearted Wharf Theater sagged to the beach, serious theater returned to Provincetown.

The third playhouse-on-a-wharf has lived up to its advance billing. It reached its glory years in the late fifties and early sixties. The O'Neill Festival in 1966 sold out the house for almost every performance. At least one O'Neill play is presented each season, new playwrights are introduced from time to time, and the standards of acting and production are as high as any on the Cape. Since the latter sixties attendance and support of creative theater in Provincetown has declined drastically. More emphasis must now be given to proven hits and less to creative theater in the economic struggle to keep the doors open.

A theater colony still exists, but each time it raises its head a regrettable apathy brings it down. In 1966 the exceptional Act IV Café Experimental Theater began producing plays by unknown playwrights with unknown actors. With little money and a small basement playhouse it introduced dozens of plays over a four-year span. One, *The Indian Wants the Bronx,* by Israel Horowitz, went straight to Broadway with the same unknown Provincetown cast. Two of its actors have achieved national recognition through leading roles in *The Godfather.* But the little theater company in Provincetown was soon forced to close when producer Robert Costa ran out of money.

It seems that the more visitors to Provincetown, the less support for its theater and the arts. Many of those who would be attracted by Provincetown's art are repelled by the wave of pseudo-Bohemians who seem to have taken over. It's so much easier to enjoy an evening at the theater in Dennis, Falmouth or one of a half-dozen other towns on the Cape.

For those willing to search it out, the Playhouse-on-the-Wharf still offers first class summer theater. Now operated by the Drama Department of the University of Massachusetts, it continues to nurse the flickering candle of creative theater in Provincetown. Talented actors and playwrights are still looking for the opportunity to develop and display their ideas. Provincetown has been such a place for close to sixty years. If it fails, an essential part of Provincetown's charm will go with it.

THE SINKING OF THE S–4

To the weatherbeaten fishermen of Provincetown, death and disaster at sea were accepted facts of life. But even they were shocked and appalled by the tragic comedy of

errors that cost the lives of the forty-man crew of the submarine S–4.

Running a familiar course on a winter afternoon in
1927, the S–4 was bound for Provincetown Harbor after
completing her sea trials. The Coast Guard cutter *Paul-
ding,* unaware of the sub's presence, was returning from
an unsuccessful rum-runner patrol. When the cutter finally sighted the sub's periscope at 75 yards in a choppy
sea, it was too late to veer off and the collision occurred
just as the S–4's conning tower broke the surface. Down
she went; water pouring through the gash in her battery
room spread to the control room, probably due to a non-
regulation attempt to rescue trapped men; and the electrical system shortcircuited, crippling the submarine in 102
feet of water about a mile off Wood End Light.

The rescue attempt quickly developed into a nightmare
of inefficiency. A Coast Guard surfboat from Wood End
spent 12 hours in rough seas grappling for the submarine
before the first salvage ship arrived. The next morning
she was hooked and a diver went down a few hours later.
The survivors signaled from within: six men alive in the
torpedo room. The navy had a choice — an air line to the
men or air to the ballast tanks. They chose the ballast
tanks in an effort to raise the sub, but soon found they
were blowing bubbles in the sea through the punctured
ribs of her hull. By the time they realized their error, the
growing sea made diving impossible — a volunteer tried
but had to be rescued himself. Nothing more was done until
the storm abated three days later, when they discovered
that their slender line had parted and the sub was lost
again! A single salvage ship grappled for hours as the
navy turned down the offer of Provincetown's dragger
fleet to comb the bottom abreast in a single sweep. Fresh
air finally reached the men four days after the sub went
down, but by then it didn't matter. When the men were
known to be dead, the navy announced that further salvage would be delayed until spring. An aroused public and
vociferous press quickly changed their mind.

The court of inquiry held the commanders of both vessels and the admiral in charge of rescue operations as equally sharing the blame. The secretary of the navy overrode this decision and placed full responsibility on the shoulders of the one who had offered no defense — the dead commander of the submarine.

The real culprit was of course the Navy Department; the lack of coordination that failed to advise each commander of the other's cruising plans was inexcusable. Government departments are too nebulous and a sin of omission too difficult to pin down, so the search for a scapegoat narrowed down to the immediate cause, the fatal mistake in a critical situation. Some say the slanting sun may have blinded the periscope eye of the submarine, others that the watch on the cutter was negligent. The navy reenacted the conditions of the accident with suitable fanfare, but forgot to consider mother nature — the sea was as placid as a mill pond.

Refloated, repaired, and refitted, the S–4 went on to complete her service as an experimental station to develop and test safety devices for the submarine service. The crew are remembered by a tablet at the Naval Academy and a memorial cross of shipwreck timbers at the Church of St. Mary of the Harbor in Provincetown.

CAPE COD NATIONAL SEASHORE

More than nine-tenths of the land area of Provincetown is included in the Province Lands sector of the Cape Cod National Seashore. For all practical purposes, the only area still under the town's jurisdiction is the long band of residential and commercial development along the shore of Provincetown Harbor. Province Lands is a seemingly unending stretch of sand dunes and beaches: geologically fragile, starkly beautiful, and undoubtedly the finest of its type to be preserved in its natural state.

Province Lands features a Visitor Center, a guide-yourself nature trail, bicycle trails, oversand routes and Race Point and Herring Cove beaches. The Visitor Center is manned from 9 A.M. to 6 P.M. daily in season; it is closed Mondays and Tuesdays from mid-October to mid-May. Its facilities include an observation deck that offers as fine a view as there is on the Cape. There is also an information desk, a Cape Cod and natural history book counter, an auditorium, and a display depicting fish and fishing in Cape Cod waters.

Many worthwhile programs are presented throughout the year in the auditorium and the outdoor amphitheater. A film on Provincetown is shown hourly in season and when attendance warrants or upon request in the off-season. Natural history, Cape Cod's heritage and National Seashore topics are featured in the amphitheater each evening during July and August. Evening slide programs are also given in the auditorium on weekends in the fall; check for current information at the desk.

If you use the telescope at the Visitor Center, you may wonder about the buildings in the distance on the dunes. The small square one dead ahead is one of three naval testing stations along the back side. To its right is the rooftop of a privately owned summer residence.

Paved bicycle trails wind for eight miles through the 4,400 acres of the Province Lands area. The trail forms a rough square with spurs on three corners. Convenient access points are at Herring Cove and Race Point beaches, the Beach Forest parking area off Race Point Road, and at the Visitor Center. The trail wanders through forests, ponds and bogs, and some of the most spectacular dunes along the Atlantic coast. A trail guide is available at the information desk.

The guide-yourself trail over the dunes for oversand vehicles begins a short way in on the inner dune route near Race Point Beach. Access to the dune trail network is also available from Herring Cove Beach, the High Head parking area and Head of the Meadow Beach in North Truro. A permit is required and a trail guide brochure should be picked up at the same time. Regulations, driving hints, and the trail maps will prove invaluable. The many miles of trails lead to all the nooks and crannies of the Province Lands. Several commercial tours are available near the wharves in Provincetown for those without oversand vehicles.

When you turn in Race Point Road toward the Visitor Center, you pass the Beach Forest Trail parking area about a half mile in on your left. Rest rooms, picnic tables and a water fountain are available here. This guide-yourself walking trail forms a 1½-mile loop through dunes, around a shallow lily pond and the beech forest beyond. Guided walks are given on a scheduled basis until mid-October. Allow about two hours for your tour.

The Beech Forest parking area is also an access point for the bicycle trail. Across the street and back a quarter mile is a convenient place to rent a bike. Up to this point we've bicycled, walked and driven the dunes. Anyone for horses? Nelson's Riding Stables not only rents bicycles but also conducts guided saddle horse tours of the dunes. Hour-long tours are scheduled every two hours from 10 A.M. to 4 P.M. in season with a two-hour sunset ride each evening at 6. Off-season they will take out groups of two or more almost any time. Bicycles and horses are both available from early March to about the end of November.

SHANKPAINTER CHILDREN'S ZOO

The first left after the traffic light on Route 6 will take you to the Children's Zoo, a short way in on Shankpainter Road on your left.

In the last century even sandy Provincetown had a few farms, with cows and horses to provide the milk and work animals for the fishing community. One of those farms was centered at the present site of the Children's Zoo. It covered many more acres in the Shankpainter Swamp area in the late 1800s; the steak house across the road used to be the dairy barn and the horses and cows grazed the scrubby beach grass on the nearby countryside. Owned and operated by the Watson family, the remaining land now serves a related purpose under the ownership of a direct descendant.

The zoo is a commercial venture, but equally important is their breeding program for endangered species. They keep a number of exotic birds and animals for display purposes only, but their real interest lies in breeding pairs — American mountain lions, Canadian lynx, ocelots, wolves, coyotes, bobcats, and rare deer. Mrs. Lynx is expecting in April 1973; her offspring and those of other pairs over succeeding years should present a worthwhile project. The zoo also maintains a "petting farm" where the youngsters can play with tame animals.

Shankpainter Children's Zoo is open from mid-May to mid-October. An admission fee is charged.

CAMPSITES AND TRAILER PARKS

About three hundred yards before the traffic light on Route 6, a right turn will take you to Dunes Edge Camp Ground in Provincetown. There are 100 fine wooded sites in this eight-acre park: 85 tent camping sites and 15 trailer sites with electrical hookups. Rest room and hot shower facilities are available at two locations. A small general store offers staples and ice. The campground is surrounded by National Seashore property yet it's convenient to town. Write to R. E. Collinson for a brochure; reservations are generally required during their season from early May to late September.

Manny Philips's Coastal Acres Camping Court is right on the edge of town. With 114 sites, about three-quarters wooded, more than half have electrical and water hookups and several have sewerage as well. Rest rooms, hot showers and dumping stations are provided. A general store is available and it is equipped to fill propane gas bottles. Reservations are suggested from Memorial Day to Labor Day. The campground is open from April to November. Write to Box 593, Provincetown, Mass. 02657, for a brochure and further information.

PUBLIC SWIMMING BEACHES

Strangely enough, the sandy village of Provincetown doesn't have an official bathing beach to call its own. The

National Seashore has two, however, as fine as any on the Cape.

Race Point Beach, to the left of the Seashore Visitor Center, and Harding Cove Beach at the end of Route 6 require the standard daily fee or season pass of all National Seashore beaches.

The harbor front along Commercial Street has numerous public landings that give access to the beach, and many enjoy not only swimming here but also walking among the old wharf pilings to gain a different perspective on the town. There are no beach facilities but the warm water attracts quite a number of bathers.

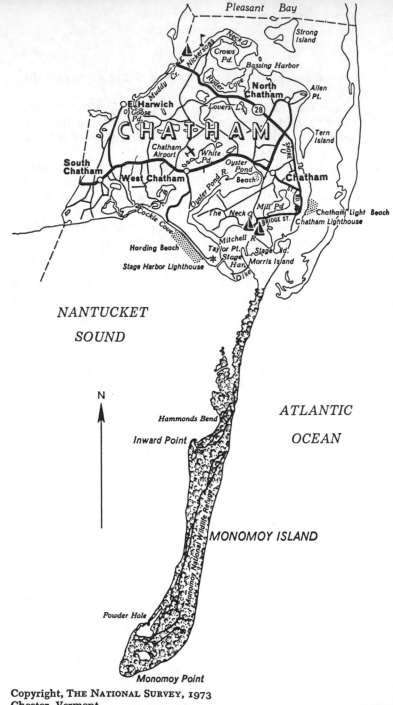

Copyright, THE NATIONAL SURVEY, 1973
Chester, Vermont

CHAPTER XII

Chatham

Chatham, almost squeezed off at the elbow of the Cape, claims a distinction that no other Cape town has been able to match: Chatham fog is unsurpassed! Indeed, the singular qualities of Chatham fog are a matter of pride in the town.

They say that Chatham housewives regularly scoop off chunks of a good "pea souper," add leftovers and heat it up for lunch. Many years ago old Somber Clark had some deep fat frying for some clam fritters when a particularly tasty high tide fog rolled in. Slicing off a few slabs, he stirred in some minced onion and a dash of bitters and gorged himself on fried fog. He soon opened up a Fried Fog Shack on the highway, but it didn't last — too much business. Somber ran short of batter in a poor summer, had to mix in a little low tide Harwich fog, and that ended that.

Legend has it that Chathamites walking home on a foggy day often found themselves going uphill and completely lost. The smart ones merely sat down on the nearest fog bank and waited. Sooner or later a familiar chimney or church steeple would peek through as the fog drifted by, and it was usually no trick for a Chatham sailor to shimmy back down to the ground. Now that the town's built up, very few get lost that way.

It seems as if Chatham were born under a cloud. Cham-

plain fought with the Indians here and the Pilgrims almost ran aground offshore, but it wasn't until the first
English settler came that the cloud really descended.

Chatham, or Monomoy as it was known then, was part
of the plantation reserved for the proprietors and old
comers. Little was done about it until 1652 when the vast
area between Old Yarmouth and Nauset was turned over
to nine proprietors, mostly Eastham residents, to negotiate
terms with the Indians. They bought much of what is now
Brewster but took no firm action on Chatham or Harwich.
There was no rush — or so they thought!

A Yarmouth man, William Nickerson, was probably
oblivious to these facts of law and high finance as he
tended his farm on Follins Pond in Yarmouth. He was a
"free-man" and a vocal one, constantly involved in land
disputes and lawsuits; he was once chided by the court to
end "his offensive speeches against the sundry of the
town." When Myles Standish came down to settle the
conflicting land claims of Yarmouth, William Nickerson
was in the thick of it. The ten acres he received were
doubtlessly less than he was bargaining for.

Single-minded and possessed with unlimited energy,
Nickerson turned his attention to the wide open spaces to
the east. On a visit to Monomoy in 1656 he struck a bargain with the Sachem Mattaquason. In exchange for a
boat, 10 coats, 6 kettles, 12 axes, 12 hoes, 12 knives, a
hat, 40 shillings in wampum, and 12 shillings in cash, he
received a large undefined tract of land in Monomoy
roughly four miles square — a shrewd deal but a bit foggy
around the edges. It was bad enough that negotiating
rights belonged to other men and that no man was permitted to trade with the Indians without the approval of
the court. It was far worse that he neglected to secure a
written deed.

The reaction from Plymouth Court was immediate and
devastating. Nickerson was found guilty, fined and his
claim dismissed. About this time Nickerson's father-in-
law died and he moved to Boston to care for the widow,

dabble in real estate, and continue his fight. Appeals and petitions led to a further decision in 1659: Nickerson could have his "farm" if he would pay a fine of £5 per acre. The fine totaled more money than existed in the Colony, enough to give pause to any man but William Nickerson.

Contentious as ever, he returned to Yarmouth in 1661. Nickerson still owned his Yarmouth farm and the law read that each man was entitled to a share in the whales beached on the shore. One of his first actions was to demand his share for his three-year absence!

Another petition to the court in 1663 brought no response so Nickerson decided to force the issue. He and eight of his married children and their families moved on to Monomoy. The court reacted quickly — the chief marshal was ordered to collect £200 as part of the penalty due, but by then no assets could be found. Nickerson then appealed to the king's representatives, who were holding sessions in Plymouth. They were sympathetic but thought his claim to a farm "four miles square" to be a bit unreasonable. The court, under the prodding of the king's counsel, finally allowed Nickerson one hundred acres of the ten thousand he claimed. Other than stimulating a series of insulting letters resulting in fines by the court, the matter rested for the next seven years.

In the same year, 1665, the court put Monomoy under the jurisdiction of Yarmouth. When Constable Thomas Howes came to collect taxes from the Nickersons he was "affronted in the execution of his office and offered divers abuses therein." The court could do little more than scold the old man and assign his unruly "naighbourhood" to Eastham.

Meanwhile Nickerson kept after a deed, even going so far as to sue Mattaquason, until he finally realized that he would have to make his peace with the nine proprietors before any real progress could come about. Substantial success came in 1672. For £90 William Nickerson received a deed from both the Indians and the proprietors to 4,000 acres, and the sole right to bargain with the Indians for the balance. Five years later a son-in-law who reportedly contributed some of the £90 sued him for a larger share of the land. Nickerson won, and his title became unassailable.

With 4,000 acres in his pocket, Nickerson quickly added the Great Neck area at a cost of two four-year-old steers, one cow, a calf, and two bushels of Indian corn. In 1679 he traded for an additional thousand acres on the west and three years later another large parcel of meadowland on Tom's Neck. He had the right to buy, but for some reason never bought the remaining few thousand acres where the village of Chatham is centered today. The rights passed on to his descendants and were bought and sold for years.

In about 1678 Nickerson conveyed a parcel or two to new settlers and almost immediately applied for town status. Without a settled minister the court could not authorize town status but promised to consider it if a minister could be secured by the next year. The persistent Nickerson couldn't arrange that for his tiny settlement but managed to talk the court into status as a constable-wick and began to exercise most of the functions of a town. When Nickerson died in 1689–1690 Monomoy was still little more than a Nickerson neighborhood. There were probably about twenty families, all farmers, well scattered around the landscape. It is interesting to note that the present bounds of Chatham are the same 16 square miles fought for and won by William Nickerson in his sixteen-year battle with the Plymouth Court.

Chatham was little more than a country farming village for many more years. In 1697 a lay preacher, Jonathan Vickery, was temporarily employed as minister and in 1700 it was voted to "bild a meten hous of 20 and 2 foot floor and 13 foot in the wall." It was noted that the "in-habbetence ded agree to take thare tornes and goo out with Edward Small to get the tember two days a pese till every man had took his torn." When completed it was plain and rough but probably the most pretentious structure in the village.

Fifty years after William Nickerson's purchase, Monomoy showed little evidence of progress. It now had a small meeting house and a tavern, but no permanent pastor. In 1711 the Reverend Hugh Adams accepted the call and immediately began to reorder the priorities of the village. First on the agenda was incorporation. Adams drafted a fourth petition, thirty-three years after the first, and it was approved by Boston in 1712 with instructions that the new town take the name of Chatham. The name, by the way, is properly pronounced "Chat-ham" not "Chat-um." It takes an old-timer to put just the proper amount of "ham" in it.

The Reverend Adams was less successful in his other activities. To establish a formal church required the approval of his fellow Cape ministers. The eccentric, opinionated and argumentative Reverend Adams and his tiny congregation were rebuffed as too small to support a church. Ignoring the decision, Reverend Adams formed his church and squared off against his old foe, demon rum.

The parsonage and the tavern stood close to each other, and their owners were two of the leading citizens of the town. It wasn't tavernkeeper Hawes that the puritanical Reverend started out after, only his rum. Under attack, Hawes repeated some rumors from the Reverend's cloudy past in South Carolina and the battle was on. Libel suits and stinging sermons split the little town down the middle. After two courts ruled in favor of Hawes, the Reverend took his case to a higher court and won, but with damages of only 10 shillings. Disgusted and urged to resign, he shook off the sands of Chatham and sought a more hospitable flock in the hills of New Hampshire.

In 1718 peace and order finally began to surface in storm-tossed Chatham. After a short period following the Reverend Treat at Eastham, the Reverend Joseph Lord accepted Chatham's call. Well educated, capable and the brother-in-law of the Reverend Stone of Harwich, he had no trouble organizing a formal church. His thirty-year ministry was one of slow but steady progress. Village life, what there was of it, centered around the new meeting house built near the site of the old in 1729. Other than the church, cemetery, sundial, pound for stray cattle, windmill, and tavern, there was no village center. The fifty to a hundred families that lived in Chatham during the Reverend Lord's ministry were farmers and fishermen. Most had oxen for work animals, a horse or two for transportation and perhaps a Negro or Indian servant. Some of the farmers did carpentry, shoemaking and blacksmithing for their neighbors, but it was not until 1735 that Chatham's first merchant, Elisha Hopkins, opened his general store.

The old church on the hill, enlarged in 1774, was torn down in 1830. The center of village life in those days is the least populated area of Chatham today. Drive out to the corner of George Ryder and Old Queen Anne roads and you'll be right in the center of it.

William Nickerson's old farm was located on the southwest side of Route 28 about where it meets Crow Pond Road. It's believed that the last of the Indians and the earliest white settlers were buried on the crest of the hill behind Nickerson's homestead overlooking Ryder's Cove. A small granite-posted graveyard remains and the Nickerson family has marked it as the probable resting place of their founder. There are three old headstones in the burial ground — all smallpox victims in the epidemic of 1766. Thirty-five died that year, including seventeen in the Rider families and Dr. Samuel Lord, the town physician. To reach the old cemetery take the winding dirt lane up the hill from Route 28 about a quarter mile southeast of Crow Pond Road.

Burials from about 1700 took place beside the new meeting house west of Great Hill. The graveyard on the corner of George Ryder Road is the oldest; the one across the street was added in 1781. The earliest legible headstone in the older cemetery is that of Richard Sears, who died in 1718. It's interesting because the engraver made a spelling mistake in Sears's name, crossed it out, and engraved the correct letter above.

In about 1800 the village center began to shift to the vicinity of Chatham Light to be near the harbor and wharves, for by then fishing was far and away the chief occupation. After the Civil War and the arrival of the railroad the center again began to shift, this time inland to its present location.

Fog or no fog, Chatham is a delightful town with one of the most picturesque settings on the Cape. Very few can boast of a commercial fishing pier and a lighthouse almost in the center of town. Narrow lanes, closely set homes, and an air of money make this one of the more exclusive little pockets on the Cape. The 4,600 residents of Chatham have done well by the wily old land speculator, William Nickerson, whose descendants still pepper his old farm.

PORT FORTUNE

Had it not been for an incident at Chatham more than 350 years ago, Cape Cod might have been first settled by the French. Samuel de Champlain, the great French explorer, came to the Cape twice in 1605–1606 in search of a more hospitable climate for his colonists than Port Royal, Nova Scotia. Stage Harbor at Chatham was one of the more attractive possibilities, but the lack of local hospitality encouraged him to move on, and a few years later he founded Quebec instead.

Champlain's visit to Chatham began in a friendly enough way. Helpful Indians guided his crippled ship through a channel around Harding's Beach to an anchorage that he later called Port Fortune, now Stage Harbor. Repairs to the damaged rudder went smoothly and the French crew made itself comfortable ashore in the balmy fall weather.

Champlain was a keen observer and recorded impressions of his surroundings. The land, he noted, was very hilly, well wooded with walnut, oaks, and cedars and only a few pines. Wild grape vines and beach plum were common and game birds and shellfish, particularly oysters, were plentiful. His vessel's commander, Sieur de Poutrincourt, killed twenty-eight sea larks with one shot. Champlain reported five to six hundred savages, naked except for doe or sealskin loincloths, and adorned with feathers and beads. The men carried bows, arrows and clubs but they were basically fishermen and farmers rather than hunters. The Indians cultivated corn, beans, squash and pumpkins and milled their crude corn to bake corn cakes. The French saw nothing noble in the savage; he was considered good for nothing but thievery.

The French were enthusiastic about the site; Champlain noted that it "would be an excellent place to erect buildings and lay the foundations of a State, if the harbor were somewhat deeper and the entrance safer."

As time wore on the Indians' open welcome of the overbearing French began to wear off. Almost inevitably, an Indian stole a hatchet, and a flurry of musket fire shattered the uneasy truce. The Indians retired and the wary French recalled all men to the ship for the night. Several on shore disobeyed the order for a last sleep in the cool fresh air. When the Indians attacked at dawn, only one or two lived to regret their choice.

The English faced minor thefts by Indians many times over later years and, invariably, firm but courteous inquiry restored the property and maintained good will. This time the French bungled the theft and then returned several times over the next few weeks seeking revenge. They devised an elaborate plan to take slaves, but only succeeded in slaughtering several Indians and finally sailed away, leaving Massachusetts clear for English settlement a few years later.

Champlain's approximate landing place is marked by an engraved granite boulder about 200 yards past Bridge Street on Stage Harbor Road. The battle reportedly took place a bit farther west on the beach by Taylors Point. Champlain's Port Fortune was renamed Stage Harbor by less romantic and more practical pioneers of a later era who cured their catch on fish stages along the shore.

SQUANTO'S GRAVE

Squanto, like Iyannough of the Cummaquids, was almost indispensable to the survival of the Plymouth pioneers.

Shanghaied by Captain Hunt in 1614, Squanto escaped in Spain, sought the protection of a merchant in England and later returned to the land of his birth. English-speaking, and by then fully at home with Englishmen, he appeared at Plymouth soon after the *Mayflower* landed and acted as interpreter when the colonists drew up their peace treaty with the Sachem Massasoit. When Massasoit left, Squanto remained behind and volunteered his services to instruct the settlers in fishing, agriculture and survival in general. Had it not been for the 1621 crop produced under the guidance of Squanto, it is doubtful the colony could have survived.

Squanto was also of great assistance as a guide, interpreter and agent among the Indians still smouldering over Captain Hunt's barbarism. It was on one such mission to Chatham with Governor Bradford in 1622 that Squanto "fell sick of an Indean feavor, bleeding much at ye nose and within a few days dyed ther; desiring ye Govr. to pray for him, that he might goe to ye Englishmens God in heaven." Squanto lies in an unmarked grave near where he died, about a half mile southwest of Chatham Light.

CHATHAM LIGHT

If any particular acre of Cape soil were chosen to represent the seafaring traditions of the peninsula, I'd vote for Chatham Light. Lighthouses and lifesaving, shipwrecks and wreckers — all have left their marks on the bluffs at Chatham.

The site of lighthouses since 1808, the beautiful setting of Chatham Light turns angry in a heavy blow. In the early days, lighthouses were identified by the number of lights rather than the timing of the blinks. Chatham was represented by two lights, the so called twin sisters of Chatham. The first pair were octagonal towers of wood with lard oil lanterns to guide sailing vessels into Chatham Harbor. A pair of brick towers replaced them in 1841 and all went well until the hurricane of November 15, 1870. This great storm broke through the outer beach and the sea began a merciless pounding against the bank below the south tower. The ultimate destruction of the lighthouses was inevitable (some say the present light cannot escape a similar fate).

When the 1870 storm hit, the south tower stood 228 feet from the bank. Each succeeding no'theaster chewed away a bit more of the bluff. By 1874 the keeper, Captain Josiah Hardy, was sufficiently alarmed to begin measuring and recording each time a storm brought the raging seas a little closer. The first four years saw a loss of 38 feet, and then the rate began to accelerate. Two years later the land from the edge of the bank to the south tower had whittled away to 100 feet and Washington finally became concerned. Two months later the distance was down to 84 feet and shortly thereafter a government man arrived to lay out two new towers. Four months later, on September 6, 1877, with 59 feet between the south beacon and oblivion, the lights went on in the new towers. As it happened, the fickle sea took two more years to claim the south tower, and another eighteen months to swallow the keeper's house and the northern twin. Faint traces of the foundation of the north tower can still be seen over the bank on the east side of the road.

The present Chatham Light is one of this third pair constructed in 1877. In 1923 one twin was moved to Nauset and the remaining light equipped with an oil vapor lamp with special lenses to produce 24,000 candlepower. This revolving light was powered by weights such as those in a grandfather's clock. The keeper's duty was to clean the wicks, fuel the light, set the weights, and keep the light lit at all costs in all weather. Times have changed. The Coast Guardsman on duty now merely switches the automatic light on fifteen minutes before sunset and off fifteen minutes after sunrise. It flashes four blinks every thirty seconds and can be seen 25 miles at sea on a clear night. Its source is a 1,000-watt bulb magnified to an incredible 2,800,000 candlepower.

If the weather is acting up, in front of the light you'll see storm warning lights, flags and pennants on the steel-latticed tower by the road. A red pennant is the small craft warning, indicating winds to 38 mph or otherwise dangerous sea conditions. Two red pennants are the gale warning with winds to 54 mph. A single square red flag with a black center is a storm warning, forecasting winds to 73 mph. The hurricane warning, two square red and black flags, means it's about time to stop looking at warning flags and to scurry to shelter inland.

The bluff across the street from the light offers one of the more spectacular views on the Cape: Pleasant Bay, Nauset Beach, and the ocean beyond, the general site of more shipwrecks than any other area on the Atlantic or Gulf coasts of the United States. More than half the recorded shipwrecks on these coasts happened between Nauset and Nantucket and a few of the scars are still visible. Look to the distant southeast and you can see the rusting hulk of the tanker *Pendleton,* split in two by a storm in February 1952. The tides, currents, shoals and rocks off Chatham make this coast as perilous as any on the Cape. Typical of the tragic heroics of the sea so common to the Cape is the story behind the Mack Monument alongside the lighthouse.

On March 11, 1902, the coal barge *Wadena* stranded on Shoveful Shoal and a crew of five remained aboard to lighten the cargo. Six days later the weather turned exceptionally foul and the lifesaving crew of the Monomoy Station pulled through the surf in answer to distress signals from the *Wadena.* The eight-man crew of the rescue boat were experts and removed the men without undue difficulty. Their orders were to sit quietly and let the surfmen handle the boat. Heading ashore the surfboat shipped some water from the heavy seas and the bargemen panicked. Overcome with fright, the bargemen clung to the crew and the boat swung broadside to the breakers and capsized. One by one the survivors lost their grip and slid under as their strength gave out.

Another barge was anchored nearby and its captain, Elmer Mayo, had had enough of watching men drown before his eyes. In a tiny dory with oversized oars and improvised oarlocks, the capable captain rowed for the lifeboat. By the time he reached it only Seth Ellis of the lifesaving crew was still hanging on. The sea claimed twelve lives but Captain Mayo's exhibition of small boat handling skill cheated Davy Jones of one or two more. Both Mayo and Ellis were awarded Congressional Medals and the Mack family, who owned the barge, erected this granite memorial in memory of their son and the eleven others lost in the disaster.

At the rear of the Mack Monument is a small graveyard formerly used as a government cemetery for unidentified seamen washed ashore at Chatham. There is one lone headstone, that of Peter Campbell, who died aboard the brig *Oriska* off Chatham in 1856. The other 106 lie unknown and unmarked, victims of the raging breakers and treacherous shoals off Chatham that have plagued sailors since the *Mayflower* was forced to turn back by Tucker's Terror in 1620. They say that the hulls of sailing vessels sunk off this coast from 1887 to 1907 would form a solid wall from Provincetown to the tip of Monomoy.

The most famous rescue off Chatham is perhaps that of the Irish immigrant ship, the *George and Ann*. This vessel sailed from Dublin in 1729 with 190 immigrants bound for Philadelphia. These were the lace-curtain Irish of their day, mostly families of some means who brought a considerable quantity of gold aboard. The commander of the *George and Ann* was Captain Rymer, accused and later convicted of prolonging the voyage with the intention that all passengers would starve to death, leaving their goods and gold at his mercy.

Captain Rymer did not miss by much! Diseased and short of rations, the immigrant leaders faced up to the captain and forced him to change course and make for port. Raising the coast, a gale carried them toward the beach at Monomoy. When rescued by Chatham men, more than half the passengers had died, including 42 children and 14 servants. Captain Rymer was returned to the mother country in irons, tried and hanged.

The leader of the immigrants, Charles Clinton, went on to head the famed Clinton family of New York. His son George, the first governor of New York and later vice president of the United States, his son James, a Revolutionary War general, and his grandson DeWitt, a governor, senator and sponsor of the Erie Canal, were three of the more illustrious of the line. Another grandson, Sir Henry, was a leading British general in the Revolution and defeated his Uncle James in a memorable battle at — Fort Clinton.

Drive down the Shore Road to Chatham Light in all kinds of weather, particularly in a pea soup fog of the kind only Chatham can produce. Beautiful and moody in any season, the view from the bluff is a fine way to feel the pulse of Cape Cod.

CHATHAM FISH PIER

In Chatham as in Provincetown, fishing is serious business. Chatham fishermen account for close to five million pounds of fish each year, with about 35 long line vessels working out of Chatham Fish Pier on a regular basis.

A visitor receives special treatment at Chatham; the pier features an observation deck above the unloading area that gives the tourist and photographer a ringside seat. From about 2 to 5 each afternoon, except Fridays, the boats return and unload at the pier. The men don't fish on Friday because they've already supplied the traditional Friday market on Thursday afternoon. From the observation deck you look right down on the decks as the men pitchfork fish from deck wells into the metal conveyor bucket that lifts the headless cod and dumps them down the chute to be boxed and iced in the packing room. This local industry brought $1.8 million to Chatham in 1971.

The fishermen of Chatham leave the pier early, always before dawn, their decks lined with brilliantly colored buoys and tubs containing baited lines. Chatham's fishermen use long lines, sometimes many hundreds of feet long, that are payed out slowly over the sea. Short hooked and baited drop lines are spaced every few inches and each end of the long line is kept afloat with one of the colorful buoys. Several hours later the boat returns, hauls in each of the long lines, and stores the fish in the refrigerated deck wells.

When the boats are unloaded at the pier, the fish are iced and packed, 125 pounds to a box, loaded into refrigerated trailer trucks, and shipped on to New York, where jobbers buy them in the wee hours and have them on sale at the Fulton Fish Market less than 24 hours after they were plucked from the sea. Fishing is not as good as it used to be due to the enormous influx of foreign boats in our offshore areas. The few hundred fishermen of Chatham have joined the clamor of protest but to date little has been done to curb the huge foreign fleets raiding traditional American fishing grounds.

Those boxes of fish heads you may see on the dock were thrown to the gulls years ago, but are now sold to lobstermen to bait their traps. A few lobstermen operate out of Chatham and most of their catch finds a ready market locally. The retail fish store on the pier handles a good proportion of them.

Chatham Fish Pier has become such a visitor attraction that you'll see many of the town's street signs have an extra directional marker to help you find it. It's located about a mile north of Chatham Light on Shore Road.

ATWOOD HOUSE (1752)

Captain Joseph C. Atwood was originally an Eastham man, a pre-Revolutionary deepwater sea captain in the early days of international trade. On a voyage to Honduras in 1749 in the tiny snow *Judith,* he was cautioned to watch for Spanish warships and "to put up a manly defense" if attacked. To Chatham's good fortune, the captain's "manly defense" was never challenged.

On his return, the captain bought 30 acres in Chatham and in 1752 built his Mansion House, as the gambrel-roof cottage was referred to in his will. Passed from father to eldest son through the years, the old home was inherited by young John Atwood in about 1830. In 1832 John courted and won Miss Marjorie Smith of Chatham Port and brought her to his Mansion House. Visibly disappointed by her reaction, John admitted he might have gilded the lily a bit but explained, "Heck, that was only courting talk, Margie!" John did get cracking, however, and built on a new ell for his bride without even waiting for the first baby.

Gambrel-roof homes were rare on the Cape in the early days and the old Atwood House is a fine example of one of the earliest. The gambrel roof developed as a means of securing a spacious second story while maintaining the basic design of a typical Cape.

Atwood House today is the headquarters and museum of the Chatham Historical Society. Beautifully preserved and restored, the rooms are furnished with period antiques, while more recent wings house outstanding museum artifacts and collections. The Joseph C. Lincoln Wing is dedicated to the memory of the Cape's most famous author, a long-time summer resident of Chatham. The newer Durand Wing houses three fine collections donated by friends of the society; a beautiful grouping of seashells from all parts of the world, an exquisite collection of threaded Sandwich glass, and a fine collection of vases, figurines and busts in Parian ware, an unglazed porcelain of great beauty. On the lawn of Atwood House is mounted an early turret from one of the twin lighthouses of Chatham. The precise French lenses are mounted and operated as they were in 1923.

Atwood House is located on Stage Harbor Road a mile from the center of town. It is open from 2 to 5 P.M. on Monday, Wednesday and Friday from late spring to early fall and a nominal admission fee is charged.

CHATHAM RAILROAD MUSEUM

A major summertime attraction in Chatham is the well-known railroad museum housed in the original Victorian depot that served the town from 1887 to 1937. As might be expected, it's located on Depot Street, a few hundred yards off Old Harbor Road, just a short way from the center of town. The museum is town-owned, manned by volunteers, and open free of charge from 2 to 5 P.M. on weekdays from late June to mid-September.

Railroad buffs come from miles around to pore over the thousands of items of memorabilia. There is much here to interest almost everyone, with nostalgic memories for older folks and a real wooden caboose to delight youngsters.

Inside, the depot has the original dispatching and ticket office with the telegrapher's key clicking away and the room arranged to give the impression that the station agent just stepped out and will be back in a minute. Ticket racks are ready, timetables are posted, and except for the fact that there is only 50 feet of track outside, the three-hour scheduled run to Boston sounds inviting. The waiting room is filled with photographs, documents, equipment, models, and other bits and pieces of interest.

Chathamites were agitating for a rail spur as early as 1863. Three weeks before the Battle of Gettysburg a petition was circulated to call a special town meeting to raise $50,000 toward the project, but it was not until 1887 that the project was completed and Chatham connected by a branch to the main line at Harwich. At one time more than 22,000 passengers traveled annually and the complex included a repair shop, fuel depot, water tower, and turntable to reverse the locomotives back on the spur to Harwich.

The station was a gift to the town from a railroad buff, Mrs. Jacob Cox, wife of a rail executive, who purchased the abandoned depot in 1951. The museum has been fortunate in its volunteer management. The committee chairman, Frank Love, was associated with the New York Central for thirty-seven years and prevailed on his old employers to donate the fine old caboose now open to the public outside.

GODFREY WINDMILL (1797)

Built by Colonel Benjamin Godfrey, this grist mill had an active business career of over a hundred years. In its working days it sat farther to the southwest on Mill Hill behind Stage Harbor and also served as a major landmark for incoming fishermen. With a fair wind, a not uncommon commodity in Chatham, the old mill could reduce a bag of corn to meal in ten minutes.

The Godfred Windmill was given to the town and moved to its present location in 1956. To reach it take Cross Street from Town Hall a couple of hundred yards and turn into Shattuck Place. The old mill sits high with a fine view. It's at the head of Chase Park, which is also noted for its picnic area and bowling on the green. The mill is open daily except Sundays from 10 A.M. to 5 P.M. during July and August. Occasionally, during these months, the town will release the brakes and grind some corn just as was done in 1797.

BAND CONCERTS

Every Friday evening during July and August the Chatham Band offers free concerts in Kate Gould Park on Main Street. As many as 5,000 people attend these concerts in this beautiful little natural amphitheater. Each program includes musical numbers by the band, folk dances for the children, dance numbers for grownups, and community singing for everyone.

Members of the colorfully uniformed forty-piece band live in Chatham and surrounding towns and are joined by visiting musicians during the summer. An unpaid volunteer group supported by the town, the Chatham Band rehearses throughout the off-season to provide a professional flourish to these evenings of old-fashioned fun. Summer evenings tend to be cool, so bring some heavier wraps and a blanket or folding chair. Kate Gould Park is on Main at the corner of Chatham Bars Avenue.

THE WIGHT MURALS

Chathamites have at times been inclined to brag about their worldliness but none had ever gone so far as to claim attendance at the Last Supper. But there they were, fully recognizable, and darned if the supper wasn't baked beans and brown bread. A second mural depicts Christ Preaching to the Multitude. Christ is represented by a fisherman preaching from a boat, and the multitude are members of the Chatham parish of the First Congregational Church, c. 1932.

Mrs. Alice S. Wight painted her famous murals in 1932 and 1935. For several years they hung on the church wall and caused quite a stir. Newspapers across the country picked up the story and tourists flocked to see them in the old church. The commotion was a bit too much for the parish; perhaps it made them a bit uneasy to have their neighbors peeking over their shoulder at services (and pity the poor member who didn't show up in either scene).

For many years now, the murals have been displayed in a small barn near the end of Stage Harbor Road. About 50 yards past Bridge Street on the right is a split rail fence and path leading to the barn. Admission is free but children, canes, and umbrellas are not permitted.

SYLVAN GARDENS

A beautiful and charming display of daffodils, tulips and other spring flowers is located on the private estate of Rolf E. Sylvan, horticulturist. The setting is entirely natural; wooded paths flow with over five hundred varieties of daffodils in colorful drifts, interspersed with a wide range of choice spring plants and flowers. The garden is at its height in late April and the first week in May.

Sylvan began his gardens in about 1938, gradually expanding his plantings in harmony with the landscape throughout the several acres of rolling woodland around his home. The shady paths of Sylvan Gardens are delightful throughout the flowering season as displays of tuberous begonias and others come to the fore.

One should keep in mind that this is a private estate that the owner has been kind enough to permit the public to visit and enjoy. Please be careful where you walk and do not pick flowers or disturb the plants in any way.

Sylvan Gardens may be reached by Balfour Lane off Route 28 in Chatham, next to the Chatham furniture store. Keep bearing right and drive slowly, for children are playing in the area.

MONOMOY WILDLIFE REFUGE

Stand on the bluffs along the outer beach and you'll notice that the waves are usually coming ashore at an angle rather than head on. Ocean waves are formed by the wind, which drags against the water surface and transfers its energy into waves. In this area the largest and most active waves come from the northeast. Each northeast wave picks up sand as it comes in, and deposits it just a little farther south. The total effect is the steady erosion of the cliffs of Wellfleet and Eastham and the movement of this sand southward along Nauset and Monomoy.

Three or four thousand years ago neither Nauset Beach nor Monomoy Island existed. The movement of the sand goes on today and Monomoy grows farther and farther southward each year. Now more than eight miles long, Monomoy Island and a small part of Morris Island have been preserved as a National Wilderness Area. This assures permanent protection of the islands' primitive and unspoiled environment for this and future generations.

When the area was acquired as a wildlife refuge in 1944, Morris and Monomoy islands were attached by land. In 1960 a raging sea broke through and made a true island out of Monomoy. In time the two islands may be rejoined; in fact it is expected that they will, for they have been rejoined by the sea each of the many times they have been separated in the past.

About a hundred years ago the south end of Monomoy Island was a thriving fishing community with docks, schools and homes. The old cast iron lighthouse, no longer in use, is all that remains to remind us of this era.

Monomoy is a typical barrier beach island of sand dunes, salt- and freshwater marshes, freshwater ponds and sparse sand dune vegetation. It serves as a link in the chain of migratory bird refuges in the Atlantic Flyway, which extends from Canada to Florida and the Gulf. Over three hundred species of birds have been recorded, including nesting waterfowl, gulls and terns. Many species may be seen in bright nuptial plumage during the spring migration, which reaches its peak in May. Beginning in late July, adult shorebirds and their young may be seen in winter plumage. The Hudsonian godwit, a bird that seldom stops en route to its wintering grounds in South America, frequents the island during this fall migration.

Monomoy is important to waterfowl, particularly the black duck, Canada goose and green-winged teal, all of which nest on the refuge. During the fall and winter, hundreds of thousands of eiders and scoters congregate over mussel beds in the offshore shoal areas east of Monomoy. Animals isolated on Monomoy include the white-tailed deer, muskrat and occasionally otter, mink, raccoon and weasel.

A number of wildlife tours of Monomoy are sponsored by the Audubon Society from late May to early September. The tour is a day-long wilderness trip for those willing and able to rough it. Information about cost, schedules, and reservations may be secured from the Wellfleet Bay Wildlife Sanctuary, South Wellfleet, Mass. 02663.

Other than the Audubon tour, you must make your own boating arrangements to visit the sanctuary. Monomoy is ideally suited to nature study, surf fishing, hiking, photography and similar activities. Camping is not permitted.

MONOMOY THEATER

The many summer theaters of Cape Cod are all a bit different. Monomoy Theater on Main Street in Chatham is academic theatre at its best. Sponsored by Ohio University, the undergraduate and graduate students of Christopher Lane are guided and supported by a resident company of about twenty professionals, bringing to Chatham one of the prime showcase for university theater to be found in the country. Audiences, theater critics and professional producers are unanimous in their acclaim for the high quality of theater training and fare offered at Monomoy.

Christopher Lane's Ohio University Players came to Chatham in 1958. A typical season features a variety of eight plays running from Wednesday through Saturday evenings in July and August. Monomoy traditionally ends its season with a Shakespearian comedy produced and directed by Miss Kathleen Stafford of the Old Vic Theatre in Bristol, England. Miss Stafford is a recognized authority on Elizabethan drama and she has brought a welcome tradition to Chatham.

In recent years the theater has also presented chamber music concerts for summer audiences. The series was expanded in 1972 to five concerts spread over three weekends. Two preseason concerts took place in late June, another on a Sunday in late July and the final two on Labor Day weekend as usual. Fine professional artists present the works of a wide range of American and European composers. You can secure current information by writing to Monomoy Theater in the spring.

PUBLIC GOLF COURSE

There is one 9-hole public golf course in Chatham. Chatham Bars is a 2,325-yard, par 34 course. The pro shop and first tee are a few yards in on Seaview Avenue off Shore Road.

PUBLIC SWIMMING BEACHES

Visitors to Chatham must pay a daily parking fee or purchase a weekly or seasonal pass to use the town's four major saltwater beaches. Cockle Cove and Ridgervale beaches are located off Route 28 in South Chatham. Hardings Beach is reached from Barn Hill Road in West Chatham, and Oyster Pond Beach is on Queen Anne Road near the Chatham village center. Another dozen or so town landings provide fine swimming but parking facilities are severely limited.

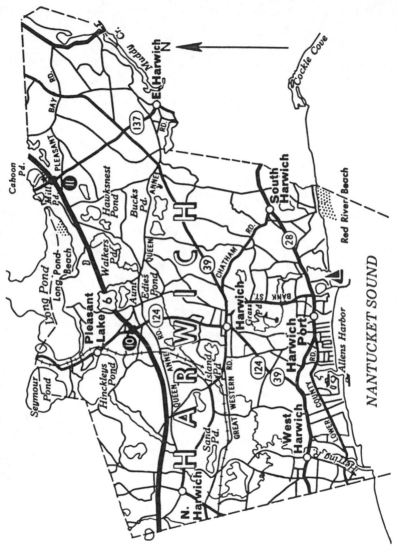

Copyright, The National Survey, 1973
Chester, Vermont

CHAPTER XIII

Harwich

Henry Ford once complained that "history is bunk." I wouldn't be surprised if the people of Harwich agree; every time this very old Cape town claims some of their history, they have to fight off a Johnny-come-lately interloper. When they speak with pride of their early settlers, Brewster quickly points out, "Well, yes, but of course they came to Brewster, even if it was called Harwich in those days." Then when they try to substantiate their valid claim to some of our earliest deepwater captains by reference to such as Captain John Kenrick, Orleans is quick to remind them that this area is now known as South Orleans. Even William Nickerson of Chatham tried to annex a few thousand acres of Harwich — it was probably the only battle he ever lost.

Old Harwich covered all the area bounded by present-day Dennis on the west and Eastham and Chatham on the east. The first recorded settler was John Wing, a substantial Sandwich Quaker who moved to the shores of present-day Brewster in 1656. John Dillingham and others soon followed and the bayside settlement was underway. Some years later a Yarmouth man, John Mecoy, was given a parcel of land on the South Shore by the local Sachem. As the tract was only 36 acres, the court confirmed his deed in 1667 rather than risk another Nickerson escapade. A year or two later Gershom

Hall established residence in the same area now known as South Harwich, the first settlement within the confines of the present town. For many years South Harwich was treated as a part of the Nickerson neighborhood, and it was the bayside village of the Wings and Dillinghams that developed into the Town of Harwich, incorporated in 1694.

When it came time for old Harwich to divide itself into two towns, it reversed the pattern of the earlier settlements. When a town spawned a new precinct, the usual process was to consider the new settlement as the candidate for town status. In Harwich, the new South Parish retained the old name and the original North Parish spun off as Brewster in 1803.

By 1744 settlers on the south side were weary of traveling the long and rough track to the meeting house in the north, and asked to be set off as a separate precinct. They were twice refused, but a petition two years later was approved by Boston despite the bitter opposition of the Reverend Stone and members of the mother parish in present-day Brewster. Work was begun on the meeting house, a small, crude two-story structure a short distance west of the present First Congregational Church in Harwich center. Its construction was along orthodox lines; even the two stairways to the gallery were segregated by the sexes lest the Lord be offended by a mixed congregation.

The Reverend Edward Pell was quickly engaged by the new south parish, his salary set at 16 bushels of Rye, 10 bushels of wheat, 100 bushels of corn and 16 cords of oak or 20 of pine "cut and drawn to his house." In 1748 he received a cost of living increase — 5 loads of hay — and further increases in following years, all in commodities. When Pell's pay was slow to come in, which was generally the case, cash equivalents were accepted in lieu of produce. This presumably accounted for what little pocket money the parson was expected to enjoy. The Reverend Pell died of illness at age forty-one, in 1752, and at his own request was buried in the north parish cemetery. He feared his own little south parish would be "overgrown with pines and overlooked at the resurrection" — such was the outlook of his day.

Reverend Pell's salary suffered not only from the seasonal vagaries of farming, but also from an ecclesiastical tug of war. Throughout his ministry the orthodox church in Harwich was under attack from numerous splinter sects eternally at odds over the payment of ministerial taxes levied by the Congregationalists. Eventually, the south parish of Harwich managed to split into fifteen different denominations, all meeting within its bounds.

In 1744 Elisha Paine of Connecticut, a zealous itinerant preacher, visited with relatives in the town. He represented a separatist sect known as the New Lights and must have converted more than a few people. A letter from him raptured that "the pine woods of Harwich ring hallelujahs and hosannas, even from babes. I never heard the like before from little ones, from six years old and upwards. God is bringing them in from the hedges." In 1749 the first New Light Church was formed in Harwich and a meeting house built in the western part of town two years later.

Harwich quickly became the center of religious unrest on the Cape. Separatists preached the doctrine of hope — salvation was there for any who would reach out for it. Men grown weary of the hellfire inevitability of Treat and Mather left the established church in droves to form New Light and Baptist societies. The Congregational Church in Harwich flickered and flamed over the years. At times the same minister preached in both the Congregational and Baptist churches; at other times the parish endured long periods without more than occasional spiritual guidance. In 1792 the divided congregation forged enough of a consensus to build a new meeting house just east of the old and attracted the Reverend Nathan Underwood as minister. Baptist sympathizers soon took exception to the orthodox parson and when Reverend Underwood retired in 1819 he had only one male member left in his tiny flock. The Reverend's major claim to fame seems to be that he crossed the Delaware with Washington. The unimpressed Baptists incorporated in 1798 and the Methodists followed suit in 1809.

By 1832 the second meeting house, although only forty years old, had become dilapidated and was deemed unfit as a house of worship. It was auctioned off in six lots: the porch for $35, the roof for $21, and the building below the roof in quarters for an average $26.50 each. The proceeds were used to fence in the graveyard.

Work began on the present church a few feet east of the old site in the same year. Despite the multitude of separatist groups, the congregation prospered and an extensive renovation was undertaken in 1854. It was at this time that the new steeple was added, soaring more than a hundred feet, and highlighting what many consider one of the most beautiful churches on the Cape.

The years prior to the Civil War saw new schisms rend the churches. Many of those debating the establishment chose their righteous motive from the antislavery issue sweeping the North. How, they asked, could one support a church that preached Christianity but condoned slavery? Those who broke away for any reason were called "Come Outers," those who remained "Standpatters" — nicknames that applied to one's politics as well as his religion.

Two Harwich sea captains of the 1840s tussled with the problem in their own way. In 1844 Captain Jonathan Walker was captured and branded as a slave stealer when he tried to smuggle slaves to freedom from Florida. Another captain, whose identity failed to survive his deed, accepted payment to run a slave to freedom but turned him in as a runaway instead. Captain Walker traveled the North as an ardent abolitionist lecturer about the same time as a group of distinguished antislavery advocates traveled to Harwich to hold an indignation meeting on the unnamed captain's home ground.

The case was stated against the proslavery captain without mentioning his name. Unawed and unbowed, the captain himself took the platform and said that a friend had just told him that he had been accused of stealing. The captain contradicted nothing, merely told the story from his own point of view. The fact that the meeting soon degenerated into an absolute riot only emphasizes the fact that the moral issues were not quite so clearcut in those days of rugged individualism as they appear in hindsight.

Come Outers, the New Lights of a later day, often led in prompting social change and higher moral values, but like most religious fanatics they sometimes indulged in antics that alternately humored and distressed their strait-laced townsmen. Kittredge reports that "frequently, when under the spell of their mania, they walked along the tops of fences instead of on the sidewalks; affected a strange, springing gait, and conversed by singing instead of by ordinary speech, in the distressing manner of characters in light opera. A favorite tune for the purpose was 'Old Dan Tucker.'" Most of the victims of Come Outerism recovered after a time, and the sect disappeared altogether after the Civil War.

The first minister of the south parish, Reverend Pell, was a bit hasty in his fear that Harwich might disappear without a trace. In the mid-1700s Harwich boasted one of the largest fishing fleets on the Cape, and as late as 1860 had eighty schooners gambling full holds of cod against the cross rips of the Georges Bank, a day's sail from home. Even before commercial fishing began its slide, many a Harwich captain came to realize that there was more money ashore farming cranberries on the marshland playgrounds of his boyhood.

Along this shore where fishing once prospered and cranberries still do, summer tourists now hold sway. Harwich has six villages in its 21 square miles with extensive frontage on warm, undertow-free Nantucket Sound. Attractive Harwich Port with its seacoast village charm and Harwich Center around the old South Parish Church draw most of the visitors today. When you're in the center look about 75 yards to the left of the library for a tiny shed with the inscription "Old Powder House. Used by the town of Harwich 1770–1864." Judging by its size, the old town counted heavily on talking its way out of trouble.

CRANBERRIES

Cranberries have long been recognized as Cape Cod's major agricultural asset. What many do not realize is that in most years, southeastern Massachusetts bogs, primarily on Cape Cod, are responsible for producing nearly half of the U.S. cranberry crop.

Harwich is still a leader in Cape cranberry production as it was when the berries were first cultivated commercially 125 years ago. The town has ideal conditions for them: extensive marshes bordering on shallow ponds, convenient sand banks, a long growing season, and a short haul to major markets.

Wild cranberries have long grown in profusion on the Cape. The Indians made little use of them except as a tonic to quiet the nerves, and as there was little sugar to use as a sweetener, the early settlers almost ignored the fruit. They did send a gift of ten barrels to Charles II in 1677 along with other local produce, for cranberries were known and appreciated in England at the time. As sugar became available "cranberry consarve" became popular, but it was not until about 1816 that Henry Hall of Dennis stumbled on a method of cultivation. A sandslide covered some of his wild cranberry vines and he noticed that they flourished as never before. The sand piles you sometimes see by today's bogs are the result of this lesson. When the bogs are drained in the spring, clean sand is spread over the plants and new green growth soon replaces the purple mantle of winter.

It was not until 1840–1845 that cranberry culture took on any commercial importance. There seems little doubt that the men of Harwich were the early leaders, but there is considerable doubt as to who the first commercial grower really was. Alvin Cahoon, Zebine Small, Nathaniel Robbins — all were pioneers, but it depends on whose relative you talk to as to who was first. Alvin Cahoon's old bog alongside Route 124 before Hinckley's Pond is given the credit by the historical society, and it's still a fine producing bog.

By 1860 it was estimated that each acre of producing bog was worth about $10,000, a good price today. These were the days of hand picking. Cord lines were drawn across the bog in the fall and men, women and children moved down the lanes on their knees. Gloved, bonneted, aproned and overalled, they stripped the sharp vines by hand. Cranberry harvest time was hard work but it was also a gala social occasion. Schools either recessed for the event or lost half their students to the bogs. Many a youngster earned little more than the cost of repairs to his torn clothes, but few wanted to miss the working picnic. The Brooks Academy Museum has a copy of the harvest orders posted by Captain Nathaniel Robbins in 1863. For those who picked neat and clean the pay was 40 cents a bushel.

Before the turn of the century the cranberry scoop came into general use, the wooden pronged scoop that is popular today as a magazine rack. Cranberry picking soon ceased to be a pleasant village reunion and became a businesslike undertaking. The industrious Portuguese were soon doing most of the work and the youngsters stayed in school.

There are now several mechanical methods of harvesting cranberries. Some machines scoop berries from dry bogs; others shake berries free in flooded bogs so that they float to the surface. Harvesting is generally done in October, but if you don't keep a sharp eye out it's all over before you notice it.

Drought and frost are the cranberry's greatest enemies. You'll notice that all the bogs are ditched and diked with sluice gates so that they can be flooded and drained as necessary. A cranberry freeze warning from the weather bureau will find them all flooded by morning. They remain that way through the winter and often serve as fine, safe hockey rinks for youngsters.

Green in summer, maroon in the autumn, and purple

over the winter, the many cranberry bogs of the Cape add colorful splashes to the landscape. You'll find them all over, but in Harwich you might visit Alvin Cahoon's old bog just north of the Mid-Cape Highway on Route 124. Others decorate the landscape on Bank Street between Harwich and Harwich Port, and when you know what you're looking for you'll spot them all over the Cape.

BROOKS ACADEMY MUSEUM

The first vocational course offered on Cape Cod was at the school of navigation established by Sidney Brooks in Harwich in 1844. Known in its day as the Pine Grove Seminary, the beautiful white-columned structure is now known as Brooks Academy and houses the Harwich Historical Society and its museum.

Pine Grove Seminary was the leading academic institution in this area for over twenty years, offering English studies, higher mathematics (including navigation and surveying), and language courses primarily for students preparing for college. Brooks closed his school in 1866 in favor of teaching on the state school ship, and sold the building to the town in 1869. Brooks Academy was used as a public school and became the town high school in 1883. In 1887 a relative, Colonel H. C. Brooks, placed $1,000 at interest "to be annually expended for a suitable medal for every school in town, to be donated once every year to the pupil in each school who is most proficient in composition and letter-writing and most excellent of behavior."

The Historical Society Museum is located on the second floor and is open Monday, Wednesday, and Friday from 1:30 to 4:30 P.M. during July and August. Admission is free. Members of the society will show you Indian artifacts, treasures brought home by Harwich sea captains, Sandwich glass, cranberry tools, toys, and many other interesting mementos of the past. You may sit and enjoy maps and pictures of Harwich in its early days, read old magazines and newspapers such as the long-defunct *Har-*

wich Independent, or perhaps glance through old diaries such as that of Mrs. Elisha Robbins who wrote of a Sunday in 1854, "Mr. Spilstead preaches on slavery? Burns the fugitive from slavery was carried back to the south about a week ago — May the Lord deliver us from the religion of this country!"

ROGERS STATUARY

In the late nineteenth century almost every home displayed some statuary in the parlor. Original works by noted sculptors were beyond the reach of most families, so John Rogers devised and patented a method of mass producing his sentimental mid-Victorian figures. At the height of his popularity many thousands were sold at prices ranging from $6 to $25. His Rogers Groups were to sculpture what Currier and Ives were to lithography. Popular from the Civil War to the turn of the century, they are much sought after by the antique collectors of today.

The second largest private collection of Rogers Groups is on display at the Brooks Library at the corner of Main and Bank streets in Harwich center. This collection was started in 1881 by Pliny Nickerson, a South Harwich native and Boston shipping tycoon who gave 40 groups to his town library. Today 68 of the 80 published groups are on display in the Rogers Wing of the library, designed as a comfortable sitting room.

John Rogers was born in Salem in 1829. He was trained as an engineer but forced by failing eyesight to work as a machinist. He began modeling in clay as a pastime and his early clay group "The Slave Auction" (December 1859) was an immediate success. Highly publicized by the abolitionists, he reproduced the piece in plaster molds and his work quickly caught on with the general public. After the war Rogers began casting in bronze and set up a factory to manufacture these delicate duplicates in clay-colored plaster at a price the public could afford.

The "People's Sculptor" produced 208 known works of all sizes and subjects of which only the eighty small

groups, none more than 30 inches high, were mass produced. These have always been known as Rogers Groups
as they are simply that — groups of ordinary people engaged in everyday activities, groups of historical figures,
and groups with a social message. His "Weighing the
Baby," "Checkers," "Coming to the Parson," and "Politics"
will tickle your fancy with their old-fashioned yet timeless
humor and sentiment. Above all, the Rogers Groups offer
an accurate record and picture of the period.

Brooks Library is open from 1 to 4 P.M. daily except
Sunday, and Tuesday and Thursday evenings from 7 to 9.

THE BRANDED HAND

In the 1840s the antislavery issue was under hot debate
in the North; abolitionists shouting for immediate emancipation, "free soilers" content to limit slavery to the
South. Cape men were vocal in their opinions and one,
Captain Jonathan Walker of Harwich, stood up to be
counted when the opportunity came his way.

Commanding a small West Indiaman, he put in at Pen-
sacola in 1844. Seven fugitive slaves begged passage to a
British port and Captain Walker took them aboard. Running contraband slaves was a serious crime well understood by the captain, but he immediately set sail,
determined to deliver his cargo to the Bahamas. Rounding
the Florida Keys he hailed a passing schooner to trade for
rations needed for his unexpected guests. It was his ill
fortune that the schooner's captain was a Southerner who
had heard of the slaves' escape and the reward for Walker.

Returned to Florida, Walker was publicly ridiculed and
abused, imprisoned in irons for eleven months, branded
as a "slave stealer" and released.

The branded "SS" on the palm of his right hand was
intended to teach the Yankee captain a lesson. It did. On
his return to New England, Captain Walker embarked on
a four-year lecture tour that inspired the abolitionists and
stirred the mind and pen of John Greenleaf Whittier in
his poem "The Branded Hand," a part of which reads:

Hold it up before our sunshine, up against our Northern air;
Ho! Men of Massachusetts, for the love of God, Look there!
Take it henceforth for your standard, the Bruce's heart of yore,
In the dark strife closing round ye, let that hand be seen before.

JOHN LONG HOUSE (1765)

The oldest house now standing in Harwich is the John Long House, at the corner of Chatham Road on the north side of Route 28 in South Harwich. A historical marker by the front door identifies the property, which is privately owned and not open for inspection.

John Long's home is a traditional full Cape beginning to show its age after more than two hundred years. According to the town record of 1765, Farmer Long's new house covered 924 square feet and included fourteen windows with 64 square feet of glass. Houses were assessed by their windows in those days and this one was valued at $500, a sizable amount.

John's wife Jane committed suicide in 1778 by hanging herself by her neckerchief in the South Harwich woods. This unhappy woman had long been considered mentally deranged by the town. The Longs' son became one of the most respected citizens of Harwich. Known as Squire John, he occupied the family homestead until his death in 1865.

WYCHMERE HARBOR

Just east of Harwich Port, past Snow Inn Road on Route 28, is a small parking area overlooking beautiful Wychmere Harbor, one of the most picturesque on the Cape.

Years ago the little harbor was called Salt Water Pond, a tiny body of water tucked in between the highway and the Sound. Retiring sea captains looking for excitement after the Civil War laid out a racetrack around the pond. It made a perfect half-mile oval and they raced their sulkies in the same spirit they used to race their ships. Fifty bushels of oats was considered a good stake.

In 1880 Rinaldo Eldridge opened the Sea View Hotel on

the north bank and attracted "summer people" and racing buffs from off the Cape to enjoy the sport. The Sea View was the first of the large summer hotels in Harwich. Quahog chowder was the house specialty, and on July 4, 1881, records show that some two thousand persons were served in the pavilion. The Sea View Hotel burned in 1892, but by then Snow Inn carried on the tradition in Harwich Port and the following year the famed Belmont Hotel went up in West Harwich.

After the Sea View burned and a storm or two had broken through the slender dike holding back the sea, the town figured it was a more suitable place to land fish than to race horses. A channel was cut and the pond dredged in 1899; summer cottages sprang up along the shore and the little toy harbor came into being. The Indians had called the area Annosarakumitt; a real estate developer felt that Wychmere better suited his purposes, and so it has been known ever since.

CROWELL BIRDS

A. Elmer Crowell, the Bird Maker of Harwich, is honored by exhibits of his art in many major museums in America and Europe. A pudgy, unassuming Cape Codder, he generally preferred to avoid the limelight and was quite content to whittle away in his little shop on Main Street, East Harwich, spinning tales of the time when he was young, skinny, and a crack shot. He would be pleased, I'm sure, with the collection of his miniatures on display at the Cape Cod Five Cent Savings Bank, Harwich Port, a Harwich institution even older than he.

Born in 1862, young Elmer Crowell had no thought of becoming an artist — his interest was shooting. When he was fifteen, he and a number of neighboring children enjoyed a summer of art lessons by Miss Emily King who was summering at "The Port," and he recalled painting among others a picture of a duck. His first finished scene was of the old Wading Place Bridge across Muddy Creek on the Chatham border. Art as a career was far from his mind.

A few years later young Elmer was caring for a private camp whose Harvard members were having trouble with their decoys — they weren't fooling the ducks. "I can make better decoys than those," said Crowell, and he did. His early duck decoys were sturdy, simplified forms with little detail, but obviously good "callers." His reputation spread and Crowell decoys rose in demand.

In later years he made fewer and fewer decoys and spent more time and skill turning out the daintier decorative birds. About seventy-five different birds made up his songless aviary, about equally divided among ducks, shore birds, and songbirds. He learned the habits and characteristics of each of his subjects and portrayed each with Audubon accuracy in pose and coloration. He soon found that highly decorated birds destined for the mantle brought a better price than those destined for the marsh.

Crowell's artistic reproductions were always carved in white cedar, cut in winter and seasoned for three to four years. He carved birds, and sometimes fish, for more than fifty years until rheumatism forced him to stop in the 1930s. His son Cleon continued in his father's trade for many years after. In trying to identify a Crowell shorebird decoy, look for two characteristics of his work: the separation of wing tips from the tail and a dark brushmark through the eyes. The most positive identification is the Crowell stamp on the base. Birds from 1900 bear an oval stamp with the words "A. Elmer Crowell Decoys, East Harwich, Mass."

There are three major Crowell collections on the Cape: this collection of miniatures at the bank and groups at the Heritage Plantation in Sandwich and the Mary Lincoln House in Centerville. Many of the best carvings depict birds in natural settings: sandpipers feeding on a piece of old driftwood, chickadees poised on a pine cone, woodpeckers hammering on a fragment of chestnut.

It's interesting that Elmer Crowell was an intimate

friend of Joe Lincoln, the Cape's foremost author. He was always quite proud of the fact that he was the prototype of Lincoln's legendary character "Queer Judson." Like Sandwich glass and Lincoln books, Crowell birds live on as symbols of the craftsmanship of Cape Cod.

HARWICH JUNIOR THEATER

Children's theater in Harwich is a delight for audiences of all ages. Each July and August the Harwich Junior Theater presents four plays drawn from a great children's repertoire: adventures from the best in children's literature, tales from other countries, classic fairy tales, and premieres of original children's plays. With a nucleus of professionals and a crew of devoted children and adult amateurs, Harwich Junior Theater introduces youngsters on both sides of the footlights to the fascinating joys of live theater. Each production runs for two weeks, on Tuesday, Wednesday and Thursday evenings.

The theater offers a variety of educational programs for youngsters. A theater workshop for children over ten teaches them just what goes into a good production. Drama workshops for grade-schoolers help them discover how to express the creativity within themselves. An apprentice program is open to high school and college students interested in special areas of theater, such as acting, theater history, and playwriting. In performance, as well as in preparation, the children work with the adults and professionals.

Harwich Junior Theater is located at the corner of Willow and Division streets in West Harwich near the Dennis Port line. Admission is nominal and the children will love this theater — just for them.

PUBLIC GOLF COURSE

There is one 9-hole golf course in Harwich open to the public. Harwich Port Golf Club is located a few hundred yards from the center of Harwich Port on the corner of

South and Forrest streets. The course is a 2,643-yard, par 35. Pull carts are available at the clubhouse.

PUBLIC SWIMMING BEACHES

Harwich boasts many fine beaches on pleasantly warm Nantucket Sound and on several of the freshwater ponds that dot the landscape. They have even squeezed one in on their short frontage on Pleasant Bay just north of the Chatham line.

Major saltwater beaches are located at the end of Pleasant and Earle roads in West Harwich, Bank Street in Harwich Port and Deep Hole Road in South Harwich, which leads to Red River Beach. Fresh water beaches are available on Long Pond north of Harwich center, Bucks Pond in the Great Sand Lake area, and on Sand Pond in North Harwich. Seasonal parking stickers may be purchased at the police station by temporary residents or a daily parking fee paid at the beach.

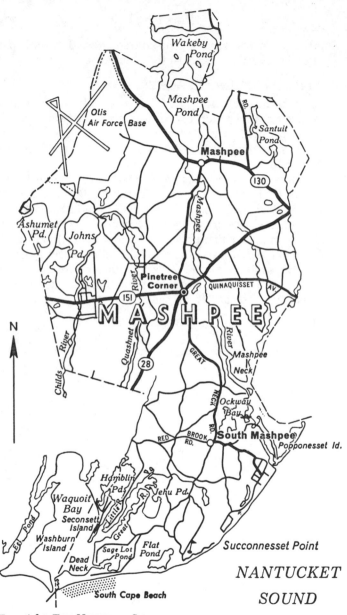

Copyright, THE NATIONAL SURVEY, 1973
Chester, Vermont

CHAPTER XIV

Mashpee

And here, fellow immigrants, is the oldest of the old Cape Cod. Cape Cod was an ancestral home of the Wampanoag Indians, and Mashpee is their last stand.

Long before the Pilgrims landed, the thirty-odd tribes of the Wampanoag Federation, probably 40,000 strong, pitched their wigwams and cultivated their crops in an orderly and organized tribal society throughout eastern Massachusetts, Narragansett Bay and Cape Cod. A part of the great Algonquin Nation, the Wampanoags' loosely related tribes and subtribes were bound by a common language and mutual dependence for subsistence and defense. Each tribe was led by a chief or Sachem and all paid homage to the great hereditary Sagamore Massasoit. It was from a tribe of the Wampanoag that Massachusetts took its name. The suffix "sett" in so many of the Indian names still used on the Cape means "by the water"; the Massachusett tribe occupied a "great hill by the water" near present-day Boston.

There were several major tribes on the Cape and many subtribes. The major tribes were the Nausets of the Lower Cape, the Mattacheese of Yarmouth and Barnstable, the Suconessetts of Falmouth, the Manomets of Sandwich and the Massipees of Mashpee. Plague brought by the white man scourged the Wampanoag Federation in 1617–1618 and the arrival of the *Mayflower* found them at a low ebb.

The Indians extended the hand of friendship and a treaty of peace and mutual assistance was concluded with Massasoit. The pact was scrupulously observed by the Cape tribes for all time — and for a somewhat shorter period by the English.

By 1646 the Indian villages around Sandwich, Barnstable, Yarmouth and Eastham had been largely displaced by settlements of the white man, and new settlers were rapidly crowding the Indians out elsewhere. The General Court in Plymouth tried to be fair with the red men but the Indians were doomed to come out second best. Shiploads of immigrants pushed the frontiers ever farther into Wampanoag territory, and the best the Pilgrim fathers could do was to disguise the struggle for land with the trappings of law and equity. The naïve Indians had little concept of land ownership. To them a sale merely permitted their white friends to farm, hunt and fish the area just as they did. When the white man fenced the Indian out, the red man found he had little left to bargain with.

Among the efforts of the General Court was a decree in 1650 that read:

> If upon good experience there shall be a competent number of Indians brought on to civilty, so as to be capable of a township, upon their request to the General Court they shall have grants of lands for a plantation as the English have.

A number of ministers and laymen had been hard at work evangelizing the Indians, and were deeply concerned as the Wampanoag homelands slipped away. The Reverend Eliot in Natick, the Mayhews of Martha's Vineyard, the Reverend Treat of Eastham, and Richard Bourne in Mashpee devoted their lives to helping the Indians to help themselves. As each witnessed the irreconcilable clash of cultures, the need for self-governing Indian communities became readily apparent.

Richard Bourne was a well-to-do layman who had settled in Sandwich in 1641. He and Thomas Tupper preached for many years in Sandwich and became concerned with the Indians' plight. Having been a representative to the General Court, Bourne was experienced in legislative affairs and his voice carried considerable weight in high places. He took up the cause of all Indians, and chose as his pulpit a hilltop along the shores of Santuit Pond in the land of the Massipee. Bourne spent the rest of his life trying to convert this pagan tribal organization into a Christian community in step with the new civilization.

By 1660 Bourne had assisted the Indians in establishing their claim to many thousands of acres — the homeland of the South Sea tribes, of which the Massipee were one. When Indian ownership of the "plantation of Marshpee" was finally ratified by the General Court it was specified "that no part or parcel of these lands might be bought or sold to any white person without the consent of all the said Indians, not even with the consent of the Court." The Indians of Mashpee now had firm title to their land but little freedom to govern it. They were wards of the state living on one of the first Indian reservations in America.

In 1665 Bourne pushed through a decree authorizing the Indians to hold their own courts, but even that experiment in self-government soon failed. The Indians may not have been competent to rule themselves in the English manner, but they quickly developed into eager and apt Christians. Bourne claimed the entire tribe as converts: four or five hundred men, women, and children. In 1670 Bourne was officially ordained as minister to the Mashpee Indian Church and continued his leadership until his death in 1685.

When the off-Cape war drums of the Wampanoag sounded in 1675, Cape and Island natives remained peaceful largely through the efforts of Bourne, Treat and Eliot. Isolated from their mainland brothers, decimated by disease, and stripped of much of their former pride and dignity, the Wampanoags of the Cape chose loyalty to the few friends they could trust — their white spiritual advisers and benefactors. Gratitude was one of the few virtues the degenerating red men could still hold high.

Bourne's first crude church was replaced in 1684 by a
new meeting house on the shore of Santuit Pond at Bryant's Neck. In 1717 this Indian church was moved to its
present site on Route 28 and remodeled as you now see it.
Bourne's successor, Simon Popmonet, was the first ordained Indian minister in New England and served his
Mashpee flock for forty years. Mashpee was blessed with
four fine pastors during the eighteenth century, both Indian and white, but even they could not stem the tide.

In 1693 all the Indian communities had been placed
under the rule of overseers with almost unlimited authority. The uneducated Indians were cheated, tricked into
debt, bound out as virtual slaves and generally kept in a
hopeless state. Grog shops flourished in Mashpee despite
the fact that they were patently illegal. In their misery, the
Indians grasped at anything that promised escape. In
1718, ostensibly to protect them from being exploited
while in a drunken stupor, they were denied the right to
make contracts, and so assumed the legal status of pau-
pers. Even their beloved rum couldn't be trusted. It became an Indian custom to sprinkle a few drops into the
fire before purchasing it. If it flamed it was indeed "fire-
water."

The Mashpee Indians were dying off as rapidly as almost any tribe on the Cape. Mashpee's status as a tax-free
reservation attracted Indian stragglers and others who
kept up the overall population, but a great dilution of their
race had begun.

Weighted down by the overseer system, in 1760 the few
educated Mashpees petitioned the new King of England,
George III, for a hearing on their "right to be treated as
other citizens rather than as slaves." King George granted
an audience and Reuben Cognehew was sent to represent
his tribe. Armed with reports prepared by Reverend Haw-
ley, Cognehew was successful and returned with a promise of self-government. Three years later "Marshpee" was
made a district empowered to elect for themselves five
overseers and other more minor officials. But it was all in

vain; no government edict could overcome a century of neglect. After twenty-five years of confusion and ineptitude, the old order was reinstated and the governor once more appointed Mashpee's overseers and guardians. The polyglot community remained poor, abject and discontented.

Flashes of a once-proud race occasionally illuminated the squalor of their existence. As the struggle for American independence approached, the Indians of Mashpee took to heart the impassioned rhetoric of freedom and liberty. Of the Mashpee men who fought in the Revolutionary War, seventy died and only three returned alive. After the tribe had sacrificed its men to America's freedom, the overseers returned in 1788 and the tribe lost its own.

During the early years of American independence, a number of Negro and mulatto refugees moved to Mashpee, and captured Hessians were sent in to oversee nonwhites working in the local salt works. Portuguese Bravas from the whaling ships soon mingled in the ethnic mixture, but despite blended blood lines, the Wampanoag strain remained paramount.

With the return of the overseer system, the Mashpees lost even the right to choose their own minister. In the 1800s two men, the Reverends Stone and Fish, were considered, but the Indians preferred one of their own, Blind Joe Amos. "Mr. Stone, he make best sermons," they observed, "but Blind Joe, he make best Christians." Of the two white men, the Indians preferred Mr. Fish, and soon regretted it.

Dictatorial in manner, Reverend Fish ruled his charges with an iron hand and for all practical purposes excluded them from their own meeting house. When a respected Connecticut Indian pastor, William Apes, paid a visit to Mashpee in 1834 he addressed the congregation in the old Indian Meeting House — and found mostly whites in the audience. William Apes decided to stay and do what he could to help. He and Blind Joe Amos joined in the New

Temperance Society, pledged to obtain freedom for the people of Mashpee.

White men from neighboring towns had long felt free to cut firewood on Indian lands. After being given advance warning to desist, one was politely relieved of his wood by a few Mashpee Indians led by Apes and Amos. The "wood-lot riot" of Mashpee — exaggerated to open rebellion by some — was quickly quelled. It had the salutary effect, however, of bringing the Indians' case before the legislature.

A white Mashpee native, the Honorable B. F. Hallet, became the Indians' advocate and champion, and in 1834 Mashpee was incorporated as a district for the second time. This time there would be no halfway measures; the district was organized just as any other township with one exception. A commissioner appointed by the governor acted as treasurer and moderated all proprietors' meetings. The Indians of Mashpee date their emancipation from this time, yet it was not until twenty-five years later that the Massachusetts legislature passed an act granting citizenship to these, the descendants of the oldest inhabitants of the State.

After years of trial and error, the District of "Marshpee" finally became the Town of Mashpee in 1870. Even so, the state was not finished with it yet. During the Depression, an Advisory Commission was appointed to regulate the town's finances. This commission died a natural death in 1969, and the town celebrated its centennial the following year, finally in control of its own destiny.

Only now and then in Mashpee is the eye caught by a leather-skinned face reminiscent of an Indian past. Racially blended now, with little resemblance to their high-cheekboned, thin-lipped, straight-haired ancestors, the Wampanoag have little left but a proud heritage and a profusion of place names all over the Cape. These names, from Annosarakumitt to Waquoit, romantic and often almost unpronounceable, are the Wampanoags' revenge.

OLD INDIAN MEETING HOUSE (1684)

It's quite appropriate, yet somehow ironic, that the old-est standing church on the Cape should be that of the Wampanoag. In all honesty one must admit that this fine historic monument, remodeled once and reconditioned several times, has survived through the ages primarily because its poverty-stricken congregation could not afford the grander structures of a later day. Having survived, the Old Indian Meeting House is now a historical treasure.

English philanthropists, eager to convert the pagan savage, consigned a special shipment of hand-hewn lumber to Plymouth for Richard Bourne's praying Indians of Mashpee. It was hauled overland by ox cart and the new meeting house was raised on the shores of Santuit Pond in 1684.

Concern for the Indians ran strong in England, and in 1711 the Reverend Daniel Williams left Harvard College a bequest of "sixty pounds per annum to be paid to a person of prudence and piety who could preach to what pagans and blacks may be neglected there." This sum, large in its day, is still distributed annually to three Wampanoag Indian Baptist churches. In Mashpee the stipend now goes toward the salary of the pastor of the Mashpee Baptist Church, who also officiates at special services at the Old Indian Meeting House.

In 1717 the Old Indian Church was moved to its present site on Route 28, east of Meetinghouse Road, and remodeled. An old mill stone from the local grist mill now graces the doorway. Inside are rows of simple box pews with a diminutive organ gallery overhead.

For many years the Old Indian Church was always left unlocked, but vandalism and neglect took a heavy toll. In the 1960s the present Sachem of the Wampanoag, Chief Mittark (Lorenzo Jeffers), and the Sachem of the Mash-pees, Chief Flying Eagle (Earl Mills), led the fund drive to restore the old building. The church, surrounded by its

ancient burial ground, is now usually open about five days
a week, including weekends and holidays, from Memorial
Day to late October.

The burial ground is of great interest. Unlike their ancestors, these praying Indians placed headstones over
their dead. The oldest stone still recognizable carries the
date 1770 and marks the grave of Deacon Zacheus Popmonet. Until removed by vandals in recent years, old
stones honored such as Chief Big Elk and Chief Black Ox,
but those you see today are limited to later Indians who
had assumed Christian family names. Earlier Indian burial grounds were located at Bryant's Neck and west of
Mashpee Pond.

ANNUAL INDIAN POWWOW

Visit Mashpee on the weekend after the Fourth of July
and you'll find there are more Indians left than you think!
In 1929 the Wampanoags held their first powwow in 250
years, and recently have observed this ancient tribal rite
on an annual basis. They come in full regalia but leave
their tomahawks at home — the spirit of Massasoit still
lives.

The Mashpee Powwow is more than a Wampanoag
ceremony today, as braves and squaws from other tribes
around the country are invited and made welcome. Sponsored by the Wampanoag Indian Council of Mashpee, the
event is held on the "12 acres" property overlooking Attaquin Park. Keep your eye on the newspapers for this year's
date, time and place.

The festivities begin early Saturday afternoon with traditional tribal dances of the host Wampanoag and visiting
tribes in full costume — brilliant headdresses, flaming
blankets, beaded doeskin jackets, and leather moccasins.
These tribal dances take place on and off throughout the
afternoon and evening, with time out for Indian sports
and a ham and bean supper served by the ladies of the
Mashpee Baptist Church. Keep in mind that the Indian

dancers get as much fun out of it as you do; after all, the point of the powwow is to rekindle the pride and consciousness of their own people by recreating the customs of their past.

On Sunday a special morning service is held in the Old Indian Meeting House. A highlight is the reading of the Lord's Prayer in the Wampanoag Indian dialect, just as Richard Bourne and others taught it to their ancestors more than three hundred years ago.

Sunday afternoon the tribal dancers return to Attaquin Park for another round of folk dances to the beat of tomtoms and chanting braves. Some of the costumes have reputedly been handed down through many generations. Other attractions are Indian folklore demonstrations, arts and crafts booths and refreshments. The Mashpee Powwow winds up with a late afternoon clambake — a tasty institution that no paleface should miss.

MASHPEE INDIAN MUSEUM

At this writing it appears fairly certain that Mashpee will have a town museum by the summer of 1973. The town has purchased an old half-Cape built in the mid-1700s by Joseph Bourne, great-grandson of Richard, the famed missionary to the Indians, and their minister from 1729 to 1742. A complete rehabilitation is now in progress under the supervision of the Mashpee Historical Commission.

The museum plans to concentrate on Mashpee memorabilia, particularly Wampanoag Indian artifacts. Admission will be free but donations will be cheerfully accepted to assist in the maintenance of this much-needed memorial to our earliest inhabitants.

Mashpee Indian Museum is located on Route 130 just across from the mill pond and the flumes of Mashpee's herring run. The pond, fed by the Mashpee River and backed by Mashpee and Wakeby ponds, was reportedly developed by the Bournes as the site of the village grist mill. The mill is long gone, but the herring run was for years the most important on the Cape, and still provides an exciting treat for visitors every spring.

THE LEGEND OF MAUSHOP

Many many moons ago a Wampanoag giant named Maushop lived on the south shore of the Cape. Maushop loved children and he became depressed over the depredations of an enormous eagle that invaded his domain. When the eagle saw children at play, he would swoop down and carry them away in his mighty talons. Maushop became enraged and determined to track the eagle to his nest.

Maushop stood guard over his young charges, but one day the eagle seized a stray child and carried it screaming over the sea. The mighty Indian raced to the water and waded in pursuit of the eagle. Deeper and deeper, farther and farther he went until he waded ashore on a strange island unknown to the Indians. Legend has it that the island was what we now know as Nantucket.

Searching the woods, Maushop found the bones of the many lost children under a large tree. Grief-stricken and outraged, he sat down to smoke his pipe and plan his revenge on the eagle. His tobacco was soaked in sea water so he searched the island for a substitute. Filling his pipe with poke and weeds, he rested and smoked until the billowing clouds drifted across to the mainland on a gentle breeze. On and on he smoked, until the drifting cloud obscured the sun.

That day marked the first fog on Cape Cod and there've been quite a few ever since. When a fog rolls in on the south shore you will know, as Indians have known for centuries, that old Maushop is smoking his pipe again.

THE MISH-QUE LEGEND

Cape Indian legends often take as their subject the natural phenomena around them, such as the creation of hills, islands, ponds, and streams. The Mashpee Indians tell the story of Mish-que, and the proof of it, the Santuit River, is still there for anyone to see.

Centuries ago a giant trout lived in the South Sea. He was known as Mish-que by the Wampanoag — the great red fish. Mish-que was thousands of years old and beginning to feel his years. In his old age he wanted most of all to reach quiet water and live in peace. He remembered the perfect place, a placid harbor on the Bay across the Cape. At his age he was wary of the long swim and stormy waters around the tip of the Cape, so he rested off Mashpee and considered his dilemma.

An Indian girl watched from the beach and guessed his predicament. "Old Mish-que! Go find the quiet water, where you belong now. You are as bad, my friend, as some of our braves in the tribe, who never know when they are old!"

"I am not like your old men in the tribe," Mish-que replied. "If I could get to the quiet water, I would go there."

The girl laughed and taunted him. "Come, old fish!" she cried and urged him ashore. Old Mish-que's pride won out over his better judgment, as the laughing girl jumped astride his back and rode him inland. The girl teased him on as he wiggled through the sand but before long his strength failed him and he knew he'd never make it. He spied a pond and dove in, the merry maid of the Wampanoag on his back. Neither girl nor the great red fish was ever seen again.

The pond is still called Santuit, "place for the aged," and Mish-que's gully to the sea the Santuit River.

LOWELL HOLLY RESERVATION

In years past, the lakes of Mashpee were a favorite haunt of some of the most renowned and ardent trout fishermen of the day. Clear, cold and spring fed, the 770 acres of Wakeby and Mashpee ponds still provide fine fishing and a taste of the rugged, wooded beauty that attracted the sportsmen of bygone days.

Daniel Webster was a constant visitor in the 1830s and 1840s, and such as General Leonard Wood and Charles Dana Gibson enjoyed the fishing here early in this century. Those who left the most lasting imprint on the town, however, were three late-nineteenth-century sportsmen and a president of Harvard University. The sportsmen, President Grover Cleveland, actor Joseph Jefferson, and editor Richard Watson Gilder were fishing cronies and came year after year to Mashpee. Each owned one of the three islands on Wakeby Pond and the islands soon assumed Indian names in the Mashpee idiom: Comtoit. Stayonit and Getoffit. Some of these men were frequent guests at the famed Hotel Attaquin, a Mashpee landmark from 1840 until it burned in 1964.

Harvard president Abbott Lawrence Lowell was more interested in natural beauty than in wading for trout and bass. He purchased the beautiful peninsula, Conaumet Neck, that forms the dividing line between the two ponds. These 130 acres, almost completely surrounded by water, were donated by Lowell as a nature reservation in 1943.

Lowell Holly Reservation features a magnificent stand of native American holly (*ilex opaca*). It's a fine wooded area with beech trees, red maples and black birches framing rhododendron and mountain laurel planted by Lowell. Picnicking is encouraged and an excellent nature trail skirts the shore of Conaumet Neck. Many visitors launch boats at Mashpee landing, leaving the landlubbers ashore to enjoy the fine swimming and natural beauties of the reservation while they fish, water ski, or merely cruise this lake, one of the largest bodies of fresh water on the Cape.

To reach the Lowell Holly Reservation from Route 130, take South Sandwich Road for two-thirds of a mile; the entrance is on your left. The reservation is open from 8 A.M. to sunset from late May through mid-October. A nominal parking fee is charged on weekends and holidays.

CAMPSITES AND TRAILER PARK

Mashpee's commercial trailer park is not for the tent camper. Otis Trailer Village is a family travel home community catering to permanent and vacationing travel trailers and mobile homes only. It is situated on wooded terrain bordering trout-stocked John's Pond. A natural sandy beach, convenient boat ramp and rental boats of all kinds invite fine swimming, boating and fishing. This 45-acre trailer park provides about 60 mobile homes and 75 travel trailer sites, all with water, electrical and sewerage hookups. Rest rooms, showers and coin-operated laundry facilities are provided. Leashed pets are accepted. Travel trailer sites are open from mid-May to mid-October.

Otis Trailer Village is just southeast of Otis Air Force Base. To reach it take Route 151 in a couple of miles from either junction with Route 28. Turn north at Sandwich Road and follow the signs for about 2½ miles. Like all trailer parks on the Cape, Otis Trailer Village is heavily booked in the summer season and advance reservations are strongly recommended. Write to Craig Green at Box 586, Falmouth, Mass. 02541, for a brochure.

PUBLIC GOLF COURSE

There is only one place to play golf in Mashpee, but the two 18-hole courses of The Country Club of New Seabury are two of the most beautiful on the Cape. Follow the signs to New Seabury from the Mashpee Route 28 rotary and you'll find the clubhouse in the residential maze ahead.

New Seabury's Blue Course is a 7,175-yard par 72. Part of it borders on and much of it overlooks beautiful Nantucket Sound. The Green Course, a less challenging 5,930 yard par 70, is only slightly less scenic. New Seabury offers all the facilities of a fine country club open to the public.

PUBLIC SWIMMING BEACHES

The Indians were shortchanged on many things over the years, and beachfront was one of them. What little they had was largely gobbled up by developers, leaving only one remote stretch of saltwater frontage for town use. You'll find Mashpee's South Cape Beach off toward New Seabury down at the end of Great Oak Road.

Mashpee does have, however, one of the finest freshwater beaches. From Route 130 take Lake Avenue a short way in past the Mill Pond and you'll find Attaquin Park and its sandy beach on beautiful Mashpee Pond. When the town was clearing the parking area here years ago they found the remains of a major Indian encampment. It seems logical that this spot, the juncture of the herring river and the pond, should have been the chosen site of local Indian headquarters many years ago. The area has not yet been explored archeologically — who knows, you may be lucky enough to find an arrowhead in this ancient home of the Wampanoag.

A parking permit is required at both Mashpee beaches. Windshield stickers may be purchased at the Town Hall farther up Route 130.

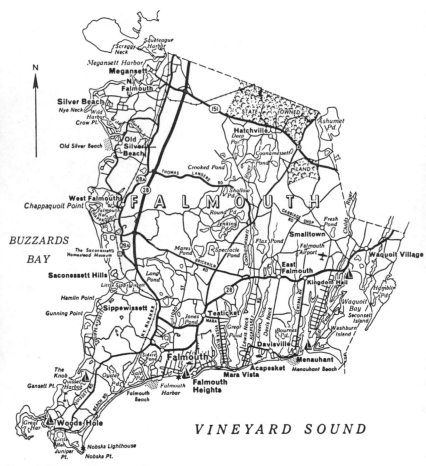

VINEYARD SOUND

Copyright, THE NATIONAL SURVEY, 1973
Chester, Vermont

CHAPTER XV

Falmouth

Daniel Webster, one of Falmouth's earlier summer visitors, once said of the town, "In point of position and in regard to prospect it is the handsomest place in these regions." Falmouth has grown considerably since Webster's day; its prospects have developed and its handsome village green preserves the best traditions of a salty Cape Cod town.

Settlement of Falmouth began in 1660 when Isaac Robinson led a group of dissatisfied Congregationalists to Succonessitt, as it was called, at about the same time that Jonathan Hatch moved in from the south shore of Barnstable. Robinson, son of the nonconformist pastor of the Pilgrim fathers in Holland, fled Barnstable in disgust at the persecution of Quakers. His new settlement attracted many of the Friends' faith and some areas, such as West Falmouth, were predominately Quaker settlements until relatively recent times.

The early proprietors built their homes near the west end of the present center of Falmouth, by the shores of Siders Pond. By 1681 they had "made provision for public preaching," probably with a rude church of some kind. Five years later the town was incorporated as Succonessitt, which was changed to Falmouth in 1693.

Samuel Shiverick, antecedent of the shipbuilders of Dennis, was the town's first minister, but he had a bad time of it and was voted out in 1703. Falmouth's first known meeting house was erected in 1708 somewhere near the Old Burying Ground off Mill Road, with Joseph Metcalfe as minister. Young Reverend Metcalfe won the town's affection with his mild manner and willingness to bend with the prevailing wind.

Like most ministers of his day, Reverend Metcalfe wore a wig — a shabby one he thought — and he took the first opportunity to replace it. He was a hard-working family man without undue personal vanity, and his choice of a new periwig was well suited to his purpose. He failed, however, to take into account the ladies of his parish, each of whom knew better than he what was appropriate to his position. The good shepherd offered to return to his old wig, but that wouldn't do — each of the ladies knew exactly which curl or lock was offensive, and each was determined to eliminate it. His new wig, snipped and clipped to remove its "unbecoming look of worldliness and pride," satisfied all but one old dame who declared all wigs a breach of the Second Commandment. The minister pointed out that the wig in its present condition "was so unlike anything in heaven above or on the earth beneath" that it could not possibly be mistaken for a graven image of anything. The Reverend Metcalfe, his gentle nature often strained by his demanding congregation, died after a ministry of sixteen years at the age of forty-two, greatly lamented by the town.

In 1749 the town fathers set aside an acre or so as a meeting house lot and a training ground forever, and in 1750 a new meeting house was raised in the town center. If there is one dominant acre that has characterized Falmouth over the years, it is this village green laid out in 1749. In those days it was simply a cleared lot — no fence, no stately trees, just an open space around the new, but very plain, meeting house. This triangular green at the west end of Main Street is the town's most attractive feature today. So much of Falmouth's history has taken place on or around the village green that the area has been designated a historic district to insure that this setting will be preserved intact.

As the Revolutionary War approached, military companies under the command of Captain John Grannis and Colonel Joseph Dimmick drilled on the little field in front of the church. The war quickly brought a British fleet to threaten Falmouth and the town lived in a state of anxiety. In 1778 marauding British vessels made a feint at Falmouth, but the ready militia discouraged them from little more than nuisance raids on small craft offshore. Tarpaulin Cove, the old pirate lair in the nearby Elizabeth Islands, was used as a base for British operations and their ships plucked any unwary Falmouth schooner from the sea. Slowly starving Falmouth fought back. After the British capture of a badly needed blockade runner, Colonel Dimmick led three whaleboats in a retaliatory raid on the cove. Dimmick and his men retook the schooner and fought their way back to Woods Hole.

Such exploits as these angered the British and they resolved to chasten the unruly town. Plans were drawn and a premature celebration held in the Elizabeth Islands home of John Slocomb, a well-known Tory. When the British spoke of burning Falmouth, Slocomb realized his true loyalty. He sent his son to warn the town, and Colonel Dimmick lost no time preparing the defense. On April 2, 1779, ten British ships anchored close to shore and sent in landing parties under cover of their warships' guns. Outnumbered and under heavy musket fire from the forewarned troops ashore, the landing parties withdrew and, after a spiteful bombardment, the invading force sailed away. In the morning another attempt was made to land at Woods Hole, but by then the coastline was well guarded and the landing parties driven off. Falmouth emerged from the Revolution with a few proud battle scars and an enviable fighting record.

With the taste of victory still on its tongue, the town took up the threads of an old intramural fight. For years they had argued over the herring run up the Coonamesset

River. Grist mills and other private rights had long en-
cumbered the run and the townspeople found themselves
pushed to support one faction or the other — free access
for the alewives or full rights to the landowners. The anti-
herring group set out to prove a vague point by firing a
cannon stuffed with herring on the village green. The
argument simmered down for a while as herring, cannon
and cannoneer all were blown to smithereens.

The church bell that tolled for the foolhardy cannoneer
was a new one, as a fine new meeting house had replaced
the old in 1796. A grand colonial, the new church on the
green boasted a bronze bell cast by Paul Revere. Revere
charged Falmouth 42 cents a pound for his work; his
receipt in the amount of $338.94 is in the vaults of the
Falmouth National Bank. The bell is inscribed: "The living to the church I call; and to the grave I summon all."
Its mellow tones still call the Congregationalist faithful of
Falmouth.

The men of Falmouth had successfully defied the British in 1779, and with war clouds approaching again they
were spoiling for another fight. An old warhorse, Captain
Weston Jenkins, organized the Falmouth Artillery Company in 1807 and talked the state into two brass cannon
for defense. The village green trembled under marching
feet again, and when war came in 1812 the company was
ready. A British fleet soon arrived to blockade the coast,
but each time they came within range the brass field
pieces of Falmouth drove them off.

Tarpaulin Cove on Naushon Island was again the British headquarters, and once again mighty Britain announced that Falmouth was about to be blown off the
map. On January 28, 1814, the British warship *Nimrod*
sailed close in and demanded the surrender of the American guns. In the best tradition of Falmouth, Captain
Jenkins retorted, "If you want these pieces, come and get
them!" With two hours' notice to clear the town, the *Nimrod* blazed away. The cannonade continued for hours, but
when the smoke cleared overall damage was found to be

slight. Several salt works were shattered, one house badly smashed, and a number of others holed by a shot or two. Several of the grapefruit-size 32-pound balls are now on display at the Historical Society Museum by the village green. Among the homes hit were the buildings now known as the Nimrod Club on Gifford and Dillingham streets and the Elm Arch Inn off Main. The Nimrod Club still proudly displays its battle scar.

Falmouth, like Orleans, showed spirit and enthusiasm in this unpopular war. When the British sailed way without the town's prized cannon, Captain Jenkins took the offensive. With thirty-one volunteers he sailed from Woods Hole in the little sloop *Two Friends* to raid the British at Tarpaulin Cove. Hiding all but two men, they sailed innocently in range of the five-gun privateer *Retaliation,* and obediently heaved to at the first shot across their bow. The confident captain of the *Retaliation* led a boarding party of six men, probably half his crew, and found himself the prisoner of his intended prize. The few left on board were an easy mark and the hated *Retaliation* sailed peacefully into Woods Hole under an American flag and Falmouth crew. From then on, the Falmouth coast was left in peace.

With peace came a bustling postwar prosperity. Whaling, trading, and manufacturing gave Falmouth a solid and diversified commercial base that continues today. The candle factory and guano plants of Woods Hole have been replaced by a sweeter-smelling oceanographic industry, and the glass works and lard oil factory have been replaced by shops and supermarkets, but the town still bustles with activity. With prosperity came the development of the village green as we know it today.

In 1832 the town agreed with Elijah Swift's request that he be allowed to plant rows of elms around the green. In 1857 the old meeting house was moved across the street to its present location. About this time the green was fenced in, and a reproduction of the original fence graces the green today. Many of the earliest old homes were torn down over the years to make way for the more substantial structures of the new aristocracy. Elijah Swift's old home was where St. Barnabas Church now stands. Consider Hatch, a descendant of one of the founders, lived just to the west. He was called Sider for short, and Siders Pond is named after him.

Many of the old homes remain, however. Along the short base of the village green triangle, Hewins Street, are three old homes owned at one time or another by Falmouth military heroes. On your left as you face them is the home built by General Joseph Dimmick's son Braddock in 1804. It was originally a Cape colonial; the porch and turret were added in later years. In the middle is the 1790 home owned in later years by Captain John Grannis, whose "thirty good, able-bodied, effective men," drilled on the green and helped to keep the British offshore. On the right lived Captain Weston Jenkins, the man who would not part with Falmouth's artillery in the War of 1812.

Across Palmer Avenue are the two homes of the Falmouth Historical Society. The imposing square-rigger with the widow's walk is the Wicks House and the smaller two-story in the half-Cape style next door is Conant House. Between the Wicks House and the First Congregational Church is the beautiful old home (1814) of Captain William Bodfish, a whaling captain. He fell in love with pretty Mary Crocker, who lived just across the green. Just after their engagement, Captain Crocker was ordered back to sea. He picked up his ship in New Bedford and arranged to have Mary and the parson standing by when he anchored briefly at Falmouth. There was time only for a short ceremony and a buggy ride around the green before Captain Bodfish kissed his bride good-bye and was off across the sea on the turn of the tide.

Falmouth was a summer refuge of the wealthy long before most Cape towns had begun to give serious consideration to that most lasting industry, the "summer people." Traditionally, Queen Awashonks of the Sagkonets was the first to recognize the summer pleasures of Falmouth. She reportedly journeyed all the way from Rhode Island to enjoy the cool breezes and beautiful views from the "Heights" — one of the first areas chosen by the white man for summer home development on the Cape. Second in size and importance only to its parent town of Barnstable, Falmouth has as varied and engaging a personality as any on the Cape. The dozen or more villages and hamlets of Falmouth and their miles and miles of waterfront offer something for every taste.

HISTORICAL SOCIETY MUSEUM

Falmouth's village green is bordered by some of the stateliest old homes on the Cape. One of the most impressive, a beautiful old square-rigged hip-roofed colonial topped by a large widow's walk now serves as the museum of the Falmouth Historical Society.

Built by Dr. Francis Wicks in 1790, the home is typical of the elegant quarters constructed by wealthy sea captains and professionals of the day. Dr. Wicks was self-taught; a medic in the Revolutionary War, he learned his science by experience and study. He is particularly noted as a driving force behind the passage of the smallpox innoculation law and for the establishment of Cape Cod's first hospital near Woods Hole. In Dr. Wicks's day, a home such as this enjoyed several servants, and it is said that Dr. Wicks also owned a slave. With eight fireplaces to keep out the chill, it was a comfortable and gracious establishment.

The fourth owner, Mrs. Julia Wood, died in 1932 and bequeathed the home to the historical society. Over the years the society has been able to gather a fine collection of Falmouth memorabilia and has arranged its treasures as though the home was lived in today. The society has recently acquired the Conant House (c. 1770) next door, which is being restored to serve as more of a museum as opposed to the furnished elegance of the Wicks House.

Members of the society welcome visitors from mid-June

to mid-September from 2 to 5 P.M. seven days a week. Allow an hour or more for the guided tour. A nominal admission fee is charged.

After the tour be sure to visit the lovely garden alongside the home. The garden is maintained by the Falmouth Garden Club and may be enjoyed at any time of the year. You are welcome to rest and relax in the gazebo or on the shaded benches scattered about the grounds. The barn of Wicks House is operated as a Thrift Shop and is open each Saturday morning in season.

"AMERICA THE BEAUTIFUL"

The third house behind Braddock Dimmick's, 16 West Main Street, is a two-story frame colonial typical of the comfortable old homes along the street and encircling the village green. This one is distinguished by a bronze tablet mounted on a boulder to honor the birthplace of Katherine Lee Bates, author of "America the Beautiful."

Bates House was built more than 160 years ago by Mayhew Hatch, a descendant of one of the founding fathers. For several years in the mid-1800s it was occupied by the Reverend William Bates, the pastor of the First Congregational Church. Katherine, or Kitty Lee as she came to be called, was born here on August 12, 1859.

Miss Bates left Falmouth at twelve and went on to attend a new school for young ladies, Wellesley College, graduating in 1880. While a sophomore in college she wrote her first poem, which was accepted by *The Atlantic Monthly*. After study at Oxford she returned to Wellesley in 1885, became professor of English literature in 1891, and is fondly remembered as a strong and inspirational campus personality until her retirement in 1925. Her famous hymn, "America the Beautiful," was written on a visit to Colorado's Rocky Mountains in 1893. It first appeared in the magazine *The Congregationalist,* on July 4, 1895, and is commemorated by murals at Wellesley.

In her many writings, Miss Bates often recalled her

childhood days in Falmouth. A stanza from one of her poems reads:

> *Never was there lovelier town*
> *Than our Falmouth by the sea.*
> *Tender curves of sky look down*
> *On her grace of knoll and lea.*

BAND CONCERTS

The Falmouth Town Band holds weekly concerts during July and August each summer. Concerts are presented each Thursday evening at 8 alongside the town marina on Scranton Avenue. A new acoustically designed band shell was built in Marine Park in 1972 and the surrounding green makes a delightful setting for this traditional American entertainment.

HIGHFIELD OF FALMOUTH

The Cape Cod Conservatory's center at Highfield is much more than just a beautiful estate. Highfield's 500 acres overlooking Vineyard Sound foster much of the cultural and artistic life of the Upper Cape (just as Conservatory studios in Barnstable and Orleans serve the mid- and lower-Cape towns). Cape Cod Conservatory is a guiding force behind the Cape's growth as a significant center of learning in music and its allied arts. Perhaps most familiar to residents as sponsors of the Cape Cod Symphony Orchestra, the Conservatory also offers instruction in music, art and the dance; frequent art exhibits and other events are free to the public, and both summer stock and off-season amateur theater are presented in the modern playhouse on the grounds of this remarkable estate.

Highfield is perhaps best known to visitors as the home of the College Light Opera Company, a musical theater group that offers an outstanding repertoire of musicals and light opera favorites from July Fourth to Labor Day. The company consists of thirty talented singers, a fifteen-piece orchestra, and a dedicated group of stage technicians. Members of the group spend their summer free of

academic responsibility and serve without pay, learning
the various techniques of music theater. Curtain time in
the air-conditioned Highfield Theater is 8:30 for the Tuesday through Saturday performances, often a Thursday
matinee is scheduled at 2:30.

During the off-season the Falmouth Theater Guild takes
over the playhouse with some of the best and most ambi-
tious amateur productions to be seen on the Cape. There
are many community theater groups in the winter on the
Cape; the Chatham Drama Guild at the Monomoy Theater
and the Barnstable Comedy Club at the Village Hall are
two other outstanding ones. Check the newspapers for
events scheduled during your visit.

Highfield Theater and the conservatory studios are located down Depot Avenue just a jog off the end of West
Main Street.

FRIENDS MEETING HOUSE

By 1658, eighteen families of Sandwich openly admitted membership in that rebellious sect, the Society of
Friends. Persecution failed to dampen the spread of the
new faith, so the authorities tried another tack. Two
orthodox Cape men were assigned to attend their meetings in 1659 with a view to persuading the Friends to
abandon their ways. To the contrary, both were converted
and later broke away to inspire Quaker meetings of their
own.

One of the two, Isaac Robinson, led a group of dissatisfied Congregationalists to Saconesset in 1660. Quaker
families soon followed and settled in what we now know
as the village of West Falmouth. Quakers predominated
in this area for more than two centuries, and summer
Sunday services, or "meetings," are still held in the old
Friends Meeting House on Route 28A in the center of
the community.

The present meeting house is the third built in West
Falmouth. The first one was constructed and the earliest
cemetery laid out in 1720. They were located a few hun-

dred yards east of the present site. To reach the early site take Blacksmith's Shop Road, just south of and across the street from the meeting house. About 200 yards in you'll see a driveway to your left. Park and walk straight in to find the iron-fenced cemetery on the right and the site of the original meeting house marked by a stone post inscribed with the date 1720 and the initials FMH on your left. This 1720 Friends Meeting House was a crude one-story structure, 30 feet square. Its pyramidal roof had a hole at the apex to draw the smoke from the charcoal fire that "centrally" heated the room. There are 69 unmarked graves in the old burial ground. It was formerly enclosed by an irregular stone wall, supplemented in 1900 by the post and rail fence now marking its bounds.

A new meeting house was built on the Main Street (Route 28A) site in 1755 and was replaced by the present structure in 1841–1842. While this meeting house was under construction the Friends held their services in the Quaker schoolhouse then across the street.

Two front entrances to the meeting house were used by men and women respectively to reach their assigned places of worship. The building is divided by a series of center partitions that were raised for common worship and lowered for separate business meetings. The sheds across the street were originally much longer. They were built in 1861 to shelter horses from the weather while their masters attended meetings.

Spare and orderly, the old Friends Meeting House and its surrounding cemetery reflect the simple ways and tastes of their founders.

SACONESSET HOMESTEAD (1678)

The Bowermans were early arrivals on the Cape, settling in West Barnstable about 1647. Thomas Bowerman was an uncompromising Quaker, and he was persecuted unmercifully for his religious faith. Many Sandwich and Barnstable Quakers of the day sought refuge in the wilderness of Saconesset. The Bowerman family retreated to

West Falmouth in 1678 and built a sturdy home of field-stone and hewn oak that has sheltered nine generations of their line and remains a splendid example of early Cape bow-roof construction.

Thomas Bowerman would not join the Congregational Church nor would he pay to support its minister. He was fined and jailed in 1705 and the Quakers of Sandwich sent him bed and bedding, "he being in prison for the Priest's Rate." Over the next twenty-five years his name crops up frequently in records as constables seized cows, hogs and sheep from his farm for his stubborn refusal to support the established church. Even after Sandwich ceased persecution of Quakers, Falmouth badgered the Bowermans and in the 1740s confiscated "one Linen wheel and one Bason, worth 20 shillings" from his son.

The ancient homestead is a delight to lovers of early American architecture. Most outstanding is its rainbow roof, its construction technique borrowed from shipbuilders. Bowed timbers added strength to the hull of a ship, so why not to the roof of a house? Saconesset Homestead features five fireplaces, the largest one able to handle a six-foot log. The great chimney is stone rather than brick, flat, gray schist split from glacial boulders gathered from the nearby hills. Be sure to visit the attic; the curved hand-hewn rafters give the interior a spacious effect out of proportion to the actual space gained by the bow roof.

In 1787 the Bowermans became the millers of West Falmouth. (The old windmill was sold and moved about forty years ago.) Until recently the old house served its original purpose — as the Bowerman family home.

Saconesset Homestead is open to the public from late May to late October, 10 A.M. to 6 P.M. daily, and on Wednesday and Thursday evenings until 9 during July and August. An admission fee is charged. Several special events are held at the homestead during the season. Sheep are sheared in the first week of July and country auctions are held each month during the season.

To reach Saconesset Homestead take Route 28A and

look for signs on the west side as you approach Sippewissett.

ASHUMET HOLLY RESERVATION

Little known and off the beaten path, the Audubon Society's Ashumet Holly Reservation should not be missed.

A Falmouth horticulturist, Wilfred Wheeler, was devoted to the propagation and preservation of the American holly. Over the years he transplanted hundreds of northern winter-hardy American holly trees and a broad range of European and Oriental strains and naturalized them on the gentle hillsides around Grassy Pond. The property was later purchased by Josiah K. Lilly III and donated to the Audubon Society in 1964. Now laced with sylvan trails padded by pine needles and graced by more than a thousand hollies and a wide range of native trees, shrubs and plants, the 45-acre Ashumet Reservation is worth a visit at any time of the year.

A spring visit will feature flowering ornamental trees and shrubs: dogwoods, magnolias, viburnums, rhododendrons, and woodland wild flowers. The masses of beautiful evergreen hollies furnish a continuous backdrop of rich green as spring blooms give way to the field flowers, herbs, heathers and heaths of summer. In August the pond is crowded with lotus blossoms, their three-foot stems reaching for the sun through the lily pads.

As the deciduous trees turn in the autumn, their bright foliage splashes color among the hollies to compete with the ripening berries. In late September and October the Franklinia blooms; a magnificent specimen of this rare shrub is located near the beehive on the trail. By about mid-November the evergreen hollies are at their colorful best for the winter. Their red, yellow, or orange berries and dark green foliage appear like a living Christmas card under a blanket of snow. Photographers will find a frosty fifteen minutes offers rich rewards. Keep in mind too that you're interrupting lunch for wintering robins and other birds who consider the holly berries a gourmet's delight.

Most holly trees require both sexes in the vicinity to develop fruit. The male produces the pollen and the female the berries, with their seeds inside. Most of those on the reservation have been transplanted or propagated from cuttings, but one area is marked to show three- and four-year-old seedlings started by the local wildlife. A trail map is available at the gate and a field guide to the numbered trail markers is available at a nominal charge. Benches are conveniently placed along the trail. Allow three-quarters of an hour or so for the complete walk.

The barn at the gate contains a small informative display about holly. If holly is part of your Christmas, be sure to attend the annual two-day sale of holly cuttings on an early weekend each December. Holly cuttings for planting are always available in the display area for those kind enough to make a small donation.

While Ashumet is famed for its holly, it is also an Audubon bird sanctuary. Of particular interest is its barn swallow nursery. When you enter the barn look up — dozens of nests, including a warm-hearted soul over the light fixture, snuggle in the beam joints.

Ashumet Holly Reservation is open year round from sunrise to sunset. The barn is open on Tuesday through Saturday from 8 A.M. to 4 P.M. and on Sundays from noon to 4 P.M. The reservation is located on the north side of Route 151 just over the Mashpee line. It's about 2½ miles in from the Route 28 Mashpee traffic circle or about 3 miles in from Route 28 in North Falmouth. When you visit, keep in mind Willa Cather's words: "It was the Indian's way to pass through a country without disturbing anything; to pass and leave no trace, like a fish through the water or birds through the air."

FALMOUTH PLAYHOUSE

Of the three "star house" summer theaters on the Cape, Falmouth Playhouse is the most beautiful and certainly the most luxurious. Converted to a modern theater in 1949, the theater is nestled in a country woodland setting overlooking charming Coonamesset Pond. An evening at Falmouth Playhouse can include gracious dining before the show and night club entertainment after the final curtain. If you wish to attend a glamorous production rivaling the best of New York, try Falmouth Playhouse on opening night — a dress occasion, of course.

Falmouth's season runs from early July to Labor Day and relies heavily on Broadway comedy and musical hits. The curtain goes up at 8:30 P.M. weekdays and at 6 and 9:30 P.M. on Saturday. A matinee is scheduled each Wednesday at 2:30. To reach Falmouth Playhouse take Sandwich Road south off Route 151 or north from Teaticket and follow the signs. It is located well back in the boondocks in the Hatchville area.

FALMOUTH ICE ARENA

Ice sports of every description have boomed in popularity on the Cape in recent years and the Falmouth Ice Arena just north of the town center on Route 28 is a beehive of year-round activity.

Owned and operated by the Falmouth Youth Hockey League, the primary purpose of the rink is to promote youth, school and amateur hockey in the area. Figure skaters claim their share of ice time, and hours are reserved for public skating, but the hockey fever now sweeping the Northeast continues right on through the summer months. As hockey practices and competitions tail off in the spring, hockey schools for youngsters begin. Public skating sessions are generally held on Saturday and Sunday afternoons and at various times during the week. Check current schedules at the arena, as times change with the seasons.

SIGHTSEEING TOURS

A fine way to get a first taste of the Cape is by taking one of the day-long bus sightseeing tours offered by Cape Cod Bus Lines of Falmouth. Tours leave Boston, Providence, Hyannis and Falmouth daily from the first of July to Labor Day. The Greyhound Terminals in Boston and Hyannis, Bonanza Terminal in Providence, and the Walker Street Terminal in Falmouth have current schedules and prices.

The tour travels the south shore of the Cape to Chatham, crosses to Orleans, and stops at the National Seashore Visitor Center in Eastham. The drivers are all native Cape Codders who cite the many points of interest along the way. The tour stops for 2½ hours in Provincetown for lunch and personal sightseeing and returns to the starting point by a somewhat different route, passing through many of the historic villages of the north shore. Tour buses reach their home terminals by about 6 P.M. in Hyannis and Falmouth and before 8 P.M. in Boston and Providence.

BOAT CRUISES

Martha's Vineyard and Nantucket live by their sea link to Cape Cod, and the ships of the Steamship Authority from Woods Hole provide necessary groceries and other supplies day in and day out. These vessels, along with those from Hyannis and Falmouth, also supply visitors — that other key ingredient for the islands' survival — and the ships of the Steamship Authority offer a few services their competitors can't match.

The four gleaming white steamers from Woods Hole make eight round trips to Martha's Vineyard and four to Nantucket daily during the summer season. The schedule is reduced somewhat in the off-season but there are two or more daily sailings year round unless weathered in by a severe storm. Unlike other cruise ships, you may bring along your car if you wish, and even reserve a stateroom for the trip. Steamship Authority vessels give you a choice of sports in summer on Martha's Vineyard, Oak Bluffs, the destination of other cruise ships, or Vineyard Haven. It's a 35-minute run to Oak Bluffs, 45 minutes to Vineyard Haven and about 2½ hours to Nantucket. In the off-season, cruises are limited to Vineyard Haven and Nan-

tucket. Passenger reservations are generally not required
unless you plan to bring a car during the summer season.
You'll find the Steamship Authority piers, parking area,
and ticket office on your left just as you enter the village
of Woods Hole from Falmouth.

Another smaller vessel, the 300-passenger *Island Queen*,
leaves the inner harbor at Falmouth village for Oak Bluffs,
Martha's Vineyard, on a busy daily schedule from mid-
June to early October. Seven daily round-trip sailings are
scheduled in the summer with additional cruises on weekends and holidays. When on board you may arrange for
a 2½-hour guided bus tour of the entire island with stops
along the way for browsing and picture taking. The *Island
Queen* departs from Pier 45, a short way down Falmouth
Heights Road from the Route 28 traffic circle at the east
end of town.

A visit to the "Old Gray Lady" of Nantucket and the
wild grape country of Martha's Vineyard should be high
on the list of any Cape visitor. It was, of course, an early
Cape man who was responsible for their existence. Maushop, the Indian giant of the Wampanoag, spent a restless
night sleeping in the sand many centuries ago. Upon
awakening, he found his moccasins buried deep and full
of sand. Impatiently, he threw the sand to the sea. Sand
from his left moccasin made Nantucket and from his
right, Martha's Vineyard.

NOBSKA LIGHT

On the way to Woods Hole, be sure to circle to your left
down Nobska Road to visit the lighthouse on the point. Until very recently the only light on the Cape with a civilian
keeper, Nobska lighthouse is fully automated now and
operated by the Coast Guard. The original lighthouse was
placed on the bluff in 1829; it was rebuilt extensively
about a hundred years ago and is still an important guide
for seafarers navigating the "hole" past Hedge Fence and
L'Hommedieu Shoals to Woods Hole and Falmouth.

Unlike many others, Nobska's light does not revolve, it

blinks in a fixed range every five seconds. Mariners see the light as white unless they're in the dangerous shoal areas to the east-southeast — a 26-degree arc that flashes red. Nobska Light shines from 87 feet above mean high water and is visible up to 15 miles on a clear night.

When the weather closes in you'll hear the deep, groaning tones of Nobska foghorn blasting the air with three short signals every thirty seconds. A radio beacon lends its assistance by transmitting the letter G at 292 kilocycles every three minutes when visibility drops below 10 miles. Storm warning flags and lights fly from the weather signal tower and small craft scurry to shelter.

On a pleasant day, however, Nobska Light brings out a good share of Woods Hole's armchair skippers. The bluffs of Nobska provide a fine vantage point; the island of Martha's Vineyard lies just across the narrows and the channel is one of the busiest sea traffic corners of the Cape. Boat watchers and dreamers are welcome — bring a picnic lunch and let the kids run along the rocky shore.

OCEANOGRAPHIC RESEARCH CENTER

Woods Hole houses one of the greatest concentrations of oceanographic and marine science research organizations in the world. The independent Woods Hole Oceanographic Institution (WHOI), the Marine Biological Laboratory (MBL), and the government-operated National Marine Fisheries Service (NMFS) have made this old whaling port a center of marine research and conservation.

The scientific community has replaced whaling, fishing, and fertilizer as the backbone of the Woods Hole economy. With a guano plant to windward, Woods Hole was one of the least desirable areas late into the last century. Today this tiny, teeming fishing village of narrow crooked streets is one of the liveliest on the Cape. To the marine institutions add the Steamship Authority, a major Coast Guard installation, commercial fishing facilities, a fine residential area and the usual melee of shops, motels, and restaurants — the result reminds one of a westernized Hong Kong.

The National Marine Fisheries Service came to Woods Hole in 1871. This area was chosen due to the stable salinity and purity of the sea water. The NMFS, then known as the Commission of Fish and Fisheries, built the first federal fishery laboratory in 1885 and replaced it in 1960 with the modern laboratory now in use. Of the three institutions, NMFS has the most impact on the commercial fishing industry. The Fisheries Service conducts practical programs to support commercial fishing, researches and analyzes East Coast fishing grounds, and engages in broad research programs covering various phases of oceanology, ecology, physiology and fish behavior. NMFS is also responsible for fulfilling U.S. research commitments to international commissions. Representatives of the Woods Hole laboratory were among the leaders who forged agreements with Russia regulating the use of offshore fishing grounds. It is not unusual to see vessels of the Soviet Union tied up at Woods Hole each fall.

NMFS maintains the 187-foot *Albatross* for research work. With a crew of twenty-two and a range of 9,000 miles, the *Albatross* can accommodate more than a dozen research scientists on extensive expeditions. The *Albatross* may be seen in her home port only occasionally.

The Marine Biological Laboratory is a privately endowed oceanographic institute that traces its origin back to 1873, when Louis Agassiz, the famous Harvard scientist, gathered a few students on Penikese Island off Woods Hole to study marine biology. In 1888 the Marine Biological Laboratory was established and has since become one of the most prestigious centers of research in the biological sciences.

MBL has research facilities for 375 scientists and their assistants and admits about 140 students each year for training in marine botany, marine ecology, and related subjects. It attracts the foremost men in its field from all over the world. Its vessel, the *Dolphin*, is used almost exclusively for short trips in nearby waters.

Woods Hole Oceanographic Institution was formed in 1930 and is now the largest and most famous of the three centers. Employing more than 600 people, over half of whom are scientists, WHOI operates three large laboratories and a pier for berthing its fleet of oceangoing vessels. WHOI has made many important contributions to the science of oceanography and has now established a formal education program leading to the award of a Ph.D. in oceanography. The WHOI Exhibition Center is open to the public in July and August.

The Oceanographic Institution's fleet of six vessels cruises the world's oceans and seas, studying ocean currents, bottom topography, the structure of the earth, the composition of sea water, and the interrelations of biological phenomena in the sea. By far the most popular vessel in the fleet is little *Alvin*, the deep-diving, two-man submarine. *Alvin* became famous when she located and recovered an H-bomb off Spain in 1966; she caused a few embarrassing moments for WHOI when she sank 5,000 feet in Hydrographers Canyon, 150 miles offshore, in 1968. *Alvin* has since been rescued, refitted, and is back in operation. Plans are underway for a titanium sheath that will permit *Alvin* to dive to depths of as much as 12,000 feet. *Alvin*'s mother ship is the 98-foot catamaran *Lulu*, especially designed for the oceanographic research requirements of the institution.

All these organizations are located on the same short street. Just after you cross the little drawbridge on Water Street, the Oceanographic Institution is on the left, the Marine Biological Laboratory a bit farther on the right, and the Marine Fisheries Service and its aquarium at the end of the street.

WOODS HOLE AQUARIUM

The National Marine Fisheries Service of the Department of Commerce, the first of the three scientific institutions to be established in Woods Hole, operates an aquarium that is used by research scientists throughout the year and is open free to the public 10 A.M. to 5 P.M. seven days a week from mid-June to mid-September. This modern facility replaced an earlier aquarium established by the department in 1883.

Fisheries conservation has been studied by the government for more than a hundred years, the first renewable resource to receive public attention in our country. The exhibit is entertaining and highly educational, as it deals almost exclusively with marine life in our own area.

The entertainers are out front, two harbor seals cavorting in a pool like carnival shills attracting a crowd. Inside are displays, models, and the usual array of fish tanks. These tanks are of great local interest, as each contains specimens of those fish we can expect to find in local waters — permanent resident local fish, inshore summer visitors, offshore groundfish, lobsters, local invertebrates and salt pond and salt marsh fish.

The displays and exhibits also concentrate on the natural history of the Cape and surrounding waters. There is a diorama of the Georges Banks, traditional fishing grounds for many generations of Cape Codders. Located about 150 miles offshore, it is one of the most productive fishing areas in the world: about 480 million pounds are taken from this bank annually. Another display illustrates the spawning process, another the story of the American lobster. The purposes and procedures of fish tagging are skillfully demonstrated to explain one of the many functions of the Marine Fisheries Service at Woods Hole. Another exhibit shows the shells found on Cape beaches, and still another is a model of a trap net or "weir," so important in the fishing history of Cape Cod.

The aquarium is not difficult to find in narrow, crowded Woods Hole — the difficulty is finding a place to park. Just follow the main street to the end and hope for a parking place in the small lot next door.

THE CANDLE HOUSE (1836)

A short way past the drawbridge on Water Street, the Broadway of Woods Hole, is the one building on the Cape that will probably still be standing when most others have fallen. The Candle House, built in 1836, boasts 2-foot-thick stone walls, with many of the individual boulders approaching a ton in weight.

The Candle House was built during the heyday of the whaling industry at Woods Hole. It was used primarily as a spermaceti candle factory and whaling ship chandlery. An adjoining bakery of less formidable wood construction turned out the hardtack and sea biscuits for the long whaling voyages. The bakery was converted to a carpentry shop by the Marine Biological Laboratories in 1903 and torn down in 1924. The cool Candle House was used to store fish specimens and as a summer classroom until recent years. It is now a warehouse, certainly one of the sturdiest on the Cape.

A plaque on the south wall commemorates this relic of the whaling era. Until recently, a fine model of a ship's prow jutted from the wall over Water Street. It was removed for maintenance and repair a few years ago and lies forgotten in storage. Perhaps the MBL can be encouraged to return it. It was regarded as a nostalgic landmark by visitors and residents alike.

ST. MARGARET'S GARDEN

The hustle and bustle of Woods Hole masks quiet avenues and byways of quaint old homes, magnificent estates, and secluded nooks and crannies that often elude the eye of visitors to this delightful community. One such oasis is the tiny citadel of peace and tranquillity found just across Millfield Street from St. Joseph's Roman Catholic Church.

Shaded by elms and maples, Millfield Street is an old-fashioned residential spur just north of Eel Pond, the crowded sailing harbor behind the busy little drawbridge. About halfway down the street is a lush hedge of Hickski evergreens with a wooden gate bearing the sign "Please enter but close the gate." Inside, on the bank of the pond, is the quiet beauty of St. Margaret's Garden and the monastic charm of St. Joseph's bell tower.

The flower garden and tower were a gift of Mr. and Mrs. Frank R. Lillie. Dedicated to the Virgin Mary and named for St. Margaret, patron saint of gardens, the little shrine offers a charming pause in a busy day. St. Joseph's bell tower, a 60-foot granite shaft, tolls the Angelus daily throughout the year at 7 A.M., noon and 6 P.M.

CAMPSITES AND TRAILER PARKS

Falmouth offers two commercial camping and trailer parks during the summer season. Both are family campgrounds catering to tent campers. Reservations are needed as both camps are fully booked in advance for July and August.

Paul Soza's Old Cape Cod Forest Campground is located on Thomas Landers Road, 2½ miles east of Route 28. His 50 acres include fine frontage on Round Pound, a private beach, and fishing and boating opportunities for youngsters. There are a hundred sites in the campground, about 20 with electrical hookups. Rest rooms and hot showers are available at three locations in the park. Leashed dogs are permitted, but no cats please. Old Cape Cod Forest is open from Memorial Day to Labor Day. Write to Mr. Soza at Hatchville, Mass. 02551, for a brochure and further information.

Sippewissett Cabins at 836 Palmer Avenue, Falmouth, Mass. 02540, is primarily a summer cottage colony but it also has 25 camping and tent trailer sites. Centrally located rest room and shower facilities are available. The campground is open from May through October. Write to Louis Tessier for further details.

PUBLIC GOLF COURSES

There are three 18-hole and one 9-hole golf courses in Falmouth open to the public.

Falmouth Country Club is located south of Route 151 on the back roads of East Falmouth and features a 6,373-yard, par 72 course. Carts and clubs may be rented and starting times should be booked ahead on weekends and holidays in season. A snack and cocktail bar is available for visitors' use.

Paul Harney's Golf Club is a short distance north of Route 151 in the hamlet of Hatchville. You'll see the signs as you approach the Mashpee line. Harney's is a 3,610-yard, par 60 executive course.

Clauson's Inn and Golf Resort is a bit farther down Route 151 on the south side of the highway. Clauson's is a 6,570-yard, par 72 course. Clauson's is a complete resort with fine facilities for both a casual round and a golfing vacation.

Falmouth's 9-hole executive layout is much closer to the village center. Grasmere Country Club is located on Gifford Street and easily reached from the east end of Main Street. Grasmere is a 2,740-yard, par 27 course. The operation includes a motor lodge and full restaurant facilities.

PUBLIC SWIMMING BEACHES

Beach parking stickers are available to temporary Falmouth residents from the beach house at Surf Drive Beach at the end of Walker Street. Prices vary depending on the length of your stay. You must present proof of temporary residence in order to buy one.

Those with parking permits may use Surf Drive Beach, Old Silver Beach on Quaker Road in West Falmouth, Chapoquoit Beach on Chapoquoit Road in West Falmouth, Wood Neck Beach off Sippewisset Road, Megansett Beach off County Road in North Falmouth, Falmouth Heights Beach at the end of Clinton Avenue, Menauhant Beach off Central Avenue and Menauhant Roads in East Falmouth, and Strong Beach at Woods Hole. Those without parking permits may use only the saltwater beaches at Surf Drive,

Menauhant, and Old Silver. A daily fee is charged transient visitors who wish to park at the beach.

Falmouth has one supervised freshwater beach on Grews Pond in Goodwill Park. No fees are charged and picnic facilities are available.

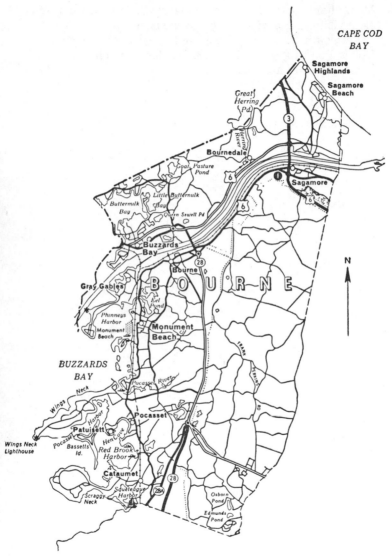

Copyright, THE NATIONAL SURVEY, 1973
Chester, Vermont

CHAPTER XVI

Bourne

Bourne is the beginning and the end — the first town to attract the expansion-minded Pilgrim fathers and the last town to be organized on the Cape. When the debt-ridden colony of Plymouth first looked toward the Cape in the 1620s, it was the waterway route almost across the peninsula at Scusset Creek that attracted their eye. After dozens of false starts and close to three hundred years, the Cape Cod Canal at Bourne now marks the beginning and the end of most visits to the Cape.

In 1624 Myles Standish, amateur engineer of the Pilgrims, noted the feasibility of a canal across the Cape at Manomet. Bradford's history wistfully considered a canal to "avoyd the compasing of Cap-Codd, and those deangerous shoulds, and so make any vioage to ye southward in much shorter time, and with far less danger." With limited means, the Pilgrims were content to settle for the portage route, and when the Dutch offered trade with New York in 1627, the water link almost across Bourne was a natural choice.

Scusset Creek and the Manomet River were only three quarters of a mile apart at one point. The last mile or two of the Scusset and the headwaters of the Manomet were merely shallow creeks, so the actual portage for the Pilgrims was three or four miles. At Aptucxet on the banks of the Manomet, the Plymouth men built a small trading post and a light sailing vessel. After signing a commercial contract with their London creditors, the first such contract drawn in America, the Pilgrims turned a tidy profit in trade with the Dutch.

Though unable to capitalize on their canal opportunity, Standish and Bradford would have agreed with a later engineer who observed the little valley flanked by small hills and commented that it "looks as though nature intended a canal to be made at this point." The three quarters of a mile between the waters was separated by a height of land only 33 feet above the low-water level at Buzzards Bay. During the hurricane of September 23, 1815, the overflowing creeks came within 18 inches of joining in a natural flow.

Once envisioned, dreams and plans for a canal were never quite forgotten. A visitor to Sandwich in 1676 inspected "the place which some had thought to cut for to make a passage from the south sea to the north." In 1697 the General Court appointed a committee to survey the possibility but there is no record of their report.

During the Revolutionary War General Washington ordered a survey of the route to "give greater security to navigation and against the enemy." His engineers recommended a double-locked 7½-mile cut at a cost of £32,148 1s 8d. A state survey fifteen years later put the cost at £70,707 10s. Neither estimator was called upon to perform at these bargain rates. Instead, the state legislature decided to invite others to risk their capital in return for reasonable tolls.

Interest in the project ebbed and flowed over the years but never died out. Potential builders petitioned the town and state for charters, and many were approved. Enthusiasm ran high in the early 1800s. Sandwich, which included present-day Bourne, always felt that a canal would put it on the map, making it a metropolis of commerce. A few dissenters speculated that strong currents and great tidal differences at each end might eventually wash away the entire Cape, but the grand plans, endless surveys and mounting cost estimates went on and on. Canal fever subsided toward midcentury as the glass industry flourished and, in 1848, the railroad arrived.

State interest revived in the 1860s and by 1870 the idea of a canal free of locks began to gain acceptance. The Ship Canal Company was chartered and ten years later the first shovelful of dirt was dug. Four gangs of over a hundred Italian laborers each worked with pick and shovel but were gone within two months. Like all before and many after, the promoters lacked nothing but cash. Grandiose plans, surveys and lurid presentations of potential savings in time, money and lives gained charters for a dozen speculators — but none could raise the money.

In 1883 the Cape Cod Ship Canal Company was chartered, backed by Boston financier Quincy Shaw. Just as Bourne became a town it appeared that the canal was on its way at last. Work was begun and in eight years the Cape Cod Ship Canal Company had excavated a 7,000-foot ditch, 13 to 42 feet deep and 180 to 230 feet wide, by moving 800,000 cubic yards of earth. At that point, the company went broke, lost its charter and was unable to continue.

Shaw's digging was of little later value but his group had made the critical purchase of 1,057 acres, only 25 or 30 acres less than the minimum needed to insure adequate rights across the Cape. He bought the land for less than $7 an acre, an accomplishment that should qualify him as at least an honorary Cape Codder.

DeWitt Clinton Flanagan of New York then took up the cause. His interest may have been inspired by his namesake's great achievement, the Erie Canal. Flanagan's Boston, Cape Cod and New York Canal Company was chartered in 1899 to build a canal 25 feet deep with a bottom width of 100 feet and a surface width of 200 feet. With the surveys completed, Flanagan's proposed banker, the Maryland Trust, became overextended elsewhere and backed out. In his search for financial backing, Flanagan was introduced to August Belmont in 1904. Belmont, a

New York financier, had a record of accepting challenges that others feared to take as well as a sentimental attachment to Bourne. He traced his ancestry through his grandfather, Commodore Matthew Perry, to the Perrys of Bourne, who moved to Manomet from Sandwich in 1663. In 1907 Belmont bought out Flanagan's Boston, Cape Cod and New York Canal Company and broke ground in June 1909, using a sterling silver shovel made by Tiffany. It took until October for the doubting *Yarmouth Register* to remark, "It begins to look like business."

Hand in hand with excavation work went the construction of two highway bridges and a railroad bridge. Bourne Bridge opened to traffic in 1911 and Sagamore Bridge two years later, both low-level drawbridges. In January 1912, after 2½ years, the company reported excavation 40 percent complete. In April 1914 the waters were joined officially and three months later the Cape Cod Canal opened for business.

Belmont's work was far from finished; it was not until 1916 that the canal reached the required 25-foot depth. It is said that every contractor on the project lost money, and a few went bankrupt. Belmont hoped to recoup his investment by toll collections. The grand opening of the canal foretold further miseries ahead, as the grand sum of $51 in tolls was rung up that day.

With shallow depth, three drawbridges, a swift current and no sea room to maneuver, expected usage of the canal did not materialize. When war broke out in 1917, the government offered Belmont $8,250,000 for his $13 million canal. They were being generous; one surveyor valued it at $2.5 million. Business improved slightly in 1918 as U-boats prowled the Atlantic, and jumped in July when the German U–156 shelled a tug and barges just off Orleans. With ownership unresolved, the government instituted condemnation proceedings and took wartime control.

The condemnation case came to trial in 1919. The company asked $25 million, the government offered $8.25

million. Belmont thought his troubles were over when the jury returned a judgment of $16.8 million. The government appealed and won, and the two parties finally agreed out of court on a price of $11.5 million; Belmont took back his canal pending congressional approval of the secretary of war's contract. It was not until 1928, four years after August Belmont's death, that Congress finally appropriated the money, shaving off $2 million in the process. Almost bankrupt, the Belmont estate was forced to accept. In the final analysis the Belmont family alone lost about $5 million on the canal, and innumerable promoters, investors, and contractors many millions more.

In 1935 new high-level highway bridges replaced the old drawbridges of Belmont's day, and a vertical-lift railroad bridge spanned a toll-free canal. Cape Cod Canal is the widest sea-level canal in the world. With a current minimum 480-foot width and 32-foot depth at mean low water, the engineers are again planning on expansion. The canal's land cut is 8.6 miles, but the Hog Island and Cleveland Ledge channels at the entrance bring the total up to 17.4 miles for the larger ships. Small vessels save 70 miles through the canal, large ships perhaps a hundred more. At the height of World War II's submarine warfare, as many as 80 merchantmen and allied warships passed through in a continuous stream each day.

The great industrial and commercial development the waterway was to stimulate has never materialized. On the contrary, the canal has turned out to be a nonstop shortcut between large maritime ports with few direct benefits to Bourne and Sandwich. It's a fascinating sight from the banks, a game fisherman's paradise, and a convenient alley for pleasure boaters, but of little other meaning to Cape Codders other than as a prominent dividing line between God's country and the outside world.

Ignoring the few villages on the mainland, Bourne and the canal are the gateway to Cape Cod. Bourne, named for its wealthy benefactor Jonathan Bourne was an active part of old Sandwich and their town histories are inseparably entwined. It was not until 1884 that this first settle-ment around Aptucxet became the last town incorporated on the Cape.

APTUCXET TRADING POST

When the Pilgrims arrived at Plymouth, they owed large debts to the mother country. The discharge of these debts came second only to the necessities of survival.

In the spring of 1627, Dutch officials in New Amsterdam wrote to Plymouth suggesting the establishment of trade relations. The old Indian trade route across the Cape up Scusset Creek to the Manomet was well known by then and, in Governor Bradford's words, they determined to take "all convenient opportunitie to follow their trade . . . they resolved to builde a small pinass at Manamet." In late summer Captain Myles Standish brought a cargo of furs up the Scusset and met the Dutch sloops on the Manomet. A trading post, more Dutch than English in design, was quickly built and a lively trade established that helped repay to the penny the speculative loans of the "merchant adventurers."

The trading post at Aptucxet — an Indian word meaning "little trap by the river" — linked them with not only the Dutch in New York but also with the French trading along the Connecticut River from Canada and the Indians from miles around. The outpost was staffed by Plymouth men who "builte a house and kept some servants, who also planted corne, and reared some swine, and were all-wayes ready to goe out with ye barke when ther was occasion." The Dutch introduced the Plymouth men to "wampum" and the traders turned a handsome profit in beaver pelts and otter skins bartered with the Indians. When the post closed in the late 1650s the colony's debt was paid and more inviting and profitable ventures beck-oned down Cape as the bayside towns began to hit their stride.

The location of the old trading post was always well known. The Perry family owned the site for more than two hundred years, but its stone foundation was largely overgrown and ignored as the new canal replaced the Manomet at its doorstep. In 1930 the Bourne Historical Society, under the leadership of Percival Hall Lombard, researched old records here and in Holland and reconstructed the Aptucxet trading post as faithfully as they could.

With the dust and debris of centuries removed, the old stone foundation disclosed a number of treasures. Most of the foundation was still intact, providing the exact dimensions they needed. The great hearthstones were in place, and further excavations revealed two root cellars below the original building. Careful archeological work turned up artifacts from the old trading post: shattered bowls, spoons, clay pipes, leaded glass, a candleholder, and a large key that was probably the key to the original front door. These and other relics are on display at Aptucxet.

The trading post is a curious design to Cape Cod eyes, with its heavily Dutch architecture. The two large rooms on the ground floor are served by fine back-to-back fireplaces. In the spring or fall there is usually a fire crackling on the 350-year-old hearth. Enough of the original handmade bricks were recovered from the site to face one end of the chimney block. The other bricks and much of the flooring and ceiling timbers were taken from a 1694 home being dismantled on the mainland. Other timbers, sills and plates came from the remains of the Sandwich Glass Works. A ladder leads to the two attic rooms under the sharply pitched roof. A guide is always on hand to conduct a tour of this early trading post, the only one to be reproduced in authentic detail on its original foundation.

The grounds around the Aptucxet trading post are being put to good use by the historical society. The entrance is marked by an old Dutch windmill brought to America by the actor Joe Jefferson, for many years a Bourne summer resident. A path from the trading post leads past the spring that supplied the fresh water for the encampment to a re-creation of a small Indian village such as might have kept company with the early traders. The Bourne 4–H Club youngsters have taken on this project, bedeviled by the animals that eat their corn patch about as fast as they plant it. Farther on is a full-size working model of the salt works that were such an important industry on the nineteenth-century Cape.

Behind the trading post overlooking the canal is a delightful picnic area. If the children don't behave just park them in the nearby stocks — they say it's a "double" but it can take four in a pinch. Aptucxet is open daily from April first to the end of October from 10 A.M. to 5 P.M., closed on Mondays in the spring and fall. An admission fee is charged. You'll find it on Aptucxet Road on the Cape side of the canal several hundred yards west of the Bourne Bridge rotary.

Many years ago a Runic stone was found in Bournedale. Its translated inscription reads "God Gives Us Light Abundantly." It is one of the few bits of solid evidence of Norse exploration on Cape Cod. The stone is displayed at the trading post until such time as Bourne realizes its dream of a museum for the many historical papers, books and artifacts now without a suitable home in the town.

OLD MONUMENT VILLAGE

In about 1663 Ezra Perry, a twenty-year resident of Sandwich, moved his family to a new homestead near the banks of the Manomet River. His home in the settlement known as Monument was the first house built in present-day Bourne.

Monument grew up around the old Aptucxet trading post and it is believed that the little community's first burial ground was near that site, but no graves were marked and no traces of it have been found. As the settlement prospered, a village center formed inland just about where Bourne village is today. A few of the older homes of the town and the second burying ground are the only traces of old Monument that still remain.

A short way south of the five-corner traffic tangle that

marks Bourne village is the Old Bourne Cemetery. About 1740 a stranger died at Falmouth and was being carried to Sandwich for burial. A blizzard made the roads impassable and the burial party could go no farther than Samuel Perry's tavern at Monument, some distance across what is now Old County Road. The burial party built a fire to soften the earth and buried the unknown stranger with his feet toward an old stone wall. That wall later became a boundary of the cemetery, but the exact burial place is lost in history. Some say it's at the front just south of the steps, others that it was closer to the tavern, in a field across the road that wasn't there in those days. Soon after, another stranger died at Perry's Tavern and he too was buried in the area. The owner of the land, Gideon Ellis, soon bowed to the inevitable and donated the land as a cemetery. For many years it was the only public burying ground between Falmouth and Sandwich, and has always been referred to in history as the "Burial place of the two strangers."

In later years the cemetery took on the formal name of Middle Monument Burying Ground, and in 1899 was incorporated as the Old Bourne Cemetery. Two of the oldest legible slate headstones belong to Samuel (1751) and Esther Perry (1749), who lie side by side on the left-hand side of the path half way from the gate.

About a third of a mile farther down Old County Road are three of the oldest homes still standing in the village. On the left is the Perry House at 111 Old County Road. This house was built by the grandson of Ezra Perry after his marriage in 1723. The exact date is not known but it is believed to have been built before 1740 as a half house. The northerly portion was added and the chimney and fireplaces rebuilt with "English brick" in 1807, resulting in a fine center chimney full Cape. The dormer and side bay window were added much later.

In the early 1800s, probably also in 1807, another Perry built the three-quarter Cape at number 103 just across the street. The front step of each house is made of a stone split in two, each house using half. This home also sports a bay window; the fad was certainly popular on Old County Road as all three of these old homes had them added in more recent times.

Just down the road on the right facing Old Dam Road is the Chamberlayne House, dating from the mid-1700s. It is recorded that Elnathan Ellis purchased the home from Thomas Bumpus, but no date is mentioned. As a bill of lading dated October 21, 1766, issued to Elnathan Ellis as master of the sloop *Greyhound*, was found in the house, it is believed he bought it about the same time. Some speculate that Bumpus was a Tory forced to sell or that his property was confiscated at the time of the Revolution.

Elnathan died in 1800 and the two-family property remained in the Ellis-Chamberlayne families until cousin Chamberlayne bought the other half from cousin Ellis in 1897. Cousin Ellis built his home next door, and a Chamberlayne still occupies Chamberlayne House.

RAILROAD BRIDGE

The two high-level highway bridges over the canal and the railroad bridge at Buzzards Bay were all constructed during the same period, from 1933 to 1935. The graceful arches of the highway spans contrast sharply with the medieval turrets of the railroad bridge. Still in operation to serve the now infrequent slow freights to the Cape, the bridge is an engineering marvel that would do credit to Rube Goldberg.

Buzzards Bay Railroad Bridge is a single-track span with a vertical clearance of 135 feet above mean high water when open and 7 feet when closed. Its span of 544 feet was until a few years ago the longest of its type in the world. The bridge can be lowered for a train in about 2½ minutes. The towers of the bridge are unanchored, resting instead on roller bearings and rockers to compensate for temperature changes and give flexibility in high winds and foul weather.

Bridgemen like to tell of the tourists that size up the

structure and ask, "How do you get the railroad cars up to the top?" The bridgemen chuckle, but the actual procedure is sometimes rather hair-raising. As there is no fixed schedule for freight trains, everyone must stay on his toes to keep vessels away when the bridge is lowered. The canal dispatcher can handle the big ships, but cruising pleasure craft often blithely ignore the warning blasts from the bridge. Two blasts mean it's coming down and four announce that the bridge is not going up for awhile. A patrol boat wards off those unimpressed by the horn.

For a fine view of the bridge visit the grounds of the Maritime Academy or the parking lot of Gray Gables Inn. With luck you may see it in operation.

GRAY GABLES

This one is less well known and publicized perhaps, but a Cape Cod home served as a summer White House long before John F. Kennedy was born. In 1890, between his first and second terms, President Grover Cleveland purchased a fishing lodge at the mouth of the Manomet River and used it as his summer home during his remaining years as Chief Executive. Gray Gables, now an inn perched on the banks of the Cape Cod Canal, was the birthplace of President Cleveland's youngest son, Richard, and the family's favorite retreat for several years. The death of his oldest daughter, Ruth, and the many memories of her at Gray Gables caused the President and his family to abandon the home after he left the White House.

President Cleveland was one of the most avid fishermen of his day. The actor Joseph Jefferson, best remembered for his role as Rip Van Winkle, and Richard Watson Gilder, editor of *Century Magazine,* were his closest vacation friends and fellow anglers. The President was a serious fisherman; conversation might be interrupted by fishing, but under no circumstances could good fishing be interrupted by conversation.

Cleveland fished most of the rivers and ponds of the upper Cape and generally asked for no comforts or favors on his treks through the woods. One evening, returning from a long and hard day's fishing, the President lost his way and was forced by a driving rain to seek shelter at a stranger's home. His knock brought the owner to an upstairs window, and the President requested permission to stay there for the night. "Well, stay there then," replied the owner — and a typical Cape Codder went back to bed.

When the President relaxed at Gray Gables he paid little attention to his clothes. The thousand acres of Gray Gables were along the path of the Cape Cod Railroad and a small substation served the estate. When a train conductor once pointed out the President of the United States on the platform to a group of passengers, one woman exclaimed, "Goodness, if I had $50,000 a year, I wouldn't dress like that."

Gray Gables was sold by the Cleveland family in 1921. It has since been subdivided and settled, leaving the gracious old home and an acre or two on the point. To reach Gray Gables take the first right over the Bourne Bridge to President's Road. Follow the winding road; the Gray Gables Inn signs clearly point the way. It's a charming location and offers a fine and different perspective on the Cape Cod Canal.

MASSACHUSETTS MARITIME ACADEMY

The 55-acre campus of the Massachusetts Maritime Academy is nestled at the end of Taylor's Point just off the busy main street of Buzzards Bay. At the Route 6 traffic rotary you'll see Academy Drive branching off toward the railroad bridge. Follow in alongside the canal to visit the oldest maritime academy in the country. MMA boasts a fine new campus right on the banks of the canal and welcomes visitors at any time.

Massachusetts Maritime Academy's purpose was and is to train young men to become officers in the United States Merchant Marine. Founded in 1891, the academy moved from Boston to Cape Cod in 1942. Graduates of Massachusetts Maritime earn a Bachelor of Science degree and pass examinations to qualify as either Third Mate or Third Assistant Engineer. In a few years' time a Third Mate can progress to Ship's Master or a Third Engineer can be licensed as Chief Engineer, although many choose administrative and executive positions with the maritime industry ashore and still others accept commissions with the U.S. Navy or Coast Guard.

The academy employs a quarter system: three quarters on campus and the summer on training cruises aboard the *Bay State*, the academy's 6,000-ton training ship. Enrollment is now about 400, but plans are underway to expand the cadet battalion to more than 800 by 1975. A new Marine Sciences Program is being inaugurated in 1973. A series of four intensive three-week courses will be presented each summer in cooperation with other Massachusetts state colleges and universities.

The *Bay State*, formerly the U.S.S. *Doyen*, earned six battle stars serving as an attack transport in the Pacific during World War II. When in port, she is open for public inspection weekdays from 8 A.M. to 4 P.M. without advance notice. Group tours may be arranged at other hours; telephone or write to the commandant of cadets or the ship's master to make plans. Groups and organizations are also encouraged to use other academy facilities such as the gymnasium and library. Massachusetts Maritime Academy generally holds an open house, primarily for prospective cadets, on a Sunday in the fall. You will, however, find a warm welcome at any time you visit.

Fishermen have long known of the fine game fishing here at the mouth of the canal. To accommodate them, the academy has beautified a fine new area, installing fishing piers and generally making the surroundings comfortable and convenient. There are plenty of stripers, cod and ground fish to be had off the piers. You can almost cast aboard the big ships as they slide by in the canal. No license is required and the comfort, convenience, and view can be matched by few other fishing holes.

BOURNE SCENIC PARK

National and state parks are not uncommon, but how
many communities can boast a town park to compete with
them? Bourne can, and the 70 acres of Bourne Scenic
Park provide superb facilities and natural advantages.

Bourne's park is designed for the overnight camper as
well as the day visitor. This beautiful wooded area along
the north bank of the Cape Cod Canal offers exceptional
swimming, fishing, camping and picnicking opportunities
in an unusual and delightful setting. There are presently
360 tent and travel trailer campsites, many of them overlooking the canal, with modern rest room, shower and
dumping station facilities strategically located at several
points. There are no electrical, water or sewerage hookups
as yet, but some are planned for the future. Campsites are
on a first-come, first-served basis, with a two-week maximum in season. Leashed pets are welcome.

Campers and day trippers alike will enjoy the park's
sea-level swimming pool, an innovation unique to Bourne.
Salt water from the Cape Cod Canal at the height of each
of its four daily tides automatically changes the water in
the pool, assuring excellent purity without chemicals or
complex filtering devices. It's an olympic-size, sand-
banked pool with lifeguards on duty and a bathhouse for
visitors. A fine playground full of swings, seesaws, and
the like is available for children.

Three stairways lead down the bank of the canal where
fishermen can cast off the riprap. The canal is noted for
its game fishing — it's a great thrill to hook a striper with
merchant ships and pleasure craft passing in review about
a hundred feet offshore.

Directly across from the park, on the south shore of the
Cape Cod Canal, are some 34 acres on which the Bourne
Recreation Authority will provide campers and others
with a fine recreational complex. Work is scheduled to
begin in the spring of 1973 on an indoor ice skating rink,
to be followed over the years by outdoor tennis courts, a

running track, baseball field, horseshoe and shuffleboard courts, and a band shell large enough to house a 50-piece orchestra with open seating in a natural amphitheater. Recreation Authority facilities in Bourne have come a long way since 1951 and promise to go a lot further.

Bourne Scenic Park is located on Route 6 just east and almost under the Bourne Bridge on the north bank of the canal. Overnight campers are charged standard rates and a nominal fee is levied on day visitors. The park is open from mid-April to late October. Write to Box 395, Buzzards Bay, Mass. 02532, for a brochure.

BOURNEDALE HERRING RUN

One of the most convenient and popular herring runs on the Cape is the run at Bournedale. When canal construction destroyed the natural stream bed, the authorities were wise to provide an artificial water course so that the alewives can still pass on to Bourne's Herring Pond at spawning time.

Driving along Route 6 on the mainland side of the Cape Cod Canal between the bridges, you'll notice a spacious parking area about a mile before the Sagamore Bridge. In April or May hundreds of people come daily to marvel at the odyssey of the alewives. The fish enter from the canal, work their way up the long concrete ladders, pass under the highway and into the resting pool tucked in by the motel across the way. From there they meander through the creeks and swamps about a mile farther in to Herring Pond, but the way is overgrown and there is little to see as you trace their journey. Contrary to the Brewster and Yarmouth runs, the best place to enjoy this one is at its saltwater source.

BURYING HILL

When the Town of Sandwich was settled in 1639, Thomas Tupper and Richard Bourne immediately began ministering to the Indians of the area. They built the first meeting house for Indians in Plymouth Colony, and it stood at the foot of Burying Hill in Bourne. When Richard Bourne pursued his destiny in Mashpee, Thomas Tupper, one of the "ten men of Saugus," remained in charge at Burying Hill. In 1696 the minister was preaching to 180 praying Indians here.

Burying Hill received its name as the ancient burying ground of the Wampanoag in Bourne. Legend says that King Saul was the last Indian to be buried here in 1810. In 1865 a cannon and flagpole were mounted on the hill. High winds brought it down, and about fifteen years later a new pole was installed. This flagpole had been the mast of the *Old Napoleon,* a ship that had foundered off Rocky Point in the Gray Gables area. Some years later this mast too came down in a storm and was replaced by the ship's mast on the hill today. The 50-foot mainmast still stands, but the 30-foot top mast lies in the underbrush, forlorn and forgotten.

The old Indian graves are unmarked and no flags fly from the mast lost in the trees on the crest of the hill. Burying Hill and the site of the first meeting house are marked by a bronze plaque in a small stone-walled park area just off Route 6 on the road leading to Herring Pond, opposite the herring run parking area. The old Indian meeting house was replaced in 1765, and we'll pick up its history in Cataumet.

CATAUMET METHODIST CHURCH (1765)

The Indians received a fine new meeting house in 1765, but there were only a few red men left to enjoy it. In disrepair and without a viable congregation, the church was moved from Burying Hill to the site of Cataumet Cemetery in 1799, and across Old County Road to its present location in 1893. Remodeled over the years and expanded in 1966, the old meeting house has been preserved and its modest colonial grace and charm remain intact. You'll find Cataumet Methodist Church on Old County Road a short way north of Shore Road, and the cemetery diagonally across the street, where tombstone buffs will find many old and historic graves.

WINDMILLS

Directly across from the church is a fine old windmill, and another is in off Old County Road about a hundred yards farther south. A third windmill is just around the corner on Shore Road on your left. All are privately owned and two have been incorporated as wings of private homes, but they are in good repair and provide excellent examples of a fascinating era.

The Red Brook area of Cataumet once supported several mills and the Shore Road windmill is known to be one of them. It was reportedly built in Bristol, Rhode Island, in 1797, dismasted and moved to New Bedford in 1821, and pushed across the ice from Fairhaven in 1853. In 1869 a hurricane broke the arms off the mill. It was restored and moved to its present site in 1906.

GENERAL LEONARD WOOD HOMESTEAD

Leonard Wood's family moved from New Hampshire to Bourne in 1867 when he was seven. His father, Dr. Charles Wood, became the village physician and built the family homestead at 866 Shore Road, Pocasset, in 1875. Leonard Wood spent his boyhood on the Cape, and in later years it was always to the Pocasset home that he returned whenever his duties permitted.

Wood graduated from Harvard Medical School in 1884 and entered the army as an assistant surgeon. In 1885 he served in Arizona in the campaigns against the Apache, commanded Theodore Roosevelt and his "Rough Riders" in Cuba in 1898, and later distinguished himself as our colonial administrator in Cuba and as governor general in the Philippines. In 1920 he was a close but unsuccessful contender for the Republican presidential nomination.

As a boy, Wood was happiest when hunting, fishing or sailing on the Cape. As a young captain he served as

President Cleveland's physician on the Cape and they often shared the tall tales of fishing and politics so fascinating to them both.

The Wood Homestead, a comfortable square-rigged hip-roof house with a widow's walk and wraparound porch, is located about a hundred yards south of Barlow's Landing Road. It is now privately owned and not open for inspection.

PAIRPOINT GLASS WORKS

Mention Sandwich to most visitors, and their reaction will most likely involve Sandwich glass. The creations of the Boston and Sandwich Glass company live on, but the factory is long gone. What few people realize is that Deming Jarves of Sandwich glass fame started a second company in 1837, and the exquisite skills of the glassmaker's art still live on only a few miles away from his old plant. Centuries-old techniques, traditions and standards of excellence still reign here in one of only two plants in the United States capable of producing at the highest levels of glass craftsmanship. Most interesting of all, you can watch the artists at work!

Deming Jarves formed the Mount Washington Glass Company in Boston as a future prospect for his eleven-year-old son. The factory moved to New Bedford under new management in 1867 and became the Pairpoint Company some years later. When this great glass house closed several years ago, one man, former manager Robert Bryden, determined to keep the Pairpoint tradition alive. After a short spell in East Wareham and a free-lance stint in Europe, Bryden returned and opened for business at Bourne. Joined by three Scots glassblowers — a sizable percentage of the experts left in the field — and a half dozen apprentices and others, Bryden and his artisans carry on the hand craftsmanship of Pairpoint glass here beside the Cape Cod Canal.

The small and ordinary cinder-block factory of Pairpoint conceals a daily devil's dance worthy of Dante.

White hot furnaces probed by pontil rods and blowing irons yield flowing balls of molten glass that are blown, twirled, twisted and snipped with a sureness and grace that lend style and order to the inferno of raging fires in the blowing room.

It takes a week to preheat the crucibles and two days more to melt the powdered mix and bring the molten lead crystal glass to a syrupy 2,400 degrees. The furnaces roar day and night and are cooled only to replace the fragile crucible that may shatter in a matter of days or a few months. Colors of glass that may be made in one crucible are limited. The different colors must be made in a sequence that cannot be reversed.

There are four stations in the blowing room, each an advance on the one before in rank and the sequence of production. The apprentice "take in boy" does the odd jobs. Glass making begins for the visitor when the "gatherer" withdraws his blowing iron from the furnace and makes the initial blown teardrop that forms the bowl of, let us say, a crystal goblet. The gatherer passes the glowing glass to the "servitor," who twirls and spins the flowing ball to make the stem and foot. He passes the work to the "gaffer" — lord of the shop — who finishes the piece with dexterous hands, a practiced eye, and a minimum of tools. After gradually cooling over a two-day period in the annealing kiln, the goblet may be decorated by yet another artist. The "engraver" cuts his design freehand — only talent and experience guide his steady hand.

Nothing is mass produced at Pairpoint. Production is limited by design; most work is done to order and many pieces are one of a kind. These skilled artisans can fashion by hand only a relatively few pieces each day and they have no intention of wasting their time and talents on novelties or the repetitious creation of easy-to-make items.

Pairpoint Glass Works is open to visitors on weekdays from 10 A.M. to 4:30 P.M. year round. A nominal admission fee is charged. You may watch the glassblowers at work from a gallery beside the workroom, and Pairpoint crystal is available for sale in a small shop on the premises. You'll find the factory on Sandwich Road in Sagamore by the south bank of the canal, almost under the Sagamore Bridge. Though greatly reduced in size from its height in the 1800s, Pairpoint still produces the highest quality of handmade lead crystal glassware.

CAMPSITES AND TRAILER PARK

Bourne offers a fine commercial camping and trailer park in addition to the facilities at the Scenic Park. Bayview Camp Grounds is a first quality family camping and trailer park located on Route 28 about a mile south of the Bourne Bridge. The high wooded plateau that makes up most of Bayview's 115 acres now provides about 250 campsites, many of them with excellent bay and canal views. An additional 200-odd campsites will be opened up over the coming years.

Campsites at Bayview are all equipped with electrical and water hookups, and most with sewerage as well. Modern rest rooms, showers, and a dumping station are provided. A supervised swimming pool, recreation hall, playground and general store are available on the premises. Ice, propane gas and firewood are among the staples sold. Bayview is one of the few campgrounds on the Cape with blacktopped roads. Leashed pets are welcome.

Bayview is always fully booked in advance from late June through Labor Day, so reservations are strongly recommended at any time during their season from mid-April to mid-October. They also provide off-season trailer storage for those who wish it. Write to Gardner Nightingale, MacArthur Blvd., Bourne, Mass. 02532, for a brochure and further information.

PUBLIC GOLF COURSE

There is one 18-hole golf course in Bourne open to the public. Pocasset Golf Club is located off County Road south of Barlows Landing Road in Pocasset. The course is a 6,300-yard par 72. Golf carts, light snacks and cocktails are available at the clubhouse.